Charging Back Up the Hill

Workplace Recovery After Mergers, Acquisitions, and Downsizings

Mitchell Lee Marks

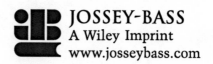

JOSSEY-BASS
A Wiley Imprint
www.josseybass.com

Published by Jossey-Bass
A Wiley Imprint
989 Market Street, San Francisco, CA 94103-1741   www.josseybass.com

An earlier version of some material was published under the title *From Turmoil to Triumph,* copyright 1994 by Mitchell L. Marks.

Jossey-Bass books and products are available through most bookstores. To contact Jossey-Bass directly call our Customer Care Department within the U.S. at 800-956-7739, outside the U.S. at 317-572-3986 or fax 317-572-4002.

Jossey-Bass also publishes its books in a variety of electronic formats. Some content that appears in print may not be available in electronic books.

Library of Congress Cataloging-in-Publication Data

Marks, Mitchell Lee.
   Charging back up the hill : workplace recovery after mergers, acquisitions, and downsizings / Mitchell Lee Marks.
      p.   cm.
Includes bibliographical references and index.
   ISBN 0-7879-6442-5 (alk. paper)
   1. Organizational change—Management.   2. Consolidation and merger of corporations.   3. Downsizing of organizations.   I. Title.
   HD58.8 .M265298 2003
   658.1'6—dc21   2002014825

REVISED EDITION

The Jossey-Bass
Business & Management Series

Contents

**Part Four: Solidifying the Context
for Workplace Recovery**

Preface

Practically every workplace and every employee has gone through a merger, acquisition, or downsizing. On the bright side, mergers and acquisitions are dynamic events that can help an organization achieve its strategic intent much more rapidly than internal growth. Downsizings have the potential to eliminate unnecessary work and refocus organizational resources to respond to economic, technological, and consumer changes. Yet in many organizations today, the old adage that "the only constant is change" rings exhaustingly true as employees are confronted by multiple waves of acquisitions, downsizings, restructurings, and other major transitions. On the dark side, it is during economic downturns that downsizings increase as executives try to show the investment community they are being proactive and taking decisive action to shore up losses. Mergers and acquisition activity revs up also, as firms with little in the way of strategic synergies or cultural fit come together in last-ditch efforts to sidestep bankruptcy.

With all of these changes, good management is the key—and given that we have been living with change in business now for some time you would think we would have solved this one. But we have not. The fact is that the vast majority of mergers, acquisitions, and downsizings are still mismanaged. Studies repeatedly show that 75 percent of mergers and acquisitions fail to achieve their intended financial and strategic objectives. Reports of downsizings rarely describe productive, regenerating, or even rebalancing results; instead, they depict reductions in force as painful, wrenching, and bloody. Although executives may have heralded the transition as the big move that will turn around the organization's fortunes, employees survey the results and find very few tangible enhancements for their workplace or themselves.

These mismanaged transitions have negative—not merely neutral—effects on workplaces and the employees who remain after the dust has settled. Senior executives lurch into a crisis mode and miss the opportunity to use the transition to build a better organization by making the cultural and human changes that could help it achieve its financial and strategic objectives. Middle managers are truly that—caught in the middle between executives who plan major transitions and subordinates who bombard them with endless questions for which there are no immediate answers. And rank-and-file employees reel at the prospect of mergers, acquisitions, and downsizings—rather than see them as opportunities to propel their workplaces toward financial and strategic goals, employees are threatened by the perceived impact of transitions on their job security and career advancement.

This is not to suggest that executives are malicious or incompetent in leading employees through transition. In my consulting I see the residual impact of mismanaged transitions everywhere—and let's face it, these are very difficult events to manage. Combining two previously independent organizations—each with its own cultures, personalities, products, and services—is no easy task. As a result, a combination that on paper looks like a marriage made in heaven turns into a living hell. Similarly, downsizings have gotten to the point where leaders are carving muscle as well as fat—one of the most difficult tasks any manager faces today is telling a decent performer that his or her services no longer are needed. So a downsizing that is supposed to breathe new life into a moribund workforce instead creates "layoff survivor sickness" as remaining employees mourn the loss of former colleagues and, of course, worry about the next swoop of the layoff ax.

The good news is that people and organizations are resilient. Over time, they will recover from the negative unintended consequences of mismanaged transitions. The bad news is that most senior executives will be too impatient to let this natural resiliency take its course. After a downturn, as the economy strengthens and executives grow increasingly optimistic about the prospects for their businesses, they will urge their employees to make a run at new opportunities. But employees will not heed the call to action. While executives are eagerly looking ahead, employees are still looking back—mourning the loss of laid-off coworkers, fretting about roadblocks to their own career expectations, dealing with having to get more work done with fewer resources, and being angry at having been kept in the dark in the past and cynical that anything will change for the better in the future.

That is where this book comes in. In it I accept—rather than deny or ignore—the reality that, one way or another, most corporate mergers, acquisitions, and downsizings have been mismanaged and that the unintended impact of these mismanaged events have to be dealt with before an organization and its workforce can move forward to capture new business opportunities. Even if an organization's leadership truly envisions great new opportunities, its workforce must work through the pain of the past before they can contribute to the fortunes of the future. In even the best-planned and most carefully managed transitions, employees need time to understand the new opportunities and how employees can play a role in achieving them. Even then, employees need more time and support to let go of attitudes and behaviors that were appropriate in the pretransition organization so they can adopt new ones more appropriate to the desired posttransition organization.

The contents of this book are based on my experience in working in more than seventy-five mergers, acquisitions, downsizings, and other major organizational transitions. They have come in all shapes and sizes—voluntary reductions in force, involuntary layoffs, friendly combinations, hostile takeovers, and even the very rare true mergers of equals. I have advised executives in organizations ranging from small high-tech start-ups to massive global conglomerates on how to plan, implement, and recover from transitions. I am fortunate to have worked in just about every industry sector—high-tech, low-tech, financial services, telecom, energy, consumer products, industrial products, professional services, health care, government, entertainment, and education.

Despite the diversity of these settings, one scenario crops up regularly: senior executives underestimate the resources required to manage and recover from transition. You see, effective transition management is not rocket science. The tools for managing mergers, acquisitions, and downsizings are the same ones that consultants and scholars have been touting for years: vision, diagnosis, transition structure, involvement, communication, and feedback. A clear *vision* is needed to align organizational resources, coordinate decision making, and inspire employees to move away from their comfort zone and make the risky yet potentially rewarding journey to the desired new state. An accurate *diagnosis* is needed to identify the gaps between the current state and the desired vision. A *transition structure*—a temporary but formal assignment of resources—is necessary to ensure that the transition is smartly planned and carefully managed. *Involvement* is needed to help people feel like architects of change rather than victims of change. *Communication* is needed to make certain that all involved are coordinated and knowledgeable regarding what is going on within and around their work situations. This communication is two-way, providing *feedback* on how well the transition is being managed, whether people understand its purpose and process, what intentional and inadvertent roadblocks stand in the way, and what essential midcourse corrections are essential for ensuring that the journey from current state to vision is successfully chartered.

Yet most organizational transitions suffer from a lack of clear vision, the denial or ignorance of current organizational dynamics, dysfunctional transition structures, minimal opportunities for involvement, poor communication, and insufficient feedback. This book takes these circumstances as the starting point for efforts to rebuild after a merger, acquisition, or downsizing and capitalize on strengthening economic conditions—people have to *recover* from the unintended consequences of mismanaged transitions before they can look ahead and capture new business opportunities. It describes how to apply the relatively simple tools of organizational change management in a context that is anything but simple: a workforce characterized by the anger, cynicism, fear, hurt, and demotivation that linger well after senior executives claim that the merger, acquisition, or downsizing is "over."

Purpose of This Book

This book began as a revision of my 1994 volume *From Turmoil to Triumph: New Life After Mergers, Acquisitions, and Downsizings.* That book was written in response to the merger mania that began in the 1980s, the wave of downsizings that followed the economic recession into the early 1990s, and the ensuing economic recovery. The premise of this book remains the same as *From Turmoil to Triumph:* senior executives will see new business opportunities emerging as the economy recovers, but employees will not be emotionally or practically prepared to grab the opportunity at hand. Thus the need for a workforce to recover from the unintended consequences of mismanaged transitions before charging ahead.

While the premise of this book remains the same as *From Turmoil to Triumph,* its context and content have changed. In addition to going through mergers, acquisitions, and downsizings, employees have been exposed to a rapid succession of demotivating news and destabilizing events in the first few years of the twenty-first century. These include the bursting of the technology bubble, a major economic recession, and widespread reports of corporate scandals, executive fraud, and accounting abuses. Employees see themselves as bearing the brunt of executive excess and corporate greed, in ways ranging from lessened job security to reduced retirement savings.

Over the next several months and years, some corporate leaders will genuinely anticipate new and greater business opportunities and see a true potential for rewards for themselves, their organizations, and their workforces. They will be energized and urge their troops to charge up the hill to capture the prize. Yet the troops will be neither ready nor willing to charge up the hill. Rather than look ahead at the opportunity, they will be unable or unwilling to let go of the pain behind them.

Unlike *From Turmoil to Triumph,* this book reflects the more prominent role of the information technology sector in organizational life today, compared to a decade ago. And it considers the changing demographic realities of the workplace and the work-force—ranging from aging baby boomers who have come to terms with a new psychological work contract and recognize that "womb to tomb" employment has gone the way of the electric typewriter to Generation Xers who know more about the get-rich-quick dreams of chasing stock options than the loyalty and commitment to building organizational capacity for the long haul.

Most important, this book presents a newly formulated process of workplace recovery. The process is very much steeped in my first-hand experience as a researcher and consultant in the area of organizational transition. But like my practice, the process described here is greatly influenced by two of the simplest yet most powerful models guiding organizational change and development: Kurt Lewin's "unfreezing-changing-refreezing" model of organizational transition and William Bridges's "ending the old–neutral zone–beginning the new" model of individual transition. In a sense, this book describes why and how I have integrated these two models into a new model describing the process of workplace recovery and how every leader and manager can benefit from it.

Content of This Book

The book is organized in four parts. Part One reviews the impact of mismanaged transitions on organizations and the people who work in them. Chapter One describes why mergers, acquisitions, and downsizings are such difficult events to manage, and Chapter Two lists the many psychological, behavioral, and business consequences of mismanaged transitions. Part Two presents the conceptual and practical underpinnings of the process of workplace recovery. Chapter Three presents Lewin's model of organizational transition and explains how, if properly managed, transitions can be used as "unfreezing events" in the first step of achieving leadership's desires for the posttransition organization. Chapter Four uses Bridges's model to describe the very normal and natural process of individual adaptation to transition—people have to let go of the old before they accept the new. Chapter Five then summarizes the process of workplace recovery that helps people end their attachments to the old (pretransition) organizational order so they can more readily accept the realities of the new (posttransition) organizational order at both the emotional and the practical business level. Chapter Five also provides the "realities" of workplace recovery that guide the design of activities to help people let go of the old and accept the new, as well as principles derived from lessons learned in designing approaches to workplace recovery.

Each of the chapters in Part Three describes how to put the four elements of workplace recovery into practice. These four elements are derived from the product of the two requirements of workplace recovery (ending the old and embracing the new) and the two levels of workplace recovery (emotional realities and business imperatives). Chapter Six addresses letting go of the emotional baggage of mismanaged transitions through the element of *empathy*—letting people know their leadership acknowledges that things have been and will continue to be difficult during and after transition. Chapter Seven moves the letting-go process to the level of business imperatives via the element of *engagement*—creating understanding and support for the need to end the old organizational order. With people's grips on the old loosened, Chapter Eight shows how to accelerate acceptance of the desired posttransition organization on an emotional level by generating the element of *energy*—getting people excited about the new organizational order and supporting them in realizing it. And Chapter Nine brings acceptance of the new to the level of the business imperatives of the desired posttransition organization through the element of *enforcement*—solidifying employee mental models that are congruent with the new organizational order.

The book concludes with a single chapter in Part Four on solidifying the context for workplace recovery. Chapter Ten highlights the ways in which senior executives lead the recovery process and middle managers contribute to its success.

Intended Audience for This Book

This book is written primarily for leaders of organizations and work teams who have gone through transitions, as well as their successors who inherit organizations that are reeling from the aftereffects of mismanaged transitions. I intend a broad definition of the term *leader* to include not just senior executives like CEOs, business unit presidents, and function heads but also managers through the ranks who lead departments or work teams. Although workplace recovery always benefits from the understanding and support of the most senior executives, I have seen it occur as a result of the commitment and hard work of middle managers who recognize they have a job to do in helping their team members let go of the effects of transitions before moving ahead to accept new workplace challenges and opportunities.

The book is also intended for the professionals who assist executives and managers in changing workplaces. This includes human resources and communications specialists, internal and external consultants, and strategic planners and other staff specialists who see the impact of mismanaged transitions and recognize that there is a job to do in ending the old before people can consider moving forward. And the book is helpful to individual employees who have lived through a merger, acquisition, or downsizing and can benefit from knowing that their reactions of anger, insecurity, and uncertainty are perfectly normal. But even though the old organizational order may feel comfortable to them, they have to recognize that their workplace has changed and they must inevitably change with it. Finally, I hope the book is of value to students and professors who study organizational life, as it documents a link between theory and practice in the fields of organizational psychology, organizational behavior, and organizational change and development.

Acknowledgments

Many people have contributed to the content and quality of this book. This includes the several resourceful and spirited internal "co-conspirators" from client organizations who have provided settings for studying and conducting workplace recovery. It also includes a wonderfully creative and fun set of fellow external consultants who, in addition to making important contributions to the challenging work of transition management, have been a real joy to work with. I especially want to thank Philip H. Mirvis for his intellectual and personal guidance all these many years. The fine staff at Jossey-Bass with whom I have worked over the years—and more recently senior editor Susan Williams and senior production editor Mary Garrett—have made this a much better offering than it otherwise would have been. Finally, I want to thank my family and friends for their love and support in being my source of recovery from the rigors of the workplace.

San Francisco, California   Mitchell Lee Marks
January 2003

The Author

Mitchell Lee Marks heads JoiningForces.org in San Francisco and San Diego. His areas of expertise include corporate culture, team building, organizational effectiveness, management development, executive coaching, senior team development, human resource management, and the strategic planning and implementation of organizational change. He works extensively with firms planning and implementing mergers, restructurings, downsizings, and other transitions. He is recognized internationally for developing innovative approaches to achieving desired business results during and after transition.

Marks is a consultant to a broad range of organizations, from small start-ups to large multinational firms. Current or past clients include Pfizer, America Online, Intel, Motorola, AT&T, Lockheed Martin, Unisys, Hewlett-Packard, Lucent Technologies, Abbott Laboratories, KPMG Peat Marwick, Imperial Oil of Canada, BP Amoco, Phillips Petroleum, Molson Breweries, SBC, Bank of America, Citibank, American Airlines, Delta Airlines, Seagram, Kaiser Permanente Medical Care Program, Blue Shield of California, Los Angeles County, the March of Dimes, and others in the financial, manufacturing, health care, entertainment, high-technology, professional services, government, publishing, consumer products, and communications industries.

Marks earned his bachelor's degree in psychology and communication from the University of California at Santa Cruz and his master's and doctoral degrees in organizational psychology from the University of Michigan. Prior to establishing his own firm, he was national practice group leader in human resource management for William M. Mercer, Inc., and senior director at the Delta Consulting Group. He was founding director of the doctoral program in organizational psychology at the California School of Professional Psychology and served on the faculties of the University of California, Irvine, and California State University. He has lectured at Harvard Business School and the Smithsonian Institution and regularly presents to business, academic, and professional and business groups.

Marks is the author of four books in addition to this one—*Joining Forces: Making One Plus One Equal Three in Mergers, Acquisitions, and Alliances* (with Philip H. Mirvis); *Resizing the Organization: Managing Layoffs, Divestitures, and Closings—Maximizing Gain While Minimizing Pain* (with Kenneth P. De Meuse); *From Turmoil to Triumph: New Life After Mergers, Acquisitions, and Downsizing;* and *Managing the Merger*—along with numerous articles in management and scholarly journals. His work has been reported frequently in the *Wall Street Journal, Fortune, The Economist, U.S. News and World Report, Business Week,* the *New York Times,* the *Washington Post,* and *Sports Illustrated,* as well as on the *PBS News Hour, NBC Nightly News,* CNBC, and other television programs.

PART ONE

The Costly Impact of Transitions on Organizations and Their People

1

Organizational MADness

When Dan left his job as a reporter on a daily newspaper to become a technical writer at a dot-com start-up in October 1999, he was energized by his prospects: he loved technology and looked forward to working in that fast-growing business sector; daily newspapers, he predicted, would soon be replaced by people getting their morning news on the Internet. His new employer had a laid-back culture of sandals, Friday beer busts, and pets welcome in the office; suits and ties were required in the stodgy world of journalism. And no small matter, the dot-com offered a slew of stock options to sway him to jump ship; rumors regularly circulated around the newsroom that headquarters back east was about to make some cuts in the bloated staff.

Dan figured his timing couldn't have been better. For a while, he was right. The dot-com's reputation, stock price, and staffing grew rapidly throughout 2000 and into 2001. Dan felt comfortable, even as scores of other dot-coms were letting people go or shutting down completely. But by the summer of 2001, it seemed that almost every day Dan ran into someone from another firm who was either laying people off or being laid off themselves. Then the bottom fell out from under Dan and his employer. Anticipated revenues never materialized, the company's stock price fell from 80 to under a dollar, and the venture capitalists who bred life into Dan's firm were no longer willing to pay for financial life support. They sold a majority interest of the company to a European media conglomerate.

At first, the new owners made no major changes. Rather than interpret this as a positive sign, employees grew anxious. Seeing what was happening elsewhere in Silicon Valley, they wondered what was going on in their organization. The lack of action was almost unbearable. When they asked questions of their leaders, the response was always "Its business as usual—just do your job." Executive visibility and communication seemed to be much less than when Dan first joined the firm. Filling this information void, rumors of mass layoffs ran through the organization. Then, on the day before Thanksgiving 2001, the European owners made the announcement: fully 25 percent of the workforce was going to be laid off through an involuntary reduction in force. Employees became paralyzed, and work stopped as people waited to see what would transpire. Then, as Dan recalled, the cuts came:

> Around three or four o'clock every day, someone from HR would come up and talk to the department manager, and then the manager would walk up to that day's victim and hand the person an envelope. In front of everybody, the manager told the person that he or she had half an hour to clear out. A security guard was posted nearby, in case anyone stayed more than thirty minutes.
>
> Each day, right around three in the afternoon, the tension of people waiting for the HR person to come up and deliver the envelope was so thick you could cut it with a knife. Then we got a clue about how to know what your fate would be that day. Targeted people's personal computers would be shut down at 2:00 P.M. They got a message that the system was down or that log-in access was denied. The company did not want these people on the computer.
>
> The worst of it was a couple of times when the company turned off the wrong machines—people who were supposed to be staying assumed they were being booted out. Then

there was the day that the entire system went down by accident. . . .

Dan was spared from the Thanksgiving Day massacre, as surviving employees dubbed it. But rumors began to circulate in early
2002 of an impending restructuring, perhaps the merger of the dot-
com with another division of the European owner. Well into 2002,
Dan still did not feel comfortable about his position:

> The company has told us nothing. People are learning what
> they know from industry magazines. Everyone is paralyzed
> again. And there is tremendous anger at the Europeans and at
> our local leadership.
>   There is no loyalty here; no one is going to go the extra
> mile after this. Two years ago, we worked sixty-five-hour
> weeks. People were willing to do it, because this was a great
> place to work and we were doing something that mattered.
> Personally, I am devastated. From here on in, it's just a job for
> me. I'll put in my forty hours and that's it. People talk about
> leaving the company, but no one is hiring.
>   What really concerns me is I have to do this for thirty
> more years—put myself at the mercy of a corporation. I don't
> think I can do this.

Mismanaged Transitions

Many organizations, as they respond to bad economic news, fall
into a classic pattern of mistakes. As profits erode and they lose
market share, employers frequently worry first about the investment
community and focus their communication efforts externally rather
than internally. Likewise, when executives search for creative solutions to company business problems, they too often decline to discuss options with workers or offer any kind of outlook for the future.
Instead, company leaders lower their profile with their own employees as they grope for the right strategy or combination of actions.

The result is nervous employees who believe that management is either insensitive to their plight or fresh out of ideas. When company leaders are finally ready to talk about recovery and revitalization, their past behavior has earned them an insecure workforce more inclined to lick the wounds of the past than to move forward to capture emerging business opportunities.

Senior executives regularly make missteps when managing events like mergers, acquisitions, and downsizings. Even when relatively well planned and carefully implemented, mergers, acquisitions, and downsizings produce unintended negative consequences. These transitions have negative—not merely neutral—effects on the people, work groups, and functions that survive. That is the starting point for this book. It describes how forward-looking leaders who see economic recovery as an opportunity to build a better-performing organization must accept and acknowledge that employees are still looking behind or, at best, are still dazed from the stress, uncertainty, and chaos of living through a transition. This book shows how to apply the relatively simple tools of organizational change management in a context that is far from simple: a workforce characterized by the anger, cynicism, fear, hurt, and demotivation that linger long after senior executives claim that the merger, acquisition, or downsizing is "over." It does this by addressing transition at both the individual and organizational levels: acknowledging the very natural and normal pattern of human adaptation to transition and using the unsettledness of the posttransition organization as an opportunity to articulate and realize desired organizational change.

Leaders who have mismanaged transitions—or their successors who inherit organizations that are reeling from the aftereffects of mismanaged transitions—have a job to do in reenergizing their people and revitalizing their organizations. If they do not realize this, these executives are in for a big surprise. CEOs, business unit heads, and team leaders may be personally energized by the opportunities that lay ahead. This makes very good sense, because they are at the helm and in control of their organizations, they determine the strategies, and they allocate the resources. Leaders may be motivated by the potential of financial growth, organizational success, and personal reward. Their spirits are buoyed by new business opportunities—perhaps the adoption of a new strategy, the introduction of a new technology or product or service, the strengthening of the economy, or even the elimination of a competitor. They anticipate that after a long and difficult struggle, victory in a decisive battle is just at the top of the next hill. They see the goal and will confidently rally their troops around the mission at hand. Then the cry will come for the troops to charge up the hill and take the prize.

Unfortunately, the troops will be neither ready nor willing to charge up the hill. Rather than focus on the opportunity ahead of them, they will be unable to let go of the pain behind them. Their vision will be obscured by the emotional residue of anger, distrust, and depression built up over years of false promises and unmet expectations. Nor will the troops have the confidence that they can take the hill—their self-esteem will be battered, their faith in their organization broken. Most significant of all, the troops will not see how any personal gain will result from taking the hill. Instead, they will fixate on memories of their fallen comrades: the casualties of layoffs and downsizings and the "walking wounded" whose careers were sidetracked by mergers and acquisitions.

Employee Worries

Fear of job loss following a merger or an acquisition was the number one worry among senior executives in the thousand largest U.S. companies in the 1990s. The timing of the survey—after merger and acquisition activity had significantly waned due to recession, the tightening of capital by major financial institutions, and a generally greater sensibility in guiding corporate combinations—makes the results all the more dramatic. Executives and other employees retain vivid memories of the trauma experienced when firms are merged or acquired, cultures clash, and coworkers who seem like decent contributors are let go merely because their positions have become redundant. Even in organizations that have not merged or been acquired, employees have learned (from firsthand experience in past jobs or vicariously from their neighbors, friends, or relatives) about the stress and anxiety associated with organizational transition.

The number two fear reported by the surveyed executives was burnout. *Burnout* entered the popular vocabulary in the 1970s after studies of mental health and other social service professionals documented that large workloads and minimal resources contributed to a sense of hopelessness in aiding clients. The "system" was not working, and these professionals grew physically tired and psychologically alienated. They expressed anger and doubt about the worth of what they were doing along with an overall lack of job interest.

Today, *burnout* signifies feelings of physical and emotional exhaustion, alienation from others, and reduced personal accomplishment. It is equally likely to occur in big corporations, small businesses, government offices, or not-for-profit agencies. In organizations that downsize through layoffs or hiring freezes, surviving employees have to work harder to cover the tasks of others. Fewer support staff or other resources are available to help get the job done. The new workplace offers scant advancement opportunities as management levels are eliminated and career paths are obscured. The recession that began this century has limited pay increases and bonus pools, and the deflated stock market has sunk stock options. All of this prompts people to ask what the payoff is for working so hard. One middle manager from a high-technology firm that went through a merger and two subsequent waves of downsizing within a four-year period put it this way: "I get to work early, stay late, come home, throw some food down my throat, put the kids to bed, do some more work, fall asleep, and get up and do it all over again. What kind of life is this? Yeah, I've kept my job while many people I know have lost theirs. But how could things be any worse if I lost it?"

Fears of job loss and feelings of burnout extend well beyond the executive suite. In the past decade, professional, managerial, and other white-collar employees joined blue-collar employees (the target of job cuts and wage freezes in past economic downturns) in suffering through layoffs, reduced benefits, and a falling quality of life. Though always painful, these conditions are more tolerable when one perceives them as being shared by others and leading to some payoff later on. Employees in the 1990s witnessed organizations willing to slash payrolls as deeply as necessary to satisfy short-term financial targets. And it all continues in the current decade. Employees worry about the next wave of layoffs while executives are buffered by generous golden parachute arrangements. Four thousand employees were laid off at Enron when it declared bankruptcy; five hundred of its executives divvied up $55 million in bonuses right before the filing. Meanwhile, the surviving employees saw their 401(k) accounts evaporate as the company stock fell and executives—many of whom were unloading their own shares—stipulated that employees could not sell Enron stock in their retirement plans.

People are not unwilling to work hard or to commit to the business objectives of their workplaces. Instead, they have become consumed by fear and suspicious of management declarations that "everything is under control" or "it's business as usual" when there is obvious evidence to the contrary. In many organizations, employees have grown cynical of programs under the rubric of "rightsizing" or "reengineering" that produce little in the way of real positive change. As employees feel they are receiving less from their employer, they give less in return. Listen to a manager from a large health care organization:

It's like each side takes something away, so the other reciprocates. First, the company took away our security when they downsized; there went our loyalty. Then they stopped merit pay raises when they introduced the new compensation plan, and we took away our commitment to doing creative and high-quality work. Next, career options went out the window with the delayering, so people stopped working hard because there was no payoff for it. I used to love coming to work at this place; now I show up, and it's simply a matter of them paying me for my time.

The word around many corporations today is that at the first sign of an economic recovery, people will jump ship. The best and the brightest—those with the most marketable skills—will lead the way. Others, the dazzled and disillusioned among them, will stay and work in an unimpassioned and indiscriminate manner. They will rely on antiquated skills, information, and practices that poorly equip them for the challenges at hand. A workforce without high-quality talent, a commitment to excellence, and the necessary tools for success will severely hinder any organization's ability to rebound in an economic recovery.

Organizational MADness

The development of a fearful, suspicious, and cynical workforce in many organizations is in large part due to what I refer to as organizational MADness—the impact of Mergers, Acquisitions, and Downsizings on short-term employee well-being and long-term organizational effectiveness. Mergers, acquisitions, and downsizings have become regularly occurring events in the managerial repertoire. Well over ten thousand corporate combinations occur in a typical year in the United States, and nearly two million positions have been cut in the past two years. Organizational MADness has gotten to the point where it is ingrained in the U.S. culture. The CBS news Web site, for example, invites people to interact with the "layoff tracker" and chronicles large company downsizings on the "pink slip parade." Even in Europe and Asia, where government regulations and corporate cultures have historically implied job security, organizations are downsizing.

Despite the frequency of merger, acquisition, and downsizing activity, most organizational transitions are financial and strategic failures. Repeated studies have shown that fewer than 25 percent of all mergers and acquisitions achieve their desired results—whether measured by the share price of merger active firms, the extent to which anticipated synergies and savings are actually achieved, the retention of desired talent, or the eventual divestiture of a once desired target. And most organizations that downsize fail to realize long-term cost savings or efficiencies beyond the cuts, necessitating multiple waves of layoffs and restructurings.

The Healthy Side of MADness

Certainly organizations need to "rightsize" by eliminating unnecessary work and responding to economic, legal, technological, and consumer changes. If organizations did not change, they would not remain competitive. Organizational leaders, however, must come to terms with the fact that the *way* in which organizations transformed themselves during the economic slowdown of the early 1990s and the burst of the technology bubble and ensuing recession a decade later has stifled personal motivation, hindered team performance, and damaged organizational effectiveness.

MADness does not imply that organizations are malevolent in their actions. In many cases, mergers, acquisitions, and downsizings are prudent business moves that enhance competitiveness and survivability in the ever-changing business environment. British Petroleum's acquisition of Amoco was an essential strategic move in a consolidating industry. Vivendi's acquisition of Seagram's film, television, and recording businesses—and its concurrent divestiture of the Seagram Spirits and Wine Group—catapulted it to prominence among diversified entertainment firms and kept its focus on key businesses. The airline industry's downsizing following the September 11, 2001, terrorist attacks have enhanced the likelihood that carriers, and their hundreds of thousands of remaining employees, will endure over the long haul.

A transition can be beneficial for organizations and their people. There is fat to be cut and waste to be eliminated from many corporations, even profitable ones. Companies wallowing in red ink are wise to eliminate a portion—be it 5, 10, or even 20 percent—of the workforce to strengthen the survivability of the vast majority of employees. And a serious assessment of workforce apportionment is an integral component of the introspection needed to rebalance a firm and its resources to take better advantage of emerging market trends or technological advances.

A transition can also spark organizational regeneration. A CEO with the right mix of visionary and charismatic leadership skills can rally employees around the notion that the merger, acquisition, or downsizing is not only a necessary response to business realities but also a proactive opportunity to improve how work is approached and conducted in the organization. A transition holds the potential to "unfreeze" the organization and its people, providing a rare chance to change corporate culture dramatically and reinforce a new way of doing things. I worked with a CEO who was stymied in efforts to build what he termed a "customer service" culture in his electronics firm. He sent his people to training programs and brought gurus in to give pep talks, but nothing seemed to change the mind-set of managers or the behaviors of employees. Finally, he acquired a slightly larger competitor with a reputation for having customer service second to none in the industry and folded his organization in it. When a good number of top jobs went to executives from the acquired firm, the shock waves reverberating throughout the company sent signals that the CEO was serious about change. Similarly, a middle manager or supervisor can use the unfrozen state as an opportunity to enhance teamwork, build better cross-functional relations, and identify and correct impediments to productivity in his or her work group.

And individuals can experience a personal form of renewal as a result of company transitions. Although many employees stay mired in maladaptive responses to the stress and uncertainty of a transition, others come to recognize that in crisis there is opportunity. They recognize that they cannot manage what is beyond their control and do not try; rather, they assess the situation and act in the areas they can control. These employees accept that the context within which they work is changing and proactively seek to align their tasks accordingly. And they recognize that the rules of the game have changed, that there is no "business as usual." They are energized by the opportunity to learn new skills, to test their ability to cope with stress and uncertainty, and to find creative ways to meet work requirements.

Unfortunately, however, using transition as an opportunity for personal growth, team development, or organizational renewal is very much the exception, not the rule. Reports of mergers, acquisitions, and downsizings rarely describe productive, regenerating, or even rebalancing outcomes. In contrast, they depict transitions as painful, wrenching, and bloody.

Transition

This book describes how organizations and their employees recover from transition. Transition is distinct from change. A change is a path to a known state: something discrete, with orderly, incremental, and continuous steps. Moving the start of the weekly staff meeting from 9:00 A.M. to 8:00 A.M. is an example of a change. It may cause some disruptiveness and require some adaptation—people have to leave home for work earlier or cancel other early-morning commitments—but its discrete nature allows people to know exactly what to expect and lets them get on with their lives inside and outside the organization.

A transition, by comparison, is a path to an unknown state, something discontinuous that involves many simultaneous and interactive changes and the selection of "breakthrough" ways of thinking, organizing, and doing business. Transition marks a break from the past. It involves death and rebirth; existing practices and routines must be abandoned and new ones discovered and developed. Adapting to transition is much more psychologically taxing than adapting to change. When Pfizer acquired Warner-Lambert, its CEO made a commitment to Wall Street to grow company revenues at an aggressive pace. The head of Pfizer's R&D function knew that current practices from either partner could not generate the drug pipeline required to attain such growth. He set out to transform how R&D was done in the pharmaceutical giant, rather than rely on current practices. Employees had to cope with changes in structure, staffing, and systems. Going with the tried-and-true Pfizer ways or even adopting incremental changes would have been easier to manage but unlikely to propel growth in the way transformation could.

Transition as a Way of Life

At a recent workshop on workplace recovery after transition attended by managers from major corporations, I asked participants to introduce themselves and indicate why they had come. "I'm from Sears," offered the first woman, "and we've had five restructurings in five years." Almost as if to one-up her, the next participant reported, "I'm from Verizon by way of Nynex, and we've had nine restructurings in four years. "Well," said the next, "I'm from Citicorp, and I've had seven bosses in three years."

Increasingly, people in organizations are being exposed to multiple waves of transition, often with one overlapping another. Take the case of Majestic Enterprises (a fictionalized name but a real situation). At its peak in the mid-1990s, Majestic boasted revenues of $19 billion, employed twenty-two thousand people, and had a reputation as a stable, well-managed company. It was also regarded as an excellent place to work. People took jobs there because they wanted a place of employment with stability, predictability, and growth. The typical Majestic employee had long tenure, high loyalty, and expectations of lifelong employment.

In 1995, Majestic made an opportunistic acquisition of a competitor's operations. In announcing the acquisition to employees, Majestic CEO Justin Jourdan acknowledged that there would be some redundancy in positions but promised to take care of this through attrition, assuring his troops that there would be no layoffs. As tough economic times set in toward the end of the decade, however, Majestic's debt obligation loomed larger and larger. Revenues remained flat, expenses increased, and margins eroded. Within three years, Jourdan ordered two major restructurings, the first to streamline decision making in general and the second to eliminate bureaucratic hurdles slowing the introduction of new products to market.

The restructurings changed the organization's design and reporting relationships but produced few cost savings. Still confronting debt and flat growth, the company had to cut expenses dramatically. In 2000, Jourdan announced the first reduction-in-force program in Majestic's history. It was voluntary, providing enhanced early retirement benefits for employees over age fifty-five and severance pay incentives for all other employees. Despite its voluntary nature, the program sent shock waves through the ranks of Majestic managers and employees.

A few months after the reduction-in-force announcement, Jourdan proclaimed a new vision for Majestic: it would become the "premier" company in its industry segment. Soon Jourdan initiated two projects to achieve this vision. First, he engaged McKinsey & Company to conduct a value-added work analysis. Shortly thereafter, Jourdan returned from a conference on organizational learning to announce that he had commissioned a training company to deliver a "continuous improvement process" program to all Majestic managers.

As the economy weakened in late 2000 and into 2001, Majestic managed a small operating profit but could not reduce its heavy debt load. The broader economic malaise diminished long-term prospects for revenue growth, and Jourdan concluded that severe cost cutting was necessary for his company's survival. In June 2001, he announced that Majestic would have to implement an involuntary downsizing program.

The Mind-Set of Employees

The 1995 acquisition was a turning point in the stable psychological work contract between Majestic and its employees. The merger and two subsequent restructurings in the late 1990s produced more change and disruption than Majestic employees had ever experienced or bargained for. After three major reorganizations in four years, employees were worn out from the scope and pace of change in the company. Because Jourdan had promised there would be no layoffs after the 1995 acquisition, employees felt he had betrayed them when he announced the 2000 reduction-in-force program. Even though the layoffs were voluntary, employee perceptions of management credibility hit rock bottom.

Jourdan's premier-company initiatives were intended to pump up employee morale and organizational effectiveness, but they backfired. The successive introduction of *premier company, value-added work analysis,* and *continuous improvement* into the corporate lexicon confused employees. Cynicism grew. Employees began to look out for management's "flavor of the month." They strongly criticized leadership for bringing in consultants and programs that produced little in the way of meaningful or beneficial change. The McKinsey value-added work analysis lingered on and on, but no apparent changes were made. Managers went through a weeklong continuous improvement process training, but once they were back in their work areas, they were never pressed to use what they had learned. "We didn't walk the talk," confessed one senior vice president, referring to leadership's failure to reinforce words with actions.

The most dramatic influence on the mind-set of Majestic employees was the 2001 involuntary downsizing. The program hit workers hard. They were stunned that their leaders would betray them with such a clear break in the historic ties between employer and employee.

Recovery After Transition

The Majestic case highlights how organizational transitions produce inadvertent effects. Like thousands of other companies, Majestic must focus its energies on enhancing business processes, organizational effectiveness, and employee productivity to meet ongoing competitive pressures. This implies more transition, but first the organization and its people must recover from their history of past, poorly managed transitions. Recovery entails addressing both the emotional realities and the business imperatives associated with re-grouping after a transition or a series of transitions.

Workplace recovery focuses on those who remain with the firm:

- Recovery recognizes the need to drive business success by minimizing the unintended effects of transition, gearing people up for their new roles and responsibilities, and renew-ing motivation for making a run at business challenges and opportunities.

- Recovery happens when all members of an organization have a shared sense of the direction in which they are headed and are tolerant of the pain involved in getting from the old way of doing things to the new.

- Recovery involves managers in helping their work team mem-bers rebound from the psychological trauma of transition, clarify new work roles and responsibilities, and secure the organizational capability and individual motivation needed for success.

- Recovery engages people in understanding how and why their workplace is changing and how and where they can exert control during and after the transition. It also helps them let go of frustrations and anger over things beyond their control.

These benefits revive organizations and their people by instill-ing new life and energy after the disruptiveness of transition. Re-covery prepares people to contribute to new economic opportunities through positive changes in perceptions, practices, policies, and processes. When aligned, these changes resuscitate individual em-ployee spirit, work team performance, and organizational results. The objective of workplace recovery is not merely to recuperate fol-lowing a merger, acquisition, downsizing, or other major transition but to rebound with a workforce that has an enhanced capacity to operate competitively.

Already in the twenty-first century, we have seen that organizational efforts to achieve, maintain, or enhance competitiveness have been affected by the availability of a well-trained and highly motivated workforce. Thus workplace recovery also sends a message to prospective new hires as well as to survivors of the merger, downsizing, or restructuring. How a firm handles the aftermath of a mismanaged transition directly influences perceptions of its culture, its leadership, and ultimately, its reputation as an employer.

Difficult Events to Manage

To be fair, mergers, acquisitions, and downsizings are very difficult events to manage. If they were easy to manage, 75 percent of all corporate combinations would not fail! To understand why the track record is so dismal, look at how these events transpire, in both practical and emotional terms.

Mergers and Acquisitions: Wired for Mismanagement

The very manner in which mergers and acquisitions are conceived runs counter to rules of effective leadership and management. When you think of an effective leader, what comes to mind? I think of someone with an inspiring *vision*, who *communicates* well, dedicates *resources* to achieving it, and coordinates competing individual perspectives into *teamwork* and *planning*. The fact is, none of these qualities are seen in any abundance in a merger or acquisition.

Inadequate Vision. Many mergers are done strictly for cost-cutting reasons, as when two underused hospitals in a community combine or when financial institutions join forces and eliminate redundant back-office functions. Often mergers and acquisitions are reactive events in which executives hop on the bandwagon in response to a major change in their industry, rather than proactive events intended to propel an organization toward its goals. The oil industry is one of many in which an initial major combination—British Petroleum's careful and strategic acquisition of Amoco—triggered multiple "copycat" combinations (including Exxon-Mobil, Chevron-Texaco, and Conoco-Phillips). And many mergers are done for reasons that have nothing to do with corporate strategy. An FTC survey of Wall Street bankers cited CEO ego as the number one reason driving merger and acquisition activity in the United States. Ego is not necessarily bad for doing a deal—you need a big ego to put big companies like AOL and Time Warner together or even to take a small firm and propel it to a larger size in one fell swoop. But cost cutting, bandwagoning, and ego satisfying are not sufficient for giving employees a compelling rationale for why they should sacrifice in the short run for hoped-for organizational enhancements in the long run. Successful combinations, by contrast, are driven by a sound strategy—a rationale for doing the deal that inspires people, provides a blueprint for integration planning and implementation, and counters the personal politicking that colors all combinations.

Inadequate Communication. Mergers and acquisitions are shrouded in secrecy. Executives putting a deal together have to keep a very tight lid on their intentions, for both competitive and legal reasons. If executives expressed their intention to purchase a company, another party might make a preemptive bid for the target and drive the price up. In any event, the government does not want executives announcing their interest in acquiring publicly traded firms too early, otherwise we would go out and purchase stock in the target. Of necessity, deals have to be done on a need-to-know only basis.

Inadequate Resources. Despite the 75 percent failure rate, many executives deny the difficulty of combining two previously independent firms into one entity. I know this because I regularly get calls from human resource executives who ask, "How can I convey to my CEO that he is underestimating the work of combining companies?" The reality is that lawyers and investment bankers surround the

CEO as a deal is being conceptualized. These advisers stand to make millions of dollars in fees if the deal goes through, so they whisper sweet thoughts of potential synergies in the CEO's ear. There are no human resource people and no consultants like myself at the table to alert the CEO to the fact that employee distraction from performance and culture clash are likely to interfere with achieving the hypothesized costs savings. And there are no operations managers, specialists in their areas, who can more realistically test the likelihood of achieving synergies than financial generalists. In most companies today, the word comes down that the CEO wants to get the deal done, momentum builds for going forward at any cost, and due diligence—a process that is supposed to alert the lead company to the potential pitfalls of a target—becomes anything but diligent.

Inadequate Teamwork. Mergers and acquisitions require coordination and cooperation across combining partners. Yet my research with organizational psychologist Philip Mirvis shows that individuals adopt very political behaviors in the hope of exercising control over an uncertain situation and protecting their positions, perks, projects, and perhaps people. They are not looking for the greater good—opportunities to build a postcombination organization that is more than the sum of its parts. Rather, they hold on tightly to the behaviors and attitudes that got them where they are. They go with what—and who—they know rather than reach out to the partner in an effort to realize efficiencies or enhanced ways of doing things. On an organizational level, culture clash rears up as employees notice differences in how the partners go about their work. Many CEOs deny culture clash going into a merger (Sandy Weill of Travelers and John Reed of Citibank are prime examples—when they announced their merger, they literally said there would be no culture clash; a year later, when they were interviewed for a *Business Week* cover story, they cited culture clash a half dozen times, and shortly thereafter, Reed was ousted in a boardroom battle). Research conducted at the London Business School, however, reveals that with 20/20 hindsight, CEOs report that culture clash is the biggest hindrance to achieving the financial and strategic objectives of a merger or acquisition.

Inadequate Planning. One of the oddities of mergers and acquisitions is that executives purchase companies *before* they know what they are going to do with them. For employees, it defies common sense that the buyer just paid millions or billions of dollars for their firm but has no plan for integrating it. They assume that there is a plan sitting on the CEO's desk but that the CEO is just not communicating it. Now, if you think about it dispassionately, it makes good sense that companies study what they have acquired before making integration decisions. Still, employees just assume they are receiving the classic "mushroom treatment"—being kept in the dark, fed manure, and ultimately canned.

Downsizing: The Detested Task

Firing people is one of the most difficult actions any manager has to take. It is tough enough to do when someone is let go for performance issues, so imagine how much more difficult it is when a manager has to lay people off for reasons other than their personal performance on the job. No matter which euphemism is used— reductions in force, rationalization, rightsizing, downsizing—no one likes to lay people off (except maybe for the infamous "Chainsaw" Al Dunlap, but he got his just desserts!).

We have learned a lot about how to downsize "correctly" following the first round of mass reductions in force in the 1990s. For example, we know it is better to make the cuts in as few as possible waves, rather than several small layoffs, so that surviving employees do not become zombies on the job in fear of the next swoop of the ax. Still, downsizing remains an unsavory event for even the most hardened of executives to manage, and the norms that predominate in most downsizing organizations run counter to effectively managing the reduction:

Sense of Urgency. Like gulping down bad-tasting medicine, the assumption in many organizations is that doing the cuts quickly is better than doing them carefully. "Announce the cuts and get back to work" is how one middle manager in a high-technology company was instructed to lead a downsizing in his department. That would be nice, but it isn't realistic. People in a downsizing are not like medicine—they are not "fast-acting." Instead, managers benefit from time to plan how they are going to make the cuts, how they will inform the survivors and the victims, and how they are going to get work done with fewer resources. And surviving employees need time to mourn the loss of coworkers, come to terms with what it means to work in an organization that lets people go even if they perform well, and ponder the long-term implications for their own job security and career advancement.

Fear of Violence. When managers learn that they have to lay people off, their thoughts immediately turn to fears of violent reactions by those affected. Although workplace shootings following downsizings are highly publicized, they are very rare. Whereas over one million people were laid off in 2001, the number of plant or office shootings can be counted on one hand. Obviously, the actual infrequency of violence does not justify the fear. Still, no one wants to be the exceptional case, and work team leaders distract themselves from managing the downsizing well by obsessing about what might happen.

Stigma of Failure. Even though downsizing is well ingrained in the managerial repertoire, it remains a stigma. When people hear that a company is cutting jobs, the assumption is that it is in dire financial straits. No one likes to boast that one's firm is downsizing or to mention at cocktail parties what a prudent move it is to eliminate unnecessary costs or get the company back on the road to success. This stigma prompts leaders to downplay the event, minimize communication and act like little or nothing is happening rather than communicate openly and fully about the event, its purpose, and its implications for going forward. "It was like they were talking about a child in a mental institution," recalled a department head in a downsized financial services firm. "'Don't talk too much about it, and people won't think about it' was the tone set by our senior team. Ha! It was the *only* thing people were talking about for weeks in our office." Contrast this with the comments of a business unit leader in a consumer products firm that also downsized: "We knew that people were going to linger around the water cooler and talk about the downsizing, so we tried to get ahead of the curve and give people some communications that conveyed why downsizing was a necessary step and how it would help get our company turned around. We didn't deny the painfulness of having to lay off good contributors, but we also made sure that our people knew that there was some upside for the majority of us who remained."

The Need to Recover After Transition

Some skeptics might ask why it is necessary to help organizations and their members recover from transition. These individuals either have not experienced the human pain and organizational inefficiencies that accompany mergers, acquisitions, and downsizings or have refused to acknowledge these inevitable side effects. These skeptics might question the need to attend to recovery in the following ways.

It's a lousy economy out there; aren't people glad to have a job? People certainly appreciate steady employment during difficult times. But employment that merely provides for security needs is not enough for intelligent, sophisticated workers, who want psychological along with financial rewards. The real question to ask is this: Once the economy recovers, will the best and brightest people be psychologically committed to realizing an organization's new business opportunities, or will they defect to another team?

But if these people jump ship, are there others waiting in line for their jobs? Studies show that even short periods of unemployment produce drastic changes in how executives view themselves and the world around them. Most regain their self-esteem soon after they find new jobs, but their alienation and cynicism about employers in general remain. An organization needs people's hearts and minds, not just their bones and muscle, to pull away from the pack and capitalize on emerging business opportunities. Organizations looking for human resources from the outside will not find a talent pool immune from organizational MADness. New hires will bring their baggage from mismanaged transitions with them. Leaders cannot escape the job of healing the psychological wounds caused by mismanaged transitions, generating excitement about the current organization, and recommitting people to organizational goals.

People are being coached to be free agent managers, aren't they? Articles in the popular press in recent years have been instructing individuals to be "free agent" employees, selling their services to the highest bidders. This is a sound strategy in the new economy, but most people don't value jumping from company to company. Sure, some will walk out the door for more money. Most people, however, resonate with stability. They want job security and opportunities for personal expression in exchange for a fair day's work. They also prefer working at a place where they feel they are being treated fairly, communicated with, and contributing to the attainment of a clear and inspiring vision. Even Generation Xers, the workers most known for job hunting, are not as footloose in the employment market as they are reputed to be. A study conducted in late 2000, *before* the economic downturn that made job searching harder for all age groups, found that nearly half of professionals aged twenty-six to thirty-seven would be very happy to spend the rest of their careers with their current companies.

People are resilient, aren't they? Yes, people are resilient; they can bounce back from debilitating circumstances to become productive. The extent and speed of bouncing back, however, can be influenced. An internal study at Honeywell found that, on average, employees spent two hours per day distracted from work obsessing over how they would be affected by a transition. Imagine how much time and money would be saved if that could be reduced to one hour per day per employee! Why wait months or years for a workforce to recover from a transition when it could take only weeks or months?

Don't people want to look to the future rather than dwell on the past? Psychological research is clear that people must first actively end the old before they can accept the new. Firms that engage in workplace recovery accelerate the rate at which employees both let go of outmoded perceptions, expectations, and behaviors and embrace new ones; those that don't end up retaining people who are bitterly holding on to the past.

Haven't people always dealt with change and transition in organizations? Change has been around as long as there have been work organizations. But prior to the organizational MADness that began in the 1980s, the relatively relaxed pace of organizational life in general—and of change in particular—provided a conducive setting for gradual adaptation to change. Employees could deal with the effects of coping with changes without significantly burdening organizational results. Steady increases in consumption during the 1950s, 1960s, and 1970s meant that practically all a company had to do to see revenues grow was put an "open for business" sign in the window. Distractions from productivity and profitability occurred but were offset by the momentum of increasing revenues. Moreover, the wide spacing between waves of transition ensured that people could regain their footing and composure before being upended by another swell.

Even the types of changes people had to confront were different. People faced modifications in aspects of their working life, not radical makeovers of the entire approach to doing their jobs. A clerk may have had to deal with incremental changes when word processors replaced typewriters or when the deductible rates for the company health care plan were adjusted. Today the clerk has to contend with such discontinuous transformational changes as re-engineering workflow processes or reformulating the psychological relationship between employer and employee. Yesterday's changes in specific pieces of the work situation left a mostly stable and secure foundation upon which to move forward. Today, whole worlds break up as a company is acquired and downsized and then a portion of it is spun off, only to be acquired and downsized again as it is integrated in the new owner's firm. The result is a dizzying and disarming specter of change with which to deal—a frequency and intensity of transition that overwhelms people's ability to cope and adapt. Especially when the transitions have been mismanaged by unclear visions, faulty communications, unfulfilled promises, and politics-plagued decision-making processes, people respond by holding on to the known—the tried-and-true practices that helped in the past but may not be appropriate for where leadership wants to take the organization.

Recovery

Let me be clear that I am not putting down executives for mismanaging organizational transitions. As noted, these are very tricky events to manage—the cards are stacked against executing them well. The time has come, however, to own up to this fact and pronounce how difficult they are to manage—along with acknowledging the unintended consequences of transition mismanagement—and raise up the work of workplace recovery.

When I tested the title and subtitle of this book with a few colleagues, I got some unenthusiastic feedback regarding the use of the word *recovery*. "It's so negative, people will think you are talking about recovery from drug addiction or alcohol abuse," warned one senior executive from a retail firm. "You should find a word that is more energizing," suggested a prominent consultant. But a couple of experiences in my personal life showed me that this was indeed the appropriate word to describe what organizations and their people need to do to rebound, revitalize, or, dare I say it, recover from a mismanaged transition. On my way to a weekly softball game, I picked up a teammate. Although San Francisco is a wonderful city to live in, driving a car there is made more onerous by the paucity of parking spaces. We had good "parking karma" that day, as we happened upon a spot right in front of the softball field. In my eagerness to parallel park, I cut the wheel too sharply, and my tire hit the curb well before I was in the space. I shifted the transmission into drive, cut the wheel sharply, moved forward a bit, and then backed up again—this time slipping smoothly into the spot. "Good recovery," said my teammate. Then, during the game, a line drive was hit to my position in the outfield. I raced toward the ball, but it hit my glove and fell to the ground. The batter tried to take advantage of this error by stretching his single into a double. Instinctively, I picked up the ball and threw out the opposing player as he ran from first base to second, to make the third and final out of the inning. My coach greeted me as I entered the dugout with a hearty "Good recovery!"

Recovery is not bad. Recovery is essential when life is less than perfect. The dictionary says to recover means "to get back." I got my car back into alignment to fit into the parking space. I got back the out I missed when I dropped the ball. Eventually my objectives were met, but I had to recover from my inadvertent miscues. That is exactly what organizations and their people need to do following the difficulty of mergers, acquisitions, and downsizings. Organizations have to get back to attaining their strategic focus, teams have to get back to working effectively, and individuals have to get back to realizing that they can grow and succeed along with their employers. Among the synonyms of recovery are upturn and resurgence. With the bleakest days of the economic recession behind us, organizations and their people have an opportunity for an upturn— to realize great profits, tremendous breakthroughs, and a return to meaningfulness in the workplace. The potential exists for a resurgence in organizational and personal development. But realistically, organizations and their people first need to recover from the unintended consequences of poorly planned and inadequately implemented mergers, acquisitions, and downsizings before they can experience an upturn or resurgence. Employees need help in letting go of their emotional and practical baggage before they can freely charge up the hill to capture the prize.

2

Unintended Consequences of Business Transitions

At the annual party celebrating the conclusion of our softball season, I offered to get my teammate Philip a beer while I was at the bar. "No, thanks," came his reply. "My doctor ordered me off all alcohol until he does some tests on my liver." Surprised at this response from a seemingly healthy man in his late twenties, I asked Philip what was going on. He began to tell me about his job in the accounting department of a medium-sized high-tech firm in Silicon Valley:

> The stress on my job has been unbearable. We've had a hiring freeze for over a year now. Only a few people are left in our department, and management expects us to pick up the slack. It's not the additional work that I mind; it's the intense pressure to get things done. There is no room for slippage. Everybody wants their reports done first, and if we mess up in even the slightest way, we get screamed at. We live in fear of being laid off; every day there are rumors that there are going to be another round of firings. And no one is helping me prioritize my work or the work I'm doing that used to be done by others. I don't have a problem with pitching in during tough times, but I don't think management understands what they are putting us through and how tense and stressful things are in our department.

Matthew, a thirty-one-year-old marketing executive, sacrificed his love of music to study engineering in college. To make himself even more employable, he earned a master's degree in marketing. Since then, he has found himself bobbing on a stormy sea of corporate restructuring:

I lost my first job in Kentucky at a local telecommunications company when a huge firm acquired it in 1997 and my position became redundant. About two months later, I found a job developing and marketing new products in Ohio. I moved our family to Dayton and fell in love with the city and the company. I felt I could spend my whole career there. I received two promotions and a series of excellent reviews. Then the company restructured and I was out of a job. After about six months, I heard of a company in Pennsylvania looking for marketing and product development skills. That job lasted nearly two years until the company was acquired. I landed my next job in the same city and was as enthusiastic and confident as I was in my first job out of college. The company was new-product- and marketing-driven—my specialties. The job lasted seven months until the recession hit the company's sales. I've lost four jobs in five years, despite personally performing very well. The American dream just isn't coming to me. My dream isn't to do better than my parents— it's to have security and build self-esteem for my family and myself.

On a trip to New York City, I visited former clients at a professional services firm that had acquired a similar-sized competitor two years earlier and recently had gone through a downsizing to "rationalize" staffing levels. By all accounts, the merger went swimmingly; it was touted in the business press as a rare successful combination in a business plagued by big egos. While visiting, I ran into Koreen, the head of the administrative services group, and asked her how she was doing:

We have just gone through a small downsizing; about four of our thirty administrative people were let go. But I have been going nonstop ever since the cuts. I feel like I am treading water and juggling balls at the same time. I haven't taken a lunch break in four days. I don't mind the hard work, but I don't see any relief in sight. I don't know how much longer I can go on before something gives—either me or the work.

Physical illness and disease, emotional despair and alienation, intellectual stagnation, and the acceptance that running harder only results in falling further behind—these are the experiences of the survivors of organizational transitions, the people who retain their jobs following mergers, acquisitions, and downsizings. It is on the minds and muscles of these survivors that a firm's future depends. These distressed and depressed employees are expected to help their organization triumph over difficult times brought on by economic recession, a loss of market share or profitability, a brush with bankruptcy, or a wrenching corporate transformation.

Organizational recovery cannot occur without the concurrent recovery of the people who constitute the organization, and vice versa: individual recovery cannot occur outside a context of sound strategy, prudent financial management, effective structure, and efficient and high-quality work processes. Yet executive attention must expand beyond strategic planning, research and development, and financial engineering to the human side of recovery. As has been said for many years now, a human problem requires a human solution. And the impact of transitions has clearly resulted in a human problem for organizations and their leaders.

Unintended Human Consequences

In principle, a transition should enable an organization to improve its competitiveness without impairing its ability to execute its strategy. In practice, however, a transition can exact a heavy toll on organizational effectiveness and employee well-being.

Wrenching Experience for All Involved

A transition that involves the displacement of people is a wrench-ing experience for all involved, and the norm in most organizations is to get it over with as quickly and quietly as possible. Even the toughest, most bottom-line-oriented executives find it difficult to make cuts. It is one thing to speak abstractly of the need to reduce costs and quite another to make decisions that affect people's lives. Intellectually, senior executives may rationalize that a reduction in force is necessary to regain or sustain profitability. Emotionally, however, they dread making the cuts. Few CEOs themselves actu-ally let senior staff members go, instead passing the burden on to subordinates.

Middle managers truly are middle managers—managers caught in the middle between the conflicting agendas, perspectives, and demands of those at the top and bottom of the organization. Top-level executives seem distant and remote, talking about strategy, financing, and other matters less tangible than middle managers' needs to get products or services to customers. Meanwhile, lower-level employees are looking for concrete direction and definitive answers to their questions, but middle managers have neither the direction nor answers to give.

The people who study corporate communications tell us that managers and supervisors have the most impact on employee reac-tions to a transition. Certainly, the senior executive must do a road show and press the flesh with employees. And human resources and corporate communications professions make a significant contribu-tion. But employees want to hear about transition from their imme-diate superiors, the people they know how to read and trust most in the organization. Yet managers and supervisors are poorly prepared for their role in contributing to transition success. When an orga-nization offers a voluntary approach to downsizing, for example, managers and supervisors find themselves in the awkward position of counseling employees on whether to stay or go. No one wants to tell an employee that his or her services are no longer needed, even if it is the most humane thing to do when a subsequent wave of involuntary cuts looms on the horizon. This is especially difficult for managers in large organizations engaged in multiple waves of downsizing. The obvious low performers have already been removed, leaving only good contributors who have to be shown the door.

After the cuts are made, work team leaders have to accomplish more with fewer resources. Supervisors and managers struggle to maintain productivity with fewer bodies, and those who survive are likely to be emotionally distraught from the loss of coworkers and distracted by worrying about their own fate. Lip service may have been given to how the downsizing will result in a leaner, meaner, smarter, and generally better organization. But now no one has time to think of smarter or better ways of doing things.

Support staff find themselves overwhelmed by the multiple demands placed on them during a transition. Human resource professionals are staggered by the workload involved in processing terminations and scheduling outplacement activities, preoccupied by knowing that their own department—a non-revenue-producing staff function—is likely to be one of the hardest hit and burdened by the line of employees waiting outside their door looking for information or just a shoulder to cry on.

Finally, a transition threatens the self-esteem and sense of fairness of all employees. People can rationalize layoffs based on performance issues, say, when an employee is repeatedly late to work or fails to meet production standards. But people cannot rationalize the fact that fellow employees who seem to be as hardworking as they are have lost their jobs because of an economic downturn or because they were unlucky enough to be in a redundant position in a merger. Downsizing victims blame themselves for not seeing it coming or not doing something to protect themselves. For victims and survivors, a reduction in force erodes perceptions of fairness in the workplace as they wonder why leadership did not stave off the dreaded event through some alternative course of action. Survivors see the human carnage of lost jobs and destroyed careers and wonder, "How could an organization I chose to work at do this to people?"

Some executives like to believe that downsizing survivors, grateful just to have a job, are ready to roll up their sleeves and get down to work. The real consequences, however, are very different. Survivors of mergers, acquisitions, downsizings, and other transitions experience a broad range of psychological and behavioral reactions that begin with rumors of impending change, continue through the weeks and months of transition planning and implementation, and linger long after the dust settles. These reactions have a lasting impact on employees' perceptions of the current organization and expectations for its future. Workplace recovery begins with *accepting* that there is unintended human and organizational fallout from transition, *understanding* these consequences, and *acting* as proactively as possible to rebound from them.

Psychological Reactions to Transition

Among the unintended consequences of organizational transitions are adverse psychological reactions.

Survivor Syndrome. Symptoms of the "transition survivor syndrome" have been well documented during the years of organizational MADness. Often people feel guilty for having been spared, similar to the psychological reaction of children who lose a playmate or sibling in a fatal accident. The survivor responds to the tragedy with extreme guilt and asks, "Why couldn't it have been me?" Survivors may also become depressed at their inability to avert future layoffs or disruptions to their work routine. In the short run, they become distracted from their work responsibilities. Over the long haul, employees who have been through a transition feel considerably less commitment to their employers.

Loss of Confidence in Management. One of the most enduring symptoms of transition survivor syndrome is the erosion of employee confidence in management. Several factors contribute to this. First, many employees wonder why their leaders did not take proactive steps to prevent layoffs or avoid the ugliness of postmerger culture clashes. Second, employees do not see how transitions have added any value to the workplace. Survey after survey shows that about three-quarters of all employees who remain on the job following a transition do not regard the revamped company as a better place to work and do feel less secure about their future with the firm. Third, and especially when they see no true organizational enhancements resulting from a transition, many employees conclude that their management is motivated by greed rather than by concern for customers or employees.

The irony here is that mergers, acquisitions, and downsizings can be productive tools to enhance organizational effectiveness and profitability and, as a result, job security and quality of work life. The way transitions are implemented and managed, however, often destroys workers' regard and respect for their organizations and leaders. In one national survey, nearly three-quarters of employees whose companies were *not* involved in a merger or layoff in the past year reported being confident in the long-term future of the company. In contrast, only about one-half of employees whose firms had been involved in a merger or layoff were confident about their company's future.

Cynicism and Distrust. People do not mind enduring some pain if they see a payoff for it, but this has not been the case in most mergers or downsizings. Promises that nothing will change during the transition and that effectiveness following it will be enhanced are rarely fulfilled. In many organizations, people see few benefits—for themselves or the business—resulting from the ordeal. Mismanaged transitions have contributed to employees' growing cynicism regarding executives and regarding opportunities to succeed in companies. In mergers, employees see senior executives who leave the company land on their feet thanks to generous golden parachutes and see top executives who stay offered lucrative employment contracts. In downsizings, employees in the middle and lower ranks rarely see any evidence that their pain is being shared by the people at the top.

Also contributing to employee cynicism and distrust is the specter of corporate accounting abuses.

Decreased Morale. An American Management Association survey on downsizing found that 77 percent of reporting companies experienced a decline in morale after a downsizing. Not surprisingly, the more frequently a company downsized, the worse the consequences. Yet 91 percent of chief executive officers believe that morale in their companies is just fine. Survivors are angry, both at themselves for not seeing trouble before it arrived and at their leaders for exposing people to such stressful treatment. They hurt because the sight of coworkers being dismissed is painful; so is the realization that a merger or reorganization might derail one's own career. And they are frustrated because their ability to get the job done is hampered by the confusion of the posttransition organization and because they see few signs that things are going to get better soon.

Reduced Loyalty. During transitions that involve a reduction in force, organizations often inadvertently hurt most the employees they least wish to alienate: those who are very loyal to the organization at the outset. Most people who join organizations need to feel that they are a part of and contributing to a larger collective. One outgrowth of people's need for group membership is that they expect and want to be treated fairly by the groups to which they belong. Research conducted by a Columbia University team suggests that if loyal employees believe that layoffs were unfair, their loyalty drops sharply, even more than that of survivors who are less committed at the start.

Dismal Outlook. Even for survivors who breathe a momentary sigh of relief for having retained a job, dismal signs predominate in the posttransition organization. Survivors feel sad about the past and anxious about the future. People miss their former mentors, coworkers, and other colleagues who may have exited in a downsizing. They also miss their former political connections to the powerful decision makers in the organization.

When they set their sights on the future, survivors become further dismayed. All signals point to fewer opportunities for advancement when restructurings eliminate traditional career paths and mergers bring in more competitors for fewer shots at reaching the higher rungs of the corporate ladder. People even see themselves having to work harder just to stay in the same place. And there is less fun on the job. The rhetoric of cost reductions puts a damper on the informal perks and playfulness that many people enjoy at work.

Loss of Control. What really scares survivors is the sense that they have lost control over their work lives. No matter how well they do their jobs, they could be hit in the next wave of layoffs. The rapid pace of change in today's business world means that one's position, pet project, or potential for advancement could be eliminated at a moment's notice, with nothing the individual can do about it. A middle-level manager from an acquired consumer products company exemplified the control issue during an interview a year after the merger announcement:

> I used to think that if I did my job well, completed my projects on time and in fine manner, I would be able to control my fate. That's no longer true. This merger is bigger than I am. I've seen other managers from our side—people who clearly were good, if not excellent, performers—get the shaft. I didn't ask to be acquired, but now my track record doesn't count for anything. I'm at the mercy of some bureaucrat at headquarters. I'm no longer the master of my own fate.

Although senior executives have the most at stake in a transition in terms of position, power, pay, and perks, they also have the most control over their situation. They design the combinations, fight the takeover battles, conceive the restructurings, anticipate the downsizings, and arrange for their personal financial security. Other employees cannot exert control over whether their workplace is being merged, downsized, rightsized, or restructured, and their sense of lost mastery over their fate extends well into the posttransition period.

Further eroding survivors' sense of control is the lack of clear direction and coordination in the months following the transition. Survivors want to get out of the blocks quickly and impress their new leaders. But their intentions are thwarted when they do not know what the business priorities are or where to turn for the equipment, information, or support they need.

Many top performers feel that the only way they can take control and salvage their careers is to walk away from their current employer. A research chemist who had just gone through a major restructuring was clear on her plans: "What is hard work going to get me here? All I've been hearing from this organization is that hard work is going to help me keep my job. Well, that is not good enough for me. I was raised in a time when good work was rewarded with an occasional promotion. There was a career path. Now with this restructuring, there is nowhere to go. Why should I stay here?" Another manager, from a financial services firm, had his plan set for taking back control: "Senior management must think they have us by the balls right now because the job market in banking is so poor. But I can tell you this, at the sight of the first ray of light of an upturn in the economy, I'm walking out of here and not turning back."

When remaining employees see the best and brightest performers jumping ship, it reinforces negative feelings, cynical attitudes, and dismal views for the future. And importantly, it is these highly skilled and creative individuals that an organization must hold on to to recover effectively from a transition.

Changing Psychological Work Contract. Long-term employees come to believe that there is more to their job than the money they make, just as a spouse might think there is more to a marriage than the obligation of financial support. This psychological contract commits both sides to maintaining the relationship, with the employees supplying loyalty and the company supplying steady employment.

Even though there was never any formal contract between employer and employee, there developed an implied psychological work contract that if you work hard, if you are skilled, and if you are devoted, you can expect decent pay, good benefits, steady employment, and an occasional promotion. In the era of organizational MADness, the psychological contract between employer and employee now contains more caveats: if the company remains profitable, if it does not get acquired, if the overall economy does not get too bad, if the marketplace does not change, and if technology does not progress. In other words, there are no guarantees.

The old psychological work contract, spelling out a paternalistic relationship between employer and employee, has evolved into a new one stressing self-sufficiency. As long as both sides consent, there is no problem in changing the rules of the game. Employers seemed to be ahead of employees, however, in recognizing that the contract was changing. To their credit, some organizations attempted to convey to employees through communications programs and workshops that their psychological bond had changed. But it was not until employees learned the hard way—through the merger mania of the 1980s and rightsizing rage of the 1990s—that they found out just how the rules had changed.

Behavioral Reactions to Transition

Mergers, acquisitions, and downsizings also have unintended behavioral consequences in the workplace.

Working Harder, Not Smarter. Employees in a posttransition organization often liken their situation to that of a chicken with its head cut off—frantically moving about without any sense of direction or hope for survival. Or they talk about struggling to keep their heads above water: they know what they have to do, but they are weighed down by the burden of a heavy workload with competing demands. Others, meanwhile, keep their heads in the sand like ostriches, hoping that the winds of change will blow by them.

The workload doesn't gets smaller when the workforce does. Survivors who return to work following cuts face the dismal prospect of being part of the 80 percent of the people who now have to do 100 percent of the work. All the surviving employees are working harder than before but feeling as though they are accomplishing less. Inevitably, certain tasks start falling by the wayside.

What about the promise of enhanced organizational effectiveness that accompanies the announcements of many organizational transitions? The reality is that no one has time to stop and think of creative ways to approach work. There are demands on employees from all directions—superiors, peers, and subordinates—that increase the pressure on transition survivors. "Everybody here is so worried about looking good and wants their work to take top priority," reported a staff analyst in a computer company. "My boss says to ask my internal customers if what they need in a week can instead be delivered in ten days. But I'm afraid to do that—it may cost me by being labeled as someone who can't cut it around here."

Lack of Direction. Compounding the sheer volume of work confronting people who survive a transition is a lack of direction in prioritizing which tasks to tackle first. After the merger of two health maintenance organizations, the leadership was indecisive regarding the relative merits of either aggressively pursuing growth in the membership rolls or conservatively maintaining levels of profitability. Middle managers were paralyzed by this lack of direction, waiting to see in which direction they should lead their groups. The director of operations expressed the frustration: "Does senior management want us to go out and get members, or do they want us to protect the margins? Either way is fine with me, but someone has got to let me know which way we are going. I do not want to build an organization that is headed one way and then get chastised because I was supposed to go the other way."

Risk Avoidance. Why wouldn't the operations manager and his peers just step up and make a decision on their own? Because risk taking plummets following a transition. Employees are so scared that they pressure themselves not to make waves or take risks, just at the time when innovation is needed. Further cuts may be in the offing, and no one wants a blemish on their record that might be used against them when the next list of victims gets drawn up. Instead, managers and employees go with what they know, relying on what has worked for them in the past. The problem is that what may have worked in the past is not necessarily appropriate for the posttransition organization.

Political Behavior. Politicking increases sharply in organizations following a transition. One way people shore up their sense of control is to lobby for themselves. Employees spend time promoting their value to executives and managers, as well as reminding them of any outstanding favors that may be owed. They network with friends and associates from outside the organization—a distraction from getting their work done but an important protective action to take in the event of future layoffs. Coworker relations may become strained as individuals explicitly or implicitly put down their colleagues in efforts to make themselves look better in the eyes of superiors.

Politics also prevails at the group level as work teams look out for number one. Managers erect barriers between teams, focusing on unit results rather than the big picture: in the short run, what is best for the team takes precedence over what is best for the overall organization.

Role Ambiguity. A constant problem interfering with organizational effectiveness in the posttransition organization is role ambiguity. Survivors wonder who is responsible for what and where decision-making authority lies. A lot of time is spent figuring how to prioritize work and how to operate in an environment in which direction is not forthcoming. This is especially frustrating for achievement-oriented people who want to start building a good track record in the posttransition environment. They hope to make a positive first impression on new superiors, peers, and subordinates, yet they do not always know who to go to or work with to get the job done right and on time. Ironically, these forward-looking individuals, eager to get on with things, are stymied by the confusion of the posttransition world.

Withdrawal. These psychological and behavioral reactions to transition have prompted many employees to withdraw their personal and professional energy from their jobs while making it look like they are still doing business as usual. People's bodies show up at work, but not their hearts and souls. As executives exhort their employees to boost productivity, improve quality, and be more globally competitive, more workers are simply responding with a shrug.

Stress and Performance

Stress is a necessary and life-sustaining function. Consider a caveman walking with a club dangling over his shoulder. He sees a saber-tooth tiger across the field. By nature, the caveman is thrust into a stress reaction with the singular objective of identifying the threat and eliminating it through either fight or flight. Chemicals produced in his body prompt physiological reactions, like increases in hearing and sight acuity, to better assess the threat. Blood rushes into his legs and arms to fight the threat or flee from it. If it was not for the stress reaction, the caveman would likely—and literally—be consumed by the threat.

Stress performs a similar function in modern organizations. If an employee senses a threat to his or her well being, it is perfectly normal that a stress reaction will ensue. The reason why stress has a bad reputation in our society is that our bodies can handle only small doses of the chemicals produced in the stress reaction. When they are exposed to multiple and continuing sources of stress, people develop the illnesses associated with stress. Furthermore, stress reactions are influenced by the amount of control people perceive themselves to have over the source of the stress. Unlike the caveman, who has total power to decide how to contend with the saber-toothed tiger, employees have fewer choices when facing organizational transitions.

A classic inverted-U-shaped relationship exists between stress and performance (see Figure 2.1). Performance is at its peak when a moderate amount of stress exists. Too little stress translates into too little motivation to produce; too much stress (a much more likely characteristic of organizations in transition) taxes mental and physical responses and detracts from performance. While stress increases people's vigilance in gathering information, too much of it can lead them to simplify and distort what they hear.

Leaders of posttransition organizations must contend not only with predictably high levels of anxiety and rumors but also with people's perceptions of what *might* happen. People have fertile imaginations and create worst-case scenarios based on their fears of what could happen in their workplace as well as on horror stories from other organizations. Employees learn vicariously from the plight of others—don't you think that reports of the Enron debacle made employees elsewhere question whether their leadership is leveling with them? This is one reason why effective communication is so vital to successful transition management—when executives do not take the time to make sure that employees understand the upside of transition, people fill in the void with scenarios that are inevitably worse than reality.

High levels of stress have a detrimental effect on performance both quantitatively and qualitatively. During and after a transition,

FIGURE 2.1. The Relationship Between Stress and Performance.

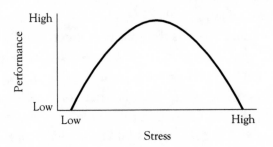

people become distracted from doing their jobs. They huddle around water coolers and coffee machines, exchanging the latest rumors. Some are at the copying and fax machines, preparing and sending out their résumés. High levels of stress also interfere with cognitive processes in intellectual tasks and with the quality of work produced in manual tasks. People respond in robotlike ways instead of thinking creatively or strategically about the situation at hand. One vice president for quality control at an aerospace firm involved in repeated waves of downsizing and restructuring described it as "like waiting for an earthquake—you do not know when the next shocks will be felt, but you know they will be coming. And you do not know if this will be the big one or not."

Sources of Stress

Organizational transition prompts stress reactions in employees in a variety of ways. The *loss* of someone or something to which people are attached is painful, and it necessitates a period of mourning or depression while they make adjustments in their lives. The potential for loss abounds in a transition—people may lose their job, coworkers, title, status, or perks. They may also lose the opportunity to realize their career aspirations and their sense of personal competence.

One key to understanding the consequences of transition is to realize that the *threat* of loss is as debilitating as an actual loss. Whether the threat is to a person's self-esteem or to his or her physical person, the resulting stress response is the same. Job insecurity is experienced like job loss. Worrying about not fitting into the postmerger culture, lamenting about one's track record accounting for nothing and having to prove one's worth to new superiors, or agonizing over what might happen to one's career all produce stress. In firms that experience multiple waves of downsizing, it is common for surviving employees to be envious of the victims—at least they can get on with their lives rather than wait around to see what happens.

Stress is based on *subjective perceptions*, not objective realities. It matters not what senior management *intends* to do but rather what people fear their leaders *might* do. Even if leadership thinks that this is the merger or restructuring that will truly turn a failing firm's fortunes around, employees who are still licking their wounds from previous transitions—or who fixate on horror stories from other organizations—will view this event as a threat and not an opportunity.

Another source of stress is the *frustration* experienced when anyone or anything even potentially prevents people from meeting basic needs or getting what they want. People who feel helpless to do anything about their situation experience this stress. So do individuals who feel competent to act but are thwarted by confusion and ambiguity in the posttransition organization. Larger workloads during and following transition do not necessarily create higher levels of stress, but a high degree of pressure coupled with a perceived lack of control do.

Finally, the critical mass of *uncertainty* in a transition contributes to stress. The announcement of a merger, acquisition, downsizing, or restructuring usually produces more questions than answers. When employees do not know what to expect, they generally anticipate the worst. Some may have new duties to master, new systems and procedures to learn, new bosses and peers to adapt to, and a new culture to assimilate. For others, there is the more palpable uncertainty about job security and company identity.

Cumulative Effects of Stress

The stress of an event is determined by the amount of change it implies, not necessarily whether the change will be beneficial or detrimental. Experts on stress tell us that marriages and births can be as stressful as divorces and deaths. Both disrupt the status quo, entangle family and friends, and require that people adapt to new circumstances. After they get over the initial reaction of how the transition might adversely affect them, most employees settle into seeing the event as a mixed bag of costs and benefits. A downsizing may be painful but also lay the foundation for enhanced business results. A culture change in a historically paternalistic organization may distort people's hopes for security but encourage them to take responsibility for their own career development. The arrival of a visionary CEO following an acquisition may inject enthusiasm and inspire greatness in an underperforming target but also produce many changes in protocol and processes.

Thus even positive changes induce stress. This is important to consider because the effects of stress are cumulative. A series of small, seemingly innocuous changes can add up to a large and significant change in the eyes of people. Multiple waves of transition—merger followed by downsizing, restructuring, and changes in everything from benefits to how to answer the phone—overwhelm people's capacity to cope with stress.

It is commonplace in organizations engaged in transition to see people handle stress through the "fight or flight" reaction. Anger and aggression are prominent in takeover targets, but they can also be found in friendly acquisitions and in internal reorganizations. Interviews conducted with employees during or soon after transitions are laced with seething indictments of managerial ineptness and examples of strained working relations across groups. By contrast, lethargy, detachment, withdrawal, and other signs of escapism can be found among acquired and reorganized professionals and managers whose work keeps them out of political power circuits.

Fight or flight reactions should be expected during and after a transition, but they can be costly. Angry managers cannot work for the common good because they are spoiling for a fight and will poison the attitudes of their subordinates. Professionals who remain in body but not spirit after the transition cannot be counted on to contribute fully to fact finding or decision making, but they will surely gripe openly about the resulting decisions.

Stress also takes a toll on people's well-being. Increased drug and alcohol abuse is common among workers surviving a transition. Calls to employee assistance programs skyrocket, and reports of a variety of psychosomatic reactions to stress are frequent: trouble falling asleep at night, headaches and back pain, smoking again after having kicked the habit, and increased tension and conflict at home and on the job.

Rates of illness and absenteeism swell at workplaces in transition, and there are plenty of numbers to document the human and financial costs of organizational MADness. At an acquired Fortune 500 technology firm that organizational psychologist Philip Mirvis and I studied, incidents of high blood pressure among employees doubled, from 11 percent in the year preceding the merger to 22 percent in the year following its announcement. In a study conducted by Northwestern National Life Insurance, 65 percent of employees surveyed reported that they suffered from exhaustion, insomnia, or other stress-related problems; one-third said they were close to burnout. Stress saps between $100 and $300 billion annually from the U.S. economy in the form of lost workdays and health care costs related to illnesses like exhaustion, depression, and heart attacks. Dr. Reed Moskowitz, director of the stress disorders clinic at New York University Hospital Medical Center, reported a 50 percent increase in requests for help from bankers, brokers, and others in the financial services industry during periods of consolidation and internal reorganization among banks, brokerage firms, and insurance companies.

The Saturation Effect

Organizations may operate within a context of change "at the speed of the Internet," but people can handle only so much disruption. Over time, their threshold for dealing with stress, uncertainty, and disorientation is met. Their ability to cope with all the changes is impaired, resulting in detrimental attitudes, maladaptive behaviors, disappointing performances, and the many other unintended consequences of organizational transition.

Think back to the case of Majestic Enterprises reported in Chapter One. Employees there encountered a series of transitions and changes between 1995 and 2001. As characterized in Figure 2.2,

FIGURE 2.2. The Saturation Effect.

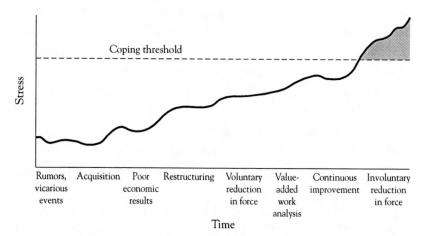

each of these events resulted in the experience of cumulative stress. After rumors of impending change and vicarious experiences of events occurring at other companies in their industry, Majestic workers were subjected to the acquisition, poor economy, restructuring, voluntary reduction in force, programs like value-added work analysis and continuous improvement, and finally the involuntary reduction in force. By then, many Majestic employees had become numbed by the dizzying course of events.

No matter how positive it was or how much potential it had, CEO Justin Jourdan could not layer another transition on this saturated workforce and hope that people would respond favorably. Instead, he had to help his people recover from the unintended consequences of previous transitions before they could move forward individually and collectively to secure new opportunities and attain new goals.

Sometimes the saturation effect occurs on an individual level and not necessarily companywide. Still, when a critical mass of people in an organization's workforce gets saturated with transition impact, it brings down the entire organization. Take the case of Elliott, age twenty-two, who moved to San Francisco in 1999 to catch dot-com fever. Elliott's first "real" job out of college was with a small high-tech start-up. He loved working there: "It was so cool, my first boss was a woman who wore leather pants and had a shaved head." A few months later, Lycos acquired the start-up. "Things changed after Lycos acquired us," recalls Elliott. "I mean, I really enjoyed working for Lycos, and the people there were really cool, but not as cool as the people I worked with before the acquisition." Then, in 2000, Spanish Internet provider Terra Networks acquired Lycos. Says Elliott, "Things really changed then. I mean, they are really cool people too, but, you know, they are more *corporate*." As the high-tech bubble burst and the economy turned sour, Elliott was the victim of a downsizing. "I was one of the last to go. I was kind of happy to go, because by the time I left, it was pretty morbid working there with all the layoffs." With two months of severance pay, Elliott did what most laid-off techies did—he hung out for a couple months. Just as his severance pay was about to run out, Terra Lycos called him back to work. "It was really odd. At first, I thought, 'This is great—I just laid low and now I don't have to worry about finding a new job.' But after I returned, the place was not the same. I mean, I like working there and I choose to work there, but the people, especially the older ones, just seem much more tense and worried, sort of like they are waiting for more layoffs. People seem scared. We still have fun at work, but it is nothing like it was before."

In many organizations like Majestic and Terra Lycos, employees have suffered an intellectual and emotional paralysis brought on by their saturated coping capacity. They are psychologically worn out, unable to get revved up about meeting new challenges. As economic recovery and the potential for a business revival arrive, people are not ready to take advantage of the situation and give a good fight.

Unintended Business Consequences

The costs of mergers, acquisitions, downsizings, and other transitions have been measured in financial as well as human terms. It is common knowledge that many mergers and acquisitions fail to achieve desired financial results. What is less well known is how few do: only about one in four mergers or acquisitions is considered to be successful, in terms of return on investment, postmerger share price, or subsequent divestiture.

Many reasons account for this high failure rate. Sometimes the reasons for doing the deal are not well founded. Kodak acquired Sterling Drugs because some analysts at headquarters figured "we use chemicals in processing film, and they use chemicals in making drugs—hey, that's synergy!" Well, there was no synergy between the firms, and Kodak soon divested Sterling for pennies on the dollar. At other times the reasons for doing the deal are sound but the process through which the organizations integrate is flawed. Personal politicking and clashes of culture interfere with people's coming together to bring the potential synergies to life. The merger of Exxon and Mobil, for example, has been described as a "political free-for-all" in which many decisions in integration teams were made based on who yelled the loudest or who dropped the highest-ranking name ("I just passed the CFO in the hall, and he told me to tell you that he really likes my proposal").

Another reason many combinations produce disappointing results is that financial analysts do a very good job of predicting the potential savings in putting two previously independent firms together but underestimate the costs it will take to realize those savings. Let's say your company and my company are merging. We both have information technology systems. The analysts tell us we can save a gazillion dollars a year by eliminating one of them. What the analysts don't consider, however, is that there is a learning curve during which one side has to be taught the other's system. Productivity will decrease because people have to take time away from their jobs to attend training sessions and then struggle with mastering new ways of doing things. And oh, by the way, we downsized the training department, so we have to pay to outsource the training. And we have to bring some temporary staff in to cover the work of people attending the training sessions. Of course people hate to learn new systems, so they will resist change, spend hours gossiping about how the old system was better than the new system, and try to hold on to their old ways. One reason people resist new things is that they feel incompetent when learning how to use them. So sick leave skyrockets when people just don't want to get out of bed and come to the office where they know they are going to have to contend with learning a new IT system. And when they do start adopting the new system, they will be embarrassed to call for help because they do not want to be cast as an incompetent. Rather than pick up the phone and call the support staff, they will ask their coworker in the next cubicle for assistance. This, of course, distracts their neighbors from doing their own work.

Firms that downsize and restructure experience their own undesirable business consequences. All the work remains, but not all the staff. Many companies are not prepared to handle the workload and, as in mergers, underestimate the costs required to cover the tasks that had been handled by laid-off employees. Among the costs downsizing firms have to contend with are increases in retraining remaining workers, using temporary workers, outsourcing functions, and paying for overtime. Some firms also lose the wrong employees—people with critical skills or needed talents take advantage of incentives to leave the company.

Health care costs incurred by organizations rise for both victims and survivors of downsizings. It is easy to see how health care costs increase for transition casualties. The psychological trauma of losing one's position or of being invited to leave through an early retirement program triggers psychosomatic ailments. Furthermore, early retirees have more time on their hands and hence more time to visit health care providers and ring up expenses. Not so obvious—but equally costly—are increased health care costs for survivors, who are also subjected to the psychosomatic effects of intense stress on the job. A study of Boeing employees found that those who experienced a high degree of emotional stress at work were more than twice as likely to file back injury claims than other employees. Working harder to cover the work of others also results in a higher accident rate. Especially problematic is when older employees return to jobs involving physical labor after being in less strenuous supervisory jobs.

A study by William M. Mercer, Inc., found that although 37 percent of the companies it tracked over a fifteen-month period reduced their headcount, one-third reported an increase in workers' compensation claims. And one in five companies said that its workers' compensation costs increased between 50 and 100 percent.

An American Management Association survey on downsizing documented just how elusive the business goals of organizational transition can be—fewer than half of the companies realized increased profits after the cuts were made, and a quarter actually experienced a decline in profitability after downsizing. While productivity increased at about a third of the companies, a similar number reported declines in employee productivity after downsizing.

Organizational MADness also has an unintended impact on customers. Following downsizings, customers complain of having to wait longer to get service and of missing familiar contacts who handled their accounts. Many banks have taken advantage of competitors' mergers to air commercials asking "why deal with closed branches, longer lines, mistakes on statements, and unfriendly, impersonal bankers when you can choose our local community bank?" Even in business-to-business transactions, customers dread hearing that suppliers or vendors are going through a merger, acquisition, or downsizing. It is common in the manufacturing sector, for example, for companies to automatically line up secondary sources of materials because they expect that there will be some problem in product quality or availability during the transition.

Learning from the MADness

Following years of mismanaged mergers, disturbing downsizings, and sunken stock options, reviving employee spirit is a daunting task. Employees are not just angry with leadership for putting them through organizational MADness. They also are fearful of the next plunge of the guillotine—it has been dropping periodically for years now, and people do not know when the MADness is going to stop. Employees need something to relieve their angst and to revive their hopes that hard work and fair play can and will be rewarded at their workplaces, both financially and psychologically.

The potential upside here is not merely to recuperate from the pain and disillusionment of recent years but to learn from the mistakes of mismanaged transitions. The factors that have created organizational MADness are going to intensify, not diminish, further driving organizations and their people mad: the pace of technological advances will become even more mind-boggling, globalization will increase as trade barriers continue to fall and advances occur in transportation and communications, and consolidation will revamp the lineup of companies in industries like telecommunications, financial services, computers, oil, entertainment, and manufacturing. Add to this the shortsightedness of Wall Street's pushing for quarter-by-quarter results. Day traders have forced buy-and-hold investors into the background. Mergers and downsizings are here to stay in the managerial repertoire. Executives will gobble up competitors and not hesitate to cut jobs along the way. We must learn from today's MADness to prevent tomorrow's.

Accepting, understanding, and responding to the unintended consequences of necessary organizational transitions can lead to the development of more effective and more rewarding workplaces, to a workforce better prepared and more confident of its ability to succeed, and to a clearer, sounder, and more mutually enriching psychological relationship between them. The yield can be organizations whose employees feel that their jobs have dignity and integrity, that their own creativity is enlivened, and that they experience the tremendous sense of accomplishment that comes when people work together to achieve goals that they could never attain on their own. And for those managers more focused on bottom-line results than on lofty possibilities, the payoff can be workers who are more productive and successful at meeting organizational objectives.

PART TWO

Laying the Groundwork for Workplace Recovery

Understanding How People Adapt to Transitions

3

The Opportunity and the Challenge

A growing number of organizational leaders have learned hard lessons from organizational MADness. They are "rightsizing" their organizations rather than "downsizing" their headcounts. That is, these chief executives and business unit heads are pressing their management teams to reformulate how work is approached rather than merely to cut out jobs without eliminating work. Similarly, senior executives are increasingly focusing their attention on corporate combinations and alliances that add strategic value and away from opportunistic mergers and acquisitions based solely on financial motives. And leaders are embracing the more complex—yet potentially more rewarding—work of transformational change over incremental change.

Still, leaders must accept that most organizational transitions in the past three decades have been poorly managed and that they have to contend with the consequences today. Employees shudder when they hear rumors that their firm is about to merge or be acquired. Work comes to a standstill when the grapevine passes on talk about an imminent wave of downsizing. People wonder why leadership is not more forthcoming with information and specifics. No executive intends to anger or alienate the workforce, yet these unintended consequences interfere with any subsequent efforts to identify and lock in desired positive enhancements as part of implementing transition. Just like parents who accept only after the fact that their behavior influenced their child's development, organizational leaders must acknowledge the imprint left on employees following transition. And just as a stepparent inherits the psychological makeup of a stepchild, executives who take over operations must accept the psychological baggage that people carry with them to work.

Fortunately, adults are more psychologically adaptive than children. They can rebound from even the most painful of situations. That is what *workplace recovery* is about: helping employees let go of the unintentional pain and consequences they experience during and after transitions while simultaneously helping organizations use transitions as opportunities to build new and better workplaces. It is about taking shell-shocked troops, rebuilding their confidence in themselves and their leaders, and preparing them to triumph in the charge up the hill, enthused and committed to achieving desired goals. By *integrating human recovery into workplace recovery*, corporations and their people can be ready to take advantage of emerging business opportunities.

Integrating Individual Recovery into Workplace Recovery

The tools to manage workplace recovery are straightforward, but their utilization is muddled over and over again. Reviving employee enthusiasm, motivation, and productivity after transition is typically hindered by a lack of understanding of the psychological roots of organizational and individual transition. Some executives are simply out of touch with the human realities of their workplaces and workforces. They deny or ignore the frailty of human spirit, the impact previously mismanaged transitions have had on employees, and the depth of effort required for removing the baggage of the past so that people can move freely forward to the future. Other organizational leaders do understand the "human side of enterprise" but are impatient or unsympathetic to the human necessity of ending old realities before accepting new ones. That is, they see the opportunity for enhancements in effectiveness and performance following transition but do not factor in the realities of individual adaptation to transition. Eagerly looking forward to capture the prize, they create unrealistic timetables and unattainable targets that frustrate employees rather than motivate them.

Organizations are nothing but people, so to achieve organizational objectives, executives need to acknowledge human realities. The opportunity that coincides with this challenge is that the *posttransition* period—the period after transition planning occurs and implementation begins in earnest—can be used to build a new and better organization. Living through a transition shakes people up; over time, they eventually will settle down. If nothing is done to manage this process, odds are that people will return to their old ways of doing things, hold on to their old perceptions, and retain their old expectations. But if the posttransition period is managed to take advantage of this opportunity, people will settle into new behaviors, perceptions, and expectations that are more in line with the new desires of senior executives and with the realities and needs of the organization following the merger, acquisition, or downsizing.

Achieving workplace recovery after transition requires intervention at two levels: organizational transition and individual adaptation. The remainder of this chapter examines organizational transition within the context of workplace recovery. The following chapter then adds an understanding of the individual adaptation process that people have to go through to contribute to desired organizational transition.

Organizational Transition

Deep, meaningful, and lasting change is a complex process. However, the most powerful model to guide the design and implementation of organizational change projects also happens to be one of the simplest: Kurt Lewin's three-step model of *unfreezing, changing,* and *refreezing* (see Figure 3.1). Suppose that your target for change is not an organization or an individual but an ice cube. If you want to convert its shape from a cube to a cylinder, you can

FIGURE 3.1. The Three-Step Model of Change Management.

proceed in one of two ways. The first is to take out a hammer and chisel; with the right skill, you could transform the ice cube into the shape of a cylinder. There is a clear cost to this approach, however: you will lose a good amount of the volume of the ice cube as you chisel it off. The alternative course of action is to unfreeze the ice cube, change its mold to that of a cylinder, and refreeze it in the shape you desire. Unless you are clumsy in pouring unfrozen water from one mold to the other or the new mold has some inherent flaw like a hole, you have the desired cylinder shape without the loss of volume.

Moving from ice cubes to organizations, the first step in the process of desired change is to unfreeze present behaviors or attitudes. For organizational change, the unfreezing event might be a severe financial loss, the introduction of a revolutionary product by a competitor, or the acquisition and integration of a target organization. The second step is changing the organization from its original behavior or perception to a new one. This means articulating and developing the desired change. In the case of disappointing financial results or looming competitive threats, this could be a change in strategy such as a greater emphasis in bringing new products to market. In mergers, once the partners are unfrozen, the new mold might take the form of a stronger customer service culture, a leaner or less hierarchical organizational structure, or the deployment of new work processes. The third step, refreezing, involves establishing processes that reinforce the desired behaviors or perceptions and lock them into the organization. This could be financial incentives that enforce desired behaviors, information systems that transport data across units of an organization, or changes in policies and procedures that support the new organization. Unless the refreezing occurs, it is all too easy for organizations and their people to slip back into familiar and accustomed patterns.

These three steps are simpler to state than they are to put into practice. Their implementation becomes even more difficult when the context is moved from a discrete case of change to a more discontinuous case of transition and yet again more difficult when dealing within a context of multiple waves of transition. The desired mold, for instance, may be in a continuous state of flux as concurrent changes and transitions tax both executive patience and employee confidence. Also, some portions of the organization may be more or less unfrozen at any given time. Senior management may be ready to charge ahead with a new program, but rank-and-file employees may remain rigidly resistant to the program—even after thorough training—if they sense signals from their immediate superiors not to bother with applying it on the job.

If properly managed, a merger, acquisition, downsizing, or other major organizational transition can be an unfreezing event (see Figure 3.2). A major transition disturbs the status quo: it jars people, changes relationships, redefines work team composition and goals, and disrupts accustomed ways of doing things. It also provides an opportunity to think in a proactive manner about what life after the transition could be like.

FIGURE 3.2. Transition as Unfreezing.

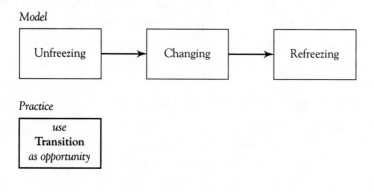

A fine example of this is the lineage of Chase Bank. Chase Bank was created by the acquisition of Chase Manhattan Bank by Chemical Bank (although the Chase name was retained, Chemical was the lead party). Chemical Bank had previously merged with Manufacturers Hanover Bank. Prior to that combination, "Manny Hanny" was plagued by flat revenue growth, problem loans to developing nations, and expense account abuses. Senior management's response was to strengthen corporate staff control over line managers. This was an appropriate reaction in light of the financial problems at hand. Ultimately, however, it resulted in a bureaucratic organization whose control mechanisms slowed decision making and diverted managerial time and attention away from business innovation.

Eventually, Manufacturers CEO John McGillicuddy and his senior team dealt with the financial problems that had necessitated the tight control. However, the bureaucracy was frozen in place through the policies, procedures, and staff positions that remained, along with an acquiescent mind-set that had settled in among employees. Operations executives were quite unhappy with this aspect of the company culture, yet senior leadership never countered the high levels of bureaucracy and inflexible staff control that had become a way of life in the bank.

When Manufacturers Hanover merged with its New York rival Chemical Bank, the Chemical name was retained, but McGillicuddy became CEO. This "merger of equals" ultimately had an unfreezing effect. (Although *mergers of equals* rarely are, the Chemical Bank–Manufacturers Hanover combination could well be described that way: it was a very friendly deal, the two banks were of approximately equal size, both CEOs remained on board, and staffing was coordinated with an eye toward balance between the two partners.) To identify integration opportunities, but also to symbolize the mutuality between the sides in merger planning, teams of managers from both banks were assigned to integration planning teams. Inevitably, issues of corporate culture edged into discussions of business strategy and operating procedures for the new bank. Unlike typical merger planning negotiations, in which managers tend to view their culture as superior to that of the other side's and defend their ways of doing things while putting down their partner's ways, participants from Manufacturers Hanover wanted a less bureaucratic postmerger organization than the one to which they were accustomed. They saw—and used—the merger as an unfreezing opportunity to rid their workplace of bureaucratic excess.

In other firms, the ways in which employees describe the transition experience give testimony to its capacity to unfreeze organizations and people:

"Everything is up for grabs," exclaimed a marketing manager after her first integration planning meeting in a computer industry acquisition.

"Leave no stone unturned," instructed a CEO to his staff as he ordered a serious cost containment program in a health care organization.

"Things aren't like they used to be around here," bemoaned a staff accountant from a utility that announced its first ever involuntary reduction in force.

What makes a transition so stressful for people—its ability to separate them from their accustomed ways of doing things—concurrently provides the benefit of unfreezing people. A transition also has the potential to put organizational structures, systems, strategies, programs, processes, and cultures "into play." Hiring guidelines, reward systems, decision-making criteria, problem-solving approaches, reporting relationships, and all other aspects of the organization are temporarily pliable and ready to be set in a new mold.

Change by Design or by Default

For change to occur at the organizational level, it must of course occur at the individual level and in particular in the ways people interpret the environment in which they operate. Individuals have limited data processing capabilities that must be used to evaluate vast amounts of information. To make sense of their world, people rely on simplified representations, or *mental models,* consisting of concepts and cause-and-effect relationships. These models are shortcuts that help people select and interpret data from all the information bombarding them. They also act as filters that reject information or actions that do not conform to the individual's ideas about his or her environment. If I get a nice annual performance review after working especially hard on a project, I might create a mental model that says, "Hard work gets rewarded here." I also am likely to discount comments from a coworker who says my boss plays favorites by concluding that my colleague is a disgruntled, bitter person.

Mental models may be updated, adapted, and improved as events occur in the workplace, but this seldom happens in a timely manner *because it takes time to unfreeze old mental models before changing them and refreezing new ones.* If I continue to work hard but am not well rewarded in my next two performance reviews and if many of the coworkers I respect transfer out of my department, I may amend my mental model to "Hard work here is not rewarded by my boss." But by then, I've wasted two years working for a jerk.

Workplace recovery after transition hinges on changing the beliefs held by employees. Changing beliefs in turn requires unlearning familiar concepts or assumed cause-and-effect relationships and replacing them with new impressions and associations. This learning occurs in a manner akin to the unfreezing, changing, and refreezing process. During *unfreezing,* old beliefs are discarded as inappropriate or useless. Once old beliefs are unlearned, new understandings about the workplace can be achieved, often through experimentation and trial-and-error learning in the *changing* phase. In the final step of *refreezing,* new belief structures ultimately become solidified as they are supported by anticipated outcomes. Of course, in today's ever-changing business world, "frozen" takes on a relative meaning.

As the shock waves of a merger, acquisition, or downsizing sub-side, people settle into patterns of thinking and acting in the post-transition organization. One of three scenarios will prevail:

- The transition experience will *not* significantly alter people's mental models, and they will retain the assumptions, percep-tions, and behaviors that served them in the pretransition organization. This is the status quo.

- The transition experience will alter people's mental models, and they will settle into and rely on assumptions, perceptions, and behaviors that were reinforced *inadvertently* during the transition. This is change by default.

- The transition experience will alter people's mental models, and they will settle into and rely on assumptions, perceptions, and behaviors that were reinforced *intentionally* during the transition. This is change by design.

Status Quo. During a transition, there is tremendous pressure on employees, especially those in busy middle management and super-visory positions, to "go with what they know." People sense so much turmoil and disruption around them—and as noted in Chapter Two, perceived threats are as stress-inducing as real changes—that they look for stability and consistency wherever they can find it. If employees' mental models have not been modified, they fall back onto their accustomed ways of conceptualizing and doing things. The transition may have temporarily unfrozen these people, but the mold did not change.

The problem with this status quo scenario is that the assump-tions, perceptions, and behaviors that served people well in the pre-transition organization may not be consistent with leadership's desires for the posttransition organization. This could be costly to an organi-zation, as in the case of the computer services firm that rearranged territories for sales support staff after it acquired and integrated a competitor. Sales people knew their preacquisition support staff could get the job done and did not want to risk alienating customers by bringing in an unproven support person. Using cases of beer as bribes, they coaxed their preacquisition staffers to work with their customers. This caused havoc in the support organization and alienated many customers who never got attended to. Holding on to the status quo after transition can also be costly to employees. Employees in a family-owned manufacturing concern with a patriarchical culture denied their vulnerability and failed to adapt when a foreign conglomerate acquired them and abandoned the no-layoff policy, eliminated tuition reimbursement programs, and replaced traditional promote-from-within practices with aggressive recruiting and hiring from outside the company.

Change by Default. Alternatively, the transition period may be so dramatic and intense that it challenges employees' existing mental models. The experience of living through a transition—including both perceived and real dynamics—may obliterate concepts or assumed cause-and-effect relationships that predominated prior to the transition and replace them with new impressions. Depending on how the transition is managed, this unlearning, changing, and relearning follows one of two patterns: new mental models emerge by default as the result of inadvertent managerial actions, or they emerge by design as the result of intentional managerial efforts to cast a new mold.

Change by default occurred following the acquisition of a small biotech company by a much larger conglomerate. The lead company recognized it was buying into an industry sector in which it had no expertise. It kept the target company's top management in place and, with the exception of changes in accounting practices to conform to its standards, mandated no changes in operations. To the outside observer, this acquisition was just mildly disruptive. However, leaders in the acquired company lurched into a crisis management mode as they experienced remorse for having sold their company, became overburdened by the joint responsibilities of running their operations and preparing mountains of financial reports for staffers from the conglomerate, and frequently met among themselves to strategize (some would later say "fantasize") how to fend off any additional overtures for change. These leaders, who had maintained close informal relationships with rank-and-file employees prior to the transition, suddenly became invisible to their workforce. Employees felt abandoned by and out of touch with their leaders. In an attitude survey conducted a year after the takeover, employees expressed how their trust toward management had plummeted and conveyed feelings that leadership was no longer concerned about the welfare of employees. When these results were reported to the leaders, they argued that they were no less concerned about employees than before the transition. Their behavior had inadvertently sent a different message, however, and the damage was done: employees launched a union drive. Although the drive was narrowly defeated, fighting it required the expenditure of tremendous resources, and employee-employer relations never returned to what they were before the acquisition.

Change by Design. In contrast to the biotech firm is the case of the merger by design of two equally sized hospitals. The senior administrator, who came from one of the partners, wanted to use the merger as an opportunity to revisit all facets of organizational life, from standard operating procedures to core competencies for managers. For example, she wanted leaders who had strong analytical skills and could operate in an adaptive manner rather than in the status quo of rigidly and uncritically applying standards. When she communicated this, she encountered tremendous cynicism: managers from her hospital assumed that they would have an edge in gaining positions in the merged operation, while those from the other side suspected that they would be at a disadvantage. Both sides were startled when they saw the chief administrator's words backed up by actions— every manager and supervisor would have to apply for jobs in the postmerger hospital and compete against counterparts from the other side and, perhaps, outside applicants.

This approach had some short-term costs, including a prevailing sense of abandonment by the administrator's former team and some interpersonal conflict among individuals vying for jobs. But in the long run, it had the intended effect of breaking down old expectations and setting the stage for designing and implementing a truly new organization.

The New Organizational Order

An organization's leadership can influence employees' new mental models and behaviors to coincide with a desired posttransition organization. This opportunity could be realized by accident, over a period of years, as desired behaviors are rewarded through annual performance reviews, promotions, assignments to favored tasks, and other forms of recognition and employees eventually get the picture. However, in today's fast-paced and competitive world, executives do not have years to craft new corporate cultures and employee mindsets. The alternative to being lucky or being languid is to be proactive and build a desired posttransition organization by design. This requires that senior leadership articulate a *new organizational order* in which people can settle after being uprooted by transition. This new organizational order is the mold that defines the changes in the middle step of the unfreezing-changing-refreezing model (see Figure 3.3). The new organizational order explicitly articulates dimensions of the desired posttransition organization:

- *Direction*—where the organization is headed
- *Mission*—the organization's purpose for being, including what distinguishes it from its competitors
- *Culture*—what matters in achieving the mission; the ways things are done in an organization and the values, attitudes, and beliefs that underlie more readily observable behaviors and practices

FIGURE 3.3. The New Organizational Order as the Mold for Change.

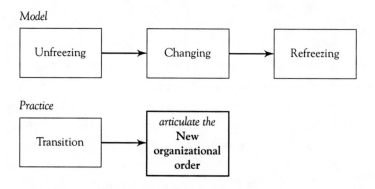

- *Psychological work contract*—the delineation of what both employer and employee bring to their relationship and what they can expect in return for their contribution

- *Core competencies*—the traits, skills, knowledge, and related attributes that an organization values and needs for success in a particular position

- *Architecture*—the design of social and work systems that make up a complex organization, including formal structure, work practices, and processes for selecting, socializing, and developing people

The new organizational order is like a vision—it paints a vivid picture of where the organization is headed. Statements of vision are important to workplace recovery. They inspire confidence among an anxious or disoriented workforce that the organization is on the path to becoming new and better. But a vision is beyond the reach of what can realistically be attained. People who already feel beat up by the bumps and bruises of a transition do not need to be confronted by something beyond their grasp. Rather, they need help in understanding how *today's* behaviors and expectations can contribute to both short-term survival and long-term revival. Thus the articulation of a new organizational order is more than a vision.

CEO Garland Cook of Pittsburgh-based Integra Bank used a new organizational order to revitalize his firm after transition. Integra grew rapidly through a series of acquisitions of banks that had focused on the specific needs of rural, suburban, or urban customers. The acquisitions were extremely friendly, but they brought together a mix of corporate cultures and diverse operating styles. Although postmerger integration was managed relatively well, the formerly independent banks were not leveraging their respective strengths. Moreover, employees were torn between conflicting management approaches and unsure of what standards were being used to judge performance on the job. Cook saw the inertia settling in among his managers and employees as competitors began to bite into market share by introducing new products and services. While intending to continue Integra's growth by acquisition, Cook recognized that the greatest flurry of takeover activity was in the past and set his attention on articulating and building a new order for the bank (see Exhibit 3.1). At a meeting of his senior management team, Cook described the changes he wanted to see:

- In contrast to the situation at most contemporary organizations, Cook wanted employees to feel that they could develop careers at Integra. He sought to replace the predominating expectation of "having a job" with one of "building a career."

- There was, in Cook's words, "considerable clutter" in the old bank—inefficient operations, unnecessary procedures, and enormous waste of money, time, and resources. He envisioned a continuous improvement orientation in the new organization in which people and teams would analyze their actions and carry forward only those that truly added value to the accomplishment of work.

- A "bankers' hours" mentality of nine-to-five service predominated. Cook preferred that employees embrace high levels of customer service, including availability on Saturdays and in evenings.

EXHIBIT 3.1. The Old and New Organizational Orders at Integra Bank.

Old Organizational Order	New Organizational Order
Jobs	Careers
Clutter	Continuous improvement
Open 9 to 5	Saturday and evening service
Tin Man	"Heart" recaptured
Constant change	Stable state
Waiting for the ax to fall	Eye on the ball

- Cook spoke passionately about his desire to recapture the "heart" of his organization. He felt that some of the fun and the humanism of the institution had been lost as its size increased over the years. He believed that his staff members were basically good people who, like the Tin Man in *The Wizard of Oz*, did not need to be given anything they did not already have. Rather, he needed to guide them in calling on the resources already within themselves.

- Anticipating a lull in acquisition and integration activity, Cook saw a new organizational order of relative stability in structure and size.

- Particularly because of this upcoming lull, Cook wanted people in the new organization to keep their eye on the ball and focus their attention on business results. In the old organizational order, the pattern of acquisitions followed by layoffs had become a way of life, and most employees were on the lookout for the next fall of the ax.

The Integra case shows that the new organizational order need not be communicated as a concrete document. Instead, it is more a fluid working draft intended to help senior executives define what they desire their posttransition organization to be like. From it may come more detailed statements of direction and mission, clear artic-ulation of cultural norms, shared expectations of the psychological work contract, common understanding of core competencies, and implementation of the desired organizational architecture.

Articulating a new organizational order helped the chief admin-istrator of the two merging hospitals convey her expectations and dreams to her subordinates. Soon after the merger announcement, she sent a letter to all employees from both institutions describing her view of what the merged hospitals could and should be. It was a fairly typical statement of direction ("Be the hospital of choice for our community"), greeted by employees in a fairly typical manner ("That's nice, but will I have a job?"). Meanwhile, as she developed her design for the postmerger organization, the administrator's think-ing focused on the teamwork necessary to achieve the new direc-tion. She acknowledged the extensive use of teams in all hospitals, but she saw them confined in the old order to single functions or routine tasks. She found little use of teamwork in such matters as resolving difficulties and exploring new ways of providing better ser-vice to patients.

The administrator envisioned a culture promoting and rein-forcing teamwork. She began to articulate this to people from the two hospitals in her formal communications—memos, newsletters, and on both organizations' intranets—and in informal visits with groups of employees. She modeled teamwork by using groups of managers from the two institutions to make decisions she had pre-viously handled on her own. She also spoke about a psychological relationship between employer and employee that went beyond pay and benefits in exchange for high-quality work: only those people who wanted to work collaboratively with employees from different departments and levels, she declared, need apply for positions in the new hospital. This was reinforced through the development of job descriptions that specified, in addition to technical and professional competencies, the ability to function in a team orientation.

All of this was done *before* any decisions were made regarding the structure or staffing of the new institution. There was considerable bickering from her managers, who felt the chief administrator was being disloyal by not giving them an edge, as well as by managers from the other hospital, who were not confident that the administrator meant what she said. During the integration process, however, the administrator stuck to her intentions and kept closely involved in the staff selection process to ensure that people with an orientation toward her desired new organizational order received positions. Once the structure and staffing had been fleshed out, the theme of teamwork became a focal point to help the postmerger staff recover from the draining work of merging operations while maintaining patient care, dealing with culture clash during integration, and overcoming anger and conflicts that spilled over from before the combination.

Refreezing the New Organizational Order

Transition survivors, by and large, are receptive to statements describing the new organizational order. Their world has been shaken up, and they engage in a vigilant search to learn what is expected of them and what they can expect from the organization. They also want to learn how to protect themselves against future fallout or, more positively, how to contribute to desired business objectives. Yet managers often fail to provide a clear and timely picture of what the posttransition organization will be like—they either haven't thought it through, assume that employees are grateful just to be employed, or are looking ahead to the next transition. This disappoints and frequently angers employees, who assume that some master plan must be sitting on the CEO's desk.

When a new organizational order is articulated, employees' responses to the statement are influenced by their experiences and perceptions molded during the transition. If management failed to "walk the talk" in abiding by its pledge to manage the transition or if promises of enhanced organizational life as a result of the transition rang hollow, people will regard the statement of the new organizational order as nothing more than management's latest castle in the sky. Conversely, if management leveled with employees about the pain of transition but provided little in the way of a new vision for the organization, surviving employees will eagerly receive a statement that clarifies where their organization—and they—are headed.

For the mold of the new organizational order to take hold, it must be refrozen (see Figure 3.4). This happens when desired actions are reinforced and employees learn new and relevant concepts and cause-and-effect relationships. This results in new mental models consistent with the new organizational order. Refreezing the desired new organization occurs by aligning systems, structures, strategies, processes, technologies, and relationships. The more consistent the messages—from the way the organization is structured, how work is approached, who gets rewarded for doing what, how people interact with one another, and so on—the more readily the desired new organizational order is realized. And when employees see that leadership's actions are consistent with its words and that there is a clear way out of the quagmire of transition, their spirit and motivation to act are revitalized along with the work team performance required to make a successful run at business opportunities.

To be clear, I am not talking about a wholesale abandonment of old mental models and the creation of countless new ones. The reality is that many mental models held by employees will be rele-

FIGURE 3.4. Refreezing Desired Change Through Recovery and Revitalization.

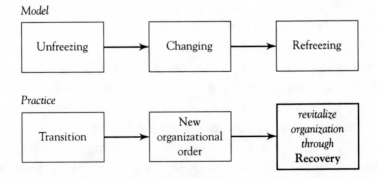

vant to both the old and new organizational orders. At the merged hospital, for example, standards like seniority counting when schedules were drawn up did not change and thus did not affect employee concepts about the importance of tenure in the organization. But to refreeze the new organizational order, changes were made in areas including the pay system (a special bonus pool was established to recognize and reward cross-unit teamwork), the selection system (candidates were assessed on their orientation toward teamwork as well as technical skills), and the structure (more cross-unit teams were built into the structure).

Opportunities in the New Organizational Order

The opportunities in the new organizational order are almost limitless. Leaders may seek to enhance teamwork, customer service, innovation, risk taking, use of technology, speed to market, or other characteristics of organizational life. The content of the new order will vary from one organization to another. However, the *process* of defining and achieving the new organizational order after transition can result in a wide range of important benefits to any work organization (see Exhibit 3.2).

Resuscitating the Human Spirit

A formal effort to recover after transition breathes life back into the moribund spirit of a workforce that has just come out of a difficult period. Building the new organizational order revitalizes exhausted employees physically and emotionally by inspiring them to high levels of individual, team, and organization achievement. This can-do attitude—and the tremendous energy that comes with it—overcomes the cynicism and depression that bring down people and their expectations of what can be accomplished after a debilitating transition. The new organizational order also focuses people on the future rather than the past. Recovery after transition energizes people further by increasing their self-confidence and capacity to act.

EXHIBIT 3.2. Opportunities in the New Organizational Order.

Resuscitating the Human Spirit
- Reenergize burned-out employees.
- Create a high level of aspiration.
- Focus people on future possibilities.
- Increase the capacity to act.

Living the Vision
- Rally people around a vision.
- Clarify their mission.
- Set operating guidelines.
- Focus people on what matters.
- Prioritize competing demands.

Renewing Human Resources
- Strengthen the pay-for-performance link.
- Enhance selection systems.
- Invest in training and development.

Helping Middle Managers
- Make sense of the chaos.
- Define the role of middle management.
- Help middle managers regain their footing.

Enhancing Work Methods
- Enhance creativity.
- Provide problem-solving skills.
- Embrace experimentation
- Increase appropriate levels of risk taking.

Promoting Organizational Learning
- Embed double-loop learning.
- Create diagnostic opportunities.
- Increase upward, downward, and lateral communication.

Living the Vision

Recovery channels individual motivation toward the needs of the organization by rallying people around a blueprint for a new and better workplace. A shared sense of where the organization is headed, along with well-communicated statements of the direction and purpose of business units or departments, dissipates much of the ambiguity that settles in the posttransition organization. Employees translate the direction and mission into operating procedures that guide their individual behavior on the job.

Enhancing Work Methods

With clear direction and priorities, employees can actually "work smarter" following transition—an often stated but rarely realized goal of transition. By sanctioning a recovery process, leadership converts its rhetoric into action by providing employees with time and resources to revise their approaches to work in line with the new organizational order. This cultivates an environment that nurtures creativity and embraces experimentation, which together boost organizational learning. It also develops problem-solving skills and contributes to a level of risk taking appropriate to the organization's need to change its pretransition ways of doing things.

Renewing Human Resources

Recovery allows an organization to make over its human resource practices and programs. Several employers have strengthened the pay-for-performance link in their compensation plans as part of building a new organizational order. Many have adjusted recruitment, selection, and hiring systems to identify and bring on board individuals with skills and competencies that fit the new organizational order. Others have also revised training and development programs to "retool" current employees to better fit the needs of the posttransition organization. In addition to providing individuals with specific skills and insights, strengthening the role of training and development sends a symbolic message to employees that they are being invested in as part of the new organizational order.

Helping Middle Managers

Although recovery after transition aids members at all organizational levels, it particularly addresses the many issues confronting middle managers, who are frightened by the disproportionate layoffs in their ranks and frustrated by the paucity of information available to help them address subordinates' concerns. First, it helps these managers make sense of the chaos that is going on in their organization and in the business environment. This strengthens their ability to communicate the whys and wherefores of transition and recovery to their employees. Second, the articulation of a new organizational order clarifies the roles and responsibilities of middle managers, in terms of both managing core business activities and contributing to a successful recovery. Third, recovery helps managers and supervisors in the middle ranks of the organization regain their footing following the wrenching transition period. Part of recovering from transition is reestablishing managers' and supervisors' self-confidence that they can lead their teams through turbulent times.

Promoting Organizational Learning

Recovery directly attacks the tendency to rely on the status quo during times of rapid change and transition. When recovery is given high-priority status, people look for—rather than filter out—data that do not confirm their old mental models, and they interpret that data in the context and needs of the new organizational order. This new perspective may allow them to see and solve long-standing problems that they never before recognized. Learning while building the new organizational order is also promoted through increased upward, downward, and lateral communication. As trust is rebuilt and experimentation is embraced, employees overcome their fears about speaking up in the posttransition organization. Managers and other leaders become more proficient at listening. Downward communication increases through the delivery of information regarding the new order, including what to expect of it and action plans for achieving it. Coordination across groups increases along with the flow of information, including the exchange of success stories to help departments and business units learn from one another's experiences.

Challenges to the New Organizational Order

Of course, there are many obstacles that interfere with recovery after transition. Three particular sources of resistance—the mindset of employees, prevailing organizational dynamics, and the manner in which the transition was managed—throw up roadblocks on the path to the new organizational order (see Exhibit 3.3).

Employee Mind-Set

Transitions affect people in various ways. Some feel like winners—they emerge with the position, project, or budget they sought. Others feel like losers—they lost something or someone important to them

---

EXHIBIT 3.3. Challenges to the New Organizational Order.

Employee Mind-Set
- Resistance to change
- Regression to primitive behaviors
- Feelings of powerlessness
- Demotivation

Organizational Dynamics
- Crisis management
- Constricted communication
- Outmoded systems

Transition Management
- Lack of consensus
- Lack of involvement
- Lack of resources

in the course of the transition. Still other employees experience transition as a mix of gains and losses as they assess how the transition affects them, their immediate work team, and the overall organization. For the vast majority of people, the perceived costs far outweigh the anticipated gains. So even though people may respond to the notion of building a new organizational order in a variety of ways, some common challenges stand in the way of building the desired posttransition organization.

Resistance to Change. Employee resistance takes many forms and can sidetrack any change effort. On the heels of a transition, people need a certain degree of stability or security in their work situation, and movement to a new organizational order presents yet another wave of anxiety-producing unknowns. Locked-in mental models prevent employees from perceiving a need for change or understanding the potential business or personal gains of the new organizational order. Old expectations and habits are difficult to give up, especially when they led to success before the transition. For example, building up a large staff may have been a source of high power and compensation in the old organizational order but may not continue to serve a manager whose superiors are looking toward a lean and mean operation.

People's resistance to change may be rooted in fear, but it may also come from a need to defend the old way of doing things. The people who created the past practices and policies are probably still in the organization. They are likely to receive the introduction of the new organizational order as a criticism of themselves as well as of their systems and approaches. If they feel attacked, they are likely to spend considerable energy attempting to preserve the status quo rather than contributing to building the new order.

Regression to Primitive Behaviors. Many people respond to organizational transition by regressing to primitive behaviors. They restrict communication or take actions that seem decisive but are not well thought out. During and following a transition, people at all levels experience an urge to hold on tightly to information. For executives, this means putting on a tough facade to give the impression that all is under control. For rank-and-file employees, this includes repressing emotion so as not to show any sign of vulnerability—in the event there is another wave of layoffs, no one wants to be tagged as a weakling who cannot handle the heat. Managers of work teams restrict decision-making authority and limit communication to a "need to know" basis. And at all levels, those who are politically inclined figure that information is power and think they are strengthening their positions by not sharing it. In general, "hard-nosed" management dominates over "humanistic" management. Consultant Harry Levinson labeled the economic recession "a blow to psychological management."

Feelings of Powerlessness. Most people experience a perceived loss of control during transition as dynamics beyond their influence take hold. Psychological research shows that when people perceive their control to be lessened, they assume it has been eliminated. The result is employee inaction and managerial paralysis. The critical mass of the unknown during a transition—unclear vision, reporting relationships, priorities, expectations, and so on—exacerbates feelings that one cannot control one's fate.

Demotivation. People behave in ways that get them the things they want, provided that they have the ability to get the job done and expect to be rewarded for doing so. The expectancy theory of motivation expresses this as a function of three factors: instrumentality (I), a person's perceived relationship between how hard he or she works and how well that work is done ("How likely is it that I can complete this task?"); valence (V), the employee's feelings about how attractive the reward is ("How much do I like or need the reward being offered for doing the work?"); and expectancy (E), the employee's expectations that doing the job will indeed be rewarded ("How likely is it that I will receive the reward?"). The employee figuratively assigns a probability between 0 (no likelihood of occurring) and 1 (total likelihood of occurring) to each factor. Being a multiplicative relationship, a low probability rating for any of the factors results in low motivation (see Exhibit 3.4).

Thus any of three perceptions may demotivate an employee after transition. First, an employee might feel unable to complete a task even when giving full effort ("How can I get everything done well and on time when there is so much to do and I do not have the information or resources I need?"). Second, the employee may not find current rewards attractive ("Why should I work so hard if all I am going to get is a merit increase of a measly few percentage points or the 'privilege' of keeping my job here, when there is more competition for fewer promotions?"). Third, the employee might conclude that the company does not deliver on its promised rewards ("Why should I bother when they reneged on giving me that promotion I was promised right before the merger?").

Organizational Dynamics

Challenges to achieving the new organizational order may also come from prevailing organizational dynamics. These include management behaviors that interfere with the exchange of valid information and organizational systems that fit the old mold rather than the new one.

Crisis Management. The uncertainty of transition, coupled with the potential for high-stakes losses and gains, leads to a crisis management orientation. Regressing to primitive management behav-

---

EXHIBIT 3.4. Expectancy Theory of Motivation.

$$\text{Motivation} = \underset{(0-1)}{E} \times \underset{(0-1)}{V} \times \underset{(0-1)}{I}$$

iors and anxious about working in an uncharted and highly political situation, top executives scurry to act decisively in commanding their domain. They focus on strategy and tactics, and their troops are supposed to fall in line like loyal foot soldiers. But the troops do not fall in line; instead, they are worried and unsure how to behave.

Studies of the handling of crises show some predictable reactions for organizations contending with high levels of uncertainty and challenge. Leaders facing a crisis centralize decision making in an authoritative mode. Much as stress leads executives to tighten up and turn inward, crisis leads an executive team in the same direction. Centralization serves many useful functions to an executive team facing a transition. It ensures that information flows to the top and that executives are able, in concert with trusted associates, to sort out possible losses and gains and map strategy for moves and countermoves. In an authoritative decision-making mode, executives have to answer only to themselves. They are not bothered by divergent viewpoints and do not have to explain themselves to subordinates who may favor other decisions. This mode of decision making proves heady to many executives and accentuates their belief that they are the masters of their organizations.

But this crisis orientation has its costs. Centralized decision making can shut the top team off from important information that might otherwise be developed in an open exchange with subordinates or, in the case of a merger, with executives from the partner organization. It can also insulate the top leaders and promote a "groupthink" mentality as strategies are considered. A crisis mentality mode hinders recovery when these reactions reduce decision quality during and after the transition.

Constricted Communication. Even in the best of times, there is static on the communication lines in most organizations. This condition worsens during times of change and crisis. Employees do not trust the messages they hear and grow cynical about management's intentions. Ironically, these employees crave information—they want proof that the transition makes sense for the company and its future, signs that it will be well managed, and answers to their endless questions of how the changes will affect them personally.

Senior executives, in turn, are wary of saying too much to employees when so little is known. They are legitimately afraid of saying something that might later be proved wrong or be used against the company in a wrongful discharge suit. Some executives wrongly assume that they have to have the "full story" before getting out in front of their people. Others say they are too busy to communicate. Still others fantasize that by not communicating about the transition they are "buffering" employees from stress. It is as if they have an image of employees blissfully whistling while they work and acting as if no news is good news. Of course, employees will tell you that no news is bad news.

Constricted communication during transition is the basis for anger, distrust, and cynicism that linger afterward. It creates a precedent and becomes ingrained in the organizational culture to the extent that upward and downward channels of communication get cut off. Most important, top executives cannot create a new organizational order that will inspire and guide people if they are out of touch with employees' views of everything from how to improve operations to what motivates them.

Outmoded Systems. Systems designed for the pretransition organization may not be appropriate for the posttransition organization. And in the case of multiple waves of change, even a new system designed with a particular vision in mind may soon lose its relevance and efficacy for coordinating work, monitoring performance, and making corrections.

An organization's reward system is a key example of how an outmoded system can interfere with building a new order. When the new order heralds enhanced teamwork but the reward system continues to reinforce individualism, employees will be confused by the conflicting messages. Of course, people's behavior will gravitate toward what is being rewarded. Unless people are moved to act in new ways, to go beyond the old organizational order, the desired new order will not be realized.

Transition Management

A final set of challenges to workplace recovery emanates from how the transition itself was managed. The process of moving through the transition can leave impressions that run counter to the desired end state. The way the transition is managed is the petri dish for growing the posttransition culture.

Lack of Management Consensus. Managers who do not share a common view of the new organizational order will pull employees in different directions. This can occur even when managers think they agree. For example, managers accede relatively easily to such broad objectives as "pushing decision making down the hierarchy." But their interpretations can vary widely. One manager in a communications conglomerate gave employees discretion to make decisions on routine business matters requiring capital expenditures below $500, another solicited employee input for decision alternatives but ultimately made the decision herself, and still another figured he would announce his unilaterally made decisions a day ahead of implementation just in case any employee had any comments.

Lack of Involvement. Unless people feel some ownership of the new organizational order, their actions to bring it to life will be half-hearted at best. In authoritarian, one-size-fits-all prescriptions for change, senior leadership knows in advance (or thinks it knows) what will be required to effect the change, and success is believed to depend on following the program. The opportunity to engage people is reduced to having them "stick with the process"—instead of action and innovation, the result is passivity and obedience. It is the difference between creating a work of art and coloring by numbers.

Reinvention is especially critical when values congruent with employee involvement are part of the new organizational order.

Implementation of a new order often demands an emotional and value-oriented commitment to change. If managers simply go through the motions of establishing a more participative management style, employees quickly recognize that the managers' behavior is insincere. When stress or controversies develop, managers revert to their traditional way of operating. The new organizational order, then, must be more of a blueprint to guide the local efforts of work teams and their leaders than a rigid program or mandate.

Lack of Resources. The most precious resource in recovering from an organizational transition is time. There is never enough of it to accommodate the dual tasks of managing the transition and running the organization. Something has to give—either the quality of transition management or the day-to-day operations of the business.

The development of a new organizational order takes time—time to conceive, communication, test, revise, and implement. Following a distracting transition, managers want to get out of the blocks quickly and show their superiors they can produce results. If there is even the slightest cynicism about leadership's intentions for creating a new organizational order, spending time on innovation and experimentation will be viewed as a wasteful distraction from core business activities. People promised organizational enhancements following a transition will look around for signs that it is living up to its billing, but they will be discouraged by the lack of time made available to design ways to work smarter or think creatively.

Other resources—people, information, tools, and equipment among them—may also be less available following transition. Cost-cutting measures often eliminate research assistants, librarians, clerical help, and other staff who provide information and other resources to managers and teams. For example, regional research centers were consolidated into one national center as part of a downsizing and restructuring effort in a large public relations firm. Although the latest technology helped, the slowed-down turnaround time that resulted alienated both current customers seeking support and executives preparing proposals to bring in new work. Sometimes even the most mundane of resources may be missing. After a defense contractor in Southern California completed waves of downsizing, one vice president wanted to remove the scores of empty desks that remained in his department's work area. His telephone calls to maintenance went unanswered, however. The person responsible for moving furniture was a victim of downsizing, and no one knew who was responsible for that now.

Transition as a Steady State

In this age of the corporate makeovers and technological upheavals, transitions can be so rapid and repetitive that organizations need to build a workforce that can change again and again. The work of establishing a new organizational order, then, may include getting and keeping people in a relatively pliable state. That is, part of refreezing a new mental model is keeping the expectation that unfreezing and remolding may—and likely will—be needed at any time.

There is no indication that the pace at which business is conducted is going to slow down anytime soon. A new economic world order has taken hold, with national economies and financial markets becoming more closely linked in a round-the-clock global economy. The life cycle of products is declining. And technological innovation continues at breakneck speed. Yet workers are lagging behind economic globalization and technical advances. Tough managers may put on a macho facade, but twenty-four-hour access to cell phones, e-mails, and faxes wears people down. And the changing economy brings as many concerns as it does opportunities.

People are not machines, and they cannot keep up the pace of change and transition without some pause and renewal. They cannot exist without some structure and stability in their lives. If they are psychologically healthy, they cannot be fulfilled human beings without having some sense of knowing what and how they are doing to contribute to the greater good. Certainly there are individuals who are totally turned on by the short-term thrill of the immediate kill. This is a small segment of the workforce, however, and it certainly is not characteristic of the vast majority of people who have a basic need for security and seek at least some stability in their employment situation.

Some managers I encounter in posttransition organizations push back and say that refreezing is counterproductive in today's business environment. Perhaps the aim for workplace recovery, then, should be a "slushy" workforce, not a frozen-solid one. That would be a workforce that has some consistency to provide stability for people but is flexible enough to contend with today's workplace realities. As we will see in the next chapter, people cannot handle a completely fluid state. They need some substance if they are to contribute to their fullest ability to economic opportunities in the new economy.

4

Individual Adaptation to Transition

Organizational transitions do not have abrupt endings. In a merger, for example, some employees may encounter immediate and substantial change, while others wait several months until an integration task force makes recommendations about their department. Then, as changes get implemented, they produce reverberations that ripple through other parts of the organization. Although many employees worry whether they will still have a job when the dust settles, the reality is that the vast majority of employees retain their positions in mergers and acquisitions. The real stress comes when survivors struggle to meet business objectives in an environment of confusion and chaos. In a downsizing, survivors mourn the loss of former coworkers and mentors and cope with getting work done with fewer resources. Over time, they develop new mental models, revise work expectations and career aspirations, and adapt to new realities.

Despite employees' ongoing need to assess and cope with transition-related changes, senior management comes to the point where it has had enough talk of merging, downsizing, or restructuring and declares the transition "over." These executives have discarded the old organizational order and are well on their way to accepting the new order. They are excited by what they see ahead—perhaps a merged operation with increased industry clout or a reduced-headcount cost structure. They do not want to hear about lingering postmerger culture clash, layoff survivor sickness, or resistance to change. They are eager to realize the improved business results expected to follow from the transition. But where are the middle managers, front-line supervisors, and rank-and-file employees? Odds are they are still holding on to the old organizational order.

This chapter examines the individual adaptation that must occur for an organizational transition to be completed. In particular, it looks at why people hold on to the old organizational order and resist the new. Some employees are so battered following a transition that they are insecure about their ability to move successfully from the old to the new. Others do not let go of the old because they lack a clear vision of what lies ahead. Still others hear the words that describe the new order but do not see how it will benefit them personally. For all employees, however, there are factors that make the known more comfortable than the unknown, even when the old has proved inadequate or obsolete and the new offers great potential and promise.

Phases of Adaptation

William Bridges's model of individual transition is both a popular and a profound representation of what people go through in the move from the old organization order to the new. Bridges's model consists of three phases (see Figure 4.1):

- *Current reality*. This is the ending of the old. It starts with recognizing the ending and saying goodbye to the status quo. People experience feelings like uncertainty, sadness, grief, loss, fear, anxiety, anger, disenchantment, and disillusionment during this phase.

- *Neutral zone*. This is the in-between phase. Once someone is able to let go of the old, he or she passes through the neutral zone. The neutral zone is a kind of no-man's land—the individual is no longer connected with the old reality but has not yet arrived at the new reality. It is confusing and often fraught

FIGURE 4.1. Bridges's Model of Individual Transition.

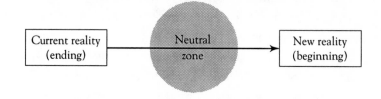

with mixed messages, a feeling of chaos, and powerful emotions. People in the neutral zone often feel lost, apathetic, listless, disoriented, foggy, distant, ungrounded, and unfocused.

- *New reality.* This is the beginning of the new state for the individual. After contending with the neutral zone, the person settles into the new reality. People who arrive at this phase feel reenergized, refocused, excited about and engaged in their situation, and grounded. Important to business organizations, they feel clear about the work that needs to be accomplished.

Not all people make it to the new reality. Some never let go of the old reality, despite all the changes that may be going on around them. Some get stuck in the quagmire of the neutral zone—they accept that the old is gone but never latch on to the new. Although individuals move through the three phases at different speeds, all go through the phases sequentially. *You cannot get to the new reality without ending the old or going through the neutral zone.*

In describing individual adaptation, Bridges highlights some key qualities of the process. Unfortunately, these realities of individual adaptation run counter to the inclinations of typical senior executives and, I believe, are at the root of why many organizational transitions are mismanaged:

- *Transitions go on within a person.* Individual adaptation is an internal process. Most executives prefer to deal with "hard" issues like structure, strategy, and finance. Despite this inclination toward concrete matters, human problems require human solutions.

• *Transitions take much longer than change.* As noted in Chapter One, change is a path to a known state (we change the meeting starting time from 9:00 to 8:00); the change may be disruptive or even undesired, but we know exactly how to deal with it. Transition is a journey to an unknown state (we downsize, but we do not know what the implications will be for getting work done or for long-term survival). Consequently, transition is much more psychologically taxing on people than change is. And adapting to it is very complex, requiring much trial-and-error learning. It takes time for people to adapt and learn as they encounter transition. Executives, however, are in a hurry to get on with things. Again and again I come across executives who develop a self-imposed sense of urgency during and after transition—they want to show financial analysts that they are in control, or they want to get the pain and disruption over with quickly. When contending with transition, however, people cannot move as quickly as executives wish.

• *Transitions start with endings.* One reason transitions take so long to work through is that people have to end the old and struggle through the neutral zone before they can accept the new. Despite this human reality, it remains the exception and not the rule for executives to acknowledge the need for people to end the current reality before they can begin the new reality.

• *Transition is a natural process.* The adaptation process that Bridges describes—ending the current reality, struggling with the neutral zone, and accepting the new reality—is a perfectly normal and to-be-expected human process. Bridges did not make it up; he observed it and wrote about it. Yet typical executives deny or ignore the psychological impact of a merger, acquisition, or downsizing. Sometimes wishful thinking is at work here—if leaders don't talk about the psychological difficulty of transition, maybe it won't be so bad or will even go away. Sometimes executives have tunnel vision on the numbers and don't consider the human realities of adaptation to transition. And sometimes executives have been isolated from what really is going on among the workforce and no one is willing to tell the emperor he has no clothes. Whatever the underlying cause, hubris of "when the going gets tough, the tough get going" and "if people are worried about keeping their job, maybe they should be" predominates. This only further alienates and discourages employees who are in the midst of a psychologically taxing transition.

A few years ago, I had a client, the CEO of a computer services firm, who refused to accept that people have to move through phases of adaptation. It made no sense to him that people had to end the old and struggle with the neutral zone before accepting the new. "Give people a vision and goals, and they will go for it," he would say. In the course of three years, his company made two major acquisitions, downsized, and restructured. These events significantly changed the composition of his senior team, so he engaged me to conduct a team-building program. Midway through the project, the CEO's best friend was diagnosed with late-stage cancer and died shortly thereafter. The CEO was not a particularly religious man, but he attended each of the Roman Catholic ceremonies to acknowledge and honor the death of his friend. These events were critically important in his adaptation process. This CEO went through a transition—aided by the ceremonies and his own acceptance of reality—by ending his attachment to his deceased best friend, struggling with the disorientation and emotions of the neutral zone, and eventually accepting the new reality of life without his friend.

Dealing with the death of a loved one is a classic example of a transition. People who experience the loss of a family member, dear friend, or important colleague just don't wake up the next day and get on with their lives. They grieve the loss of their loved one and struggle with accepting new realities. Some people take weeks to go through this natural and normal process, others take months, and still others take years. Some individuals never reach the stage of acceptance. Unlike a simple change, in which they know exactly what to expect, mourners encounter tremendous uncertainty and insecurity regarding their future—How will they go on living without their loved one? Who will they turn to for support? What will they do when they need assistance normally provided by the deceased? All of this is much more trying on a person's well-being than simply getting to a meeting that has been changed from 9:00 to 8:00.

Religions have embraced the concept of transformational change for centuries. Religious institutions have elaborate ceremonies to commemorate births, deaths, marriages, and other life transitions. These rituals are a means to help people work through a dramatic change—the loss of familiar realities—as an essential precursor to moving on to new realities.

Adaptation After Organizational Transition

So how does this very natural and normal process of adaptation apply to workplace recovery? Individual adaptation to transition occurs through three phases: holding on to the old, letting go of the old, and accepting the new. Throughout these phases, every person and organization encounters forces for maintaining the status quo and forces for change (see Figure 4.2). These forces operate counter to each other, with a constantly shifting balance. Early on, the forces for maintaining the status quo are strong and are expressed through outright resistance to change or, at best, the absence of a will to act. Over time, the forces for the new organizational order tend to dominate and provide the necessary impetus for letting go and adaptation.

In the *holding-on* phase, forces for the old order and for resisting perceived or real threats to the individual's current situation predominate. The person senses danger in the form of a threat to self-preservation. Most people respond to this perceived danger with feelings of helplessness and in some cases panic. The person feels confused, cannot fully grasp what is happening, and consequently cannot adequately cope with the situation. The threat to accustomed ways of doing things, personal position, expected cause-and-

FIGURE 4.2. Adaptation After Transition.

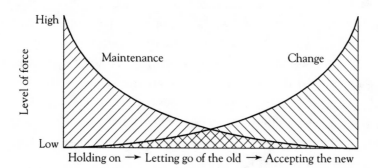

effect relationships, capability to act, and self-esteem can be over-whelming. This is why employees feel like they have little or no control during and after transition, as well as why more senior executives tend to cope a little better than those at middle and lower ranks—they have more at risk but also more control over resources.

Searching for ways to control the threat, the individual attempts to fortify old ways of doing things—trying to go on as if things have not really changed. Avoiding or denying reality, the person is likely to indulge in wishful thinking. This helps reduce anxiety, at least in the short run. During this stage, individuals' thinking becomes rigid, and they refuse to consider the possibility of change in their own behaviors, values, or goals. Any hint that the old organizational order can persist is counterproductive to recovery because it solidifies the status quo: A senior vice president who bad-mouths the new organizational order raises hopes that the old will carry on; a compensation system that reinforces the status quo helps employees rationalize behaving in old patterns.

In some organizations, the old order prevails and no movement is made toward the new organizational order. Sooner or later, however, most people encounter external forces for change, and internal forces for growth and development overcome the status quo and resistance to change, leading to the second phase, *letting go*. People discover that the coping mechanisms used to this point are not proving successful at averting the perceived threat and stress. A renewed brush with reality occurs, followed by a renewed period of personal uncertainty and stress. Intellectually, employees recognize the transition's potential for improvements in organizational competitiveness, work processes, and personal opportunities; emotionally, however, they are frightened by—or at least uncomfortable with—the specter of change. People hope to exert some control through politicking and positioning. Eventually, however, they learn that conventional coping mechanisms do not succeed at fending off the forces for change, nor does wishful thinking.

What Bridges calls the neutral zone, many of my clients have dubbed the *twilight zone*. It is dark and scary—people literally have to grope their way out of the darkness, and even when progress is being made, the daunting journey is intimidating to most employees. Employees go through a gamut of responses—feeling depressed and withdrawing some days but revving up and feeling resentful and angry on others. Some may mourn the loss of the old; others feel bitter about their losses. For all, it is a confusing and uncomfortable time.

Finally, the individual enters the third phase, *accepting the new*. More than just a weakening of the status quo, arriving at this phase requires a strengthening of the forces for change and growth. The employee embraces the new organizational order: it is understood, accepted, and even inspiring. When well communicated and supported, the new organizational order becomes a beacon for guiding employee actions toward organizational goals. On a personal level, the employee operates in the here and now and accepts new realities. When the forces for the new are strong, resolution takes the form of a new equilibrium, with the acceptances of a new vision, new attitudes, new behaviors, and a new sense of purpose.

Obviously, the more consistent the forces for change, the quicker adaptation occurs. The more that forces interfering with desired change are identified and roadblocks to adaptation are eliminated, the more readily people let go of the old. The more the forces for desired change reinforce one another—whether they come from how the organization is structured, how work is approached, who gets rewarded for doing what, how people interact with one another, and so on—the more readily the desired new organizational order is realized. And when employees see that leadership's actions are consistent with its words and that there is a clear way out of the quagmire of transition, their spirit and motivation to act are revitalized along with the work team performance required to make a successful run at business opportunities.

When they accept the new organizational order and grow comfortable with their position in it, employees report a lessening of anxiety and depression and a strengthening of hope and optimism. They develop a renewed sense of worth in the workplace, modify their self-image as a member of the organization, and build up their confidence that they can succeed in it. They are ready to charge up the hill and capture the prize.

Swinging from the Old to the New

One reason so many organizational change efforts fail (be they mergers, acquisitions, downsizings, restructurings, or culture transformations) is that the leaders who initiate these programs and the staffers who implement them fail to recognize that people have to end the old before they can accept the new. Moving through a transition is a lot like swinging on a set of rings (see Figure 4.3). The organization wants the individual to progress from the old to the new, a goal that may or may not be consistent with the employee's desire, ability, or motivation. With one hand securely clinging on to the first ring, the employee is expected to grab the next. But the individual has to let go of the old to get within reach of the new. Below, the ground is hard, and no safety net is in sight to protect from a fall. Few except the truly courageous (or truly foolish) will let go of the first ring until they have a reasonable degree of confidence that they can successfully latch onto the one ahead. The individual employee can take some actions to increase the chances of successfully moving ahead, but there is always some hang time in midair without

FIGURE 4.3. Swinging from the Old to the New.

the security of holding onto either the old ring or the new one. Some people may find this an invigorating time; for most, however, it is scary and fraught with anxiety. Fear of hitting the hard ground keeps employees holding tightly onto the old.

A variety of forces, both internal and external to the individual, influence the speed with which people swing from the old organizational order to the new. Three sets of forces are particularly significant in delaying the natural process of adaptation: dealing with loss, demotivation, and executive inattention to the letting-go process.

Dealing with Loss

Before people can contribute to the upside of a transition, they have to come to terms with what they feel they are losing as a result of it. Employees in an acquired company lose their company identity; in a downsizing, they lose coworkers and mentors; in a culture transformation, they lose accustomed ways of doing things; and in all of these, they lose expectations of everything from job security to career paths.

Accordingly, employees need to mourn the loss of their company, coworkers, and cultures. Such grieving follows the contours of reactions to death so aptly specified in the work of Elisabeth Kübler-Ross, whose studies of terminally ill patients and their families found repeatedly occurring stages. Employees regularly use these stages to describe their experience of going through an organizational transition.

First, there is denial of the loss. Executives may fantasize that a hostile raider withdraws its unfriendly takeover bid or that shareholders will not sell out. Employees may deny their vulnerability in a downsizing by reminding themselves how valuable they are to the company and how their work area could not function without them. At an acquired entertainment firm, a middle manager excitedly ran through the halls shouting, "I've got a copy of [the buying company]'s organizational chart, and there is no one who has my job! I'm going to survive this thing!" As it turned out, the buyer did not have anyone doing that job because it did not value that function, and so the manager was among the first to be laid off. Then comes a period of anger at company leaders ("How could they allow this to happen to us?"), at the acquirer ("What gives them the right to do this to people?"), and even at oneself ("Why didn't I see this coming? Why didn't I leave before things got to this point?").

Next comes strategizing and bargaining. Unrealistic schemes for maintaining the status quo and influencing others are developed in this stage. Acquired management teams often plot ways to change the acquirers before they themselves are changed; a manager in a downsizing environment may publicize how an important project is ahead of schedule and under budget in an effort to protect jobs for himself and his team. Finally comes the stage of acceptance. Only at this point are individuals ready to accept their losses realistically. In the context of death and dying, this is the achievement of an inner and outer peace: "My time has come, and I'm ready to go." In an acquisition, it is the acceptance that life as it was known in premerger days is over and a preparation for accepting the realities of the postmerger organization. In a downsizing, it is the acceptance of new realities, roles, and expectations.

As with the phases of adaptation to transition, moving through these stages is a perfectly normal and to-be-expected human reaction to loss—whether the loss of a loved one or one's working situation.

Some people move more quickly through the stages than others, and some people get stuck in denial, anger, or strategizing and bargaining without ever arriving at the stage of acceptance. An organization recovering from transition cannot eliminate the natural response of moving through these stages, but it can accelerate it.

Demotivation After Transition

Employees will resist letting go of the old when their mental models, developed within the context of the old organizational order, predict a lack of success in moving from one ring to the next. As briefly introduced in Chapter Three, the expectancy theory of motivation highlights three conditions that can reduce employee motivation to let go of the old organizational order and accept the new. Being a multiplicative relationship, a low probability rating on any of the three factors results in low motivation. As Exhibit 4.1 shows, the characteristics of typically mismanaged transitions directly affect each of these motivational factors.

First, the employee may feel incapable of making the move from one ring to the next ("Even if I give it my best shot, there is a good chance I will fall"). This assessment could be based on general and historical perceptions of one's capabilities but also on recent episodes of frustration in trying to get things done during the chaos of transition. An employee who felt unable to influence his or her situation or whose work suffered due to competing demands or the unavailability of needed resources will see less connection between how hard he or she works and how well he or she performs. This is what led Dan, the writer discussed at the opening of the book, to go from thinking about his position with the dot-com as a productive, mutually rewarding relationship to "just a job." Sixty-five-hour workweeks and success in developing an excellent reputation for the start-up's content did not reduce his vulnerability to being laid off. The result for Dan and many of his coworkers was a "why bother?" attitude, since hard work did not contribute to protecting them from layoffs.

EXHIBIT 4.1. Links Between Transition Mismanagement and Reduced Employee Motivation.

Transition Conditions	Effect on Employee Motivation
• Lack of control • Competing demands • Limited resources	Inability: employee feels unable to complete tasks even if giving best effort
• Unclear vision • Little evidence of improved organization • Heightened cynicism • Lessened confidence	Undesirability: employee does not find new organizational order attractive
• Broken promises • Changing psychological work contract • Increased distrust	Unpredictability: employee does not expect to benefit from or in the new organizational order

Second, the employee may feel that what awaits at the second ring is not worth the risk of letting go of the first one ("I can make it to the next ring, but how will I be any better off over there than I am here?"). If no clear vision of the new organizational order was developed or communicated during the transition or if little evidence was produced to back up promises of a new and better organization, the perceived attractiveness of life on the second ring will suffer to the point where employees figure, "Why make the trip?" Even if a decent rationale or business case was conveyed to employees—and if employees understood and supported the rationale—many employees will still ask, "What's it in for me if I take the risk of moving forward?"

The merger of two large energy companies provides an excellent example of how not having a clear vision of the new organizational order inhibits letting go of the old. In this case, as in all mergers and acquisitions, a clash of corporate cultures enveloped the transition period as employees from both partners came to revalue key aspects of their business and ways of doing things. Company practices and systems that had always been taken for granted became much more important as executives reflected on what they might lose in the combination. Overt politicking colored the integration decision-making process: department heads and unit leaders figured that if their side's systems or ways of doing things prevailed in the combined organization, so would their jobs.

True to form, people throughout the ranks started noticing differences between the companies' cultures and denigrating the other side while promoting their own. Managers from one partner reeled at bureaucratic controls in areas that ran untethered in the other. Managers from the side with the strong bureaucracy, in turn, worried about too little control over their freewheeling counterparts. Yet people from both sides also held out some hope that the merger would be an opportunity to replace outmoded, unproductive, or uninspiring ways of doing things. As one manager put it, "I don't necessarily support having our ways retained, but I can say for sure that I don't want to see their culture winning out. The real opportunity is to come up with something better than what either side had in the past."

Unfortunately, the combined organization's senior leadership did not articulate characteristics of a new organizational order. Senior executives were dealing with their personal transitions—many of them had a new boss, and all of them had new peers and subordinates—and learning to work with one another. As part of the terms of doing the deal, the CEO of one side agreed to hold that title in the combined company for two years and then retire and pass it on to the other side's CEO. The current CEO was satisfied with masterminding a bold move in the industry and did not see building a new postmerger culture as part of his transition management responsibility. "Why worry about that now," he mused, "when the new CEO will want to put his own stamp on the company in two years?" His point is a good one, but in the meantime, the transition drifted along, rudderless. Transition task forces floundered without a new organizational order to guide integration decision making.

Had there been a shared vision of a new organizational order, task force meetings could have been forums for assessing gaps between the current organizations and the desired postmerger organization. Instead, they were reduced to us-versus-them battles as participants held on to their old organizational orders. As reports of these unproductive and self-serving meetings moved through both companies' grapevines, employees saw no clear advantage in accepting the new and therefore kept a tight grip on the old. They also followed the behaviors modeled by their leaders of not letting go of the old. With employees seeing no personal or business benefits in moving from one ring to the next, who can blame them for holding on to their old ways, beliefs, and expectations?

A third situation that demotivates people after transition occurs when the employee does understand the potential personal benefits or rewards of the new organizational order but for whatever reason does not expect a payout for making the leap to the next ring ("Why should I bother moving forward when management won't deliver on its promises?"). If a transition is perceived to have blocked an expected promotion, prevented a desired new project, obscured a career path, changed the psychological work contract, or caused distrust toward management, the employee is apt to be suspicious of new vows.

Take the case of Martin, a talented executive with a stable position in the computer peripheral industry who was wooed away by a competitor promising an opportunity to build a new product area from scratch. Assured by the company recruiter that "this is the product we are betting our future on," Martin was totally turned on by the opportunity to build the area in his own design and have an impact on the future of the company. Still, before coming on board, Martin carefully negotiated sufficient levels of funding and autonomy in running the operation. Martin finally left his old job, leapt into the new one, hired staff, and made excellent progress in product development. Barely a year went by, however, before the company acquired another firm with a relatively mature business in Martin's new product area. Figuring that this would jump-start its entry in the area, Martin's superiors put the acquired management team in charge of Martin's product line. When Martin confronted his boss about the broken promises, he was told that the acquisition "merely confirmed the company's commitment to this product" and that he should "learn to be a team player." Martin's reaction was to withdraw psychologically:

> I went through the motions, but I really was not producing much work. A couple of times I saw where I could make a difference in what these guys were producing, but I didn't feel any ownership over what they were doing, and I just didn't bother to contribute. Yeah, it hurts my ego, but I'm being paid very well for not doing very much! I'm biding my time until another offer comes along, but I don't know what I can do to prevent getting jerked around again.

With low expectations that the new ring (the new organizational order) is attainable, is worth reaching for, or is likely to provide some personal payoff, employees are slow to move forward. This underscores the potency of unintended consequences of mismanaged transitions to linger long after the event is considered "over." In the case of blue-chip firms, the company is right to reduce the cost base and bring its relationship with its people more in line with current economic realities. These moves are necessary for long-term profitability and may eventually enhance employee job security and compensation. But they are not without costs to short-term employee motivation and productivity.

Similarly, small and medium-sized companies do not set out to hurt their employees by engaging in transitions. Martin's bosses at the computer peripheral company were extremely pleased with the pace of new product development under his watch. The company received an unsolicited offer to purchase a competitor with balance sheet problems but a strong product line. The CEO jumped at what he considered a major coup and assumed that his subordinates, including Martin, would be as excited as he was about the integration opportunities. The company made a bold move, but it did not make a concerted effort to help employees embrace the transition by showing them how they could succeed and benefit with it. What was a potential motivator on paper became a demotivator in practice.

Inattention to Letting Go

Along with the internal forces for holding on are external forces that inhibit employee progress toward letting go of the old. The legitimacy of the need for ending the old order before moving on to the new order may be denied by those with the capacity to make resources available to accelerate recovery. While human resource professionals and first-line supervisors witness the pain being experienced by employees (along with the resulting distraction from performance), executives— concerned about the future— overlook the need to let go of the old before accepting the new. Many managers are blinded by their personal agenda of getting out of the blocks quickly following a transition. In a merger, acquired managers want to impress new bosses. After a downsizing, managers hope to reduce their personal vulnerability in the event of another round of downsizing. They hold on to a fallacy of getting people's behavior in line by putting their noses to the grindstone and producing operational results. The hoped-for acquiescence, however, is invariably blocked by personal forces for holding on to the old.

In some organizations, the natural adaptation process of letting go of the old before accepting the new is understood but not wholeheartedly embraced. These employers dismiss allowing people to deal with their feelings as an inappropriate use of time and other resources. This reasoning ignores the fact that people will go through the phases of holding on, letting go, and accepting the new whether the organization likes it or not. Time and attention get diverted away from work activities in any event. Rather than deplete resources, a workplace recovery program accelerates the speed with which people come to terms with and move through their adaptation process.

Executives may also question the expenditure of money on a recovery program when the organization has just endured a painful pruning of costs. Employees sometimes echo these doubts—like the administrative assistant who asked her CEO during a lunch break at a postdownsizing grieving program, "How can you justify spending money on this hotel room, lunch for everybody, and an outside facilitator when we just laid people off and you told us we have to find even more ways of cutting costs?" The CEO gave an exemplary reply:

> While it has been a painful decision to terminate some employees, and the other financial sacrifices we have to make are substantial, we will never cut back on investing in our employees. The competition is only getting stronger out there, and if we want to be a survivor in this industry, our people have to get stronger too. We have come here today not only to help you cope with your feelings about where we have been and what we are going through but also to help you identify how to be more successful as individual contributors in the future. This is only going to help us become a more competitive organization, and I always will pay for that.

Contributing to the inattention to letting go are fears of exploring internal psychological forces. In some organizations, executives just don't feel comfortable exploring aspects of subconscious motivation or talking about feelings of helplessness, vulnerability, rejection, and anger in a work setting. Doing so is hardly congruent with the crisp, "businesslike" behavior many executives extol following transition.

Another key reason why the letting-go process is often ignored in organizations engaged in transition is that senior executives are ahead of the curve: they have typically let go of the old long before others in the organization have even begun the adaptation process. Ordinarily, senior executives have been involved in secret premerger discussions, deliberated the need for a downsizing, or pondered the cultural implications long before the transition was announced to the overall organization. In each case, they have several months' head start in the process of psychologically rejecting the old organizational order and adapting to the new.

As Figure 4.4 shows, those at the top levels in an organization begin their process of moving from holding on to letting go of the old and accepting the new well before employees at other levels. Senior executives, those with the most at stake, often have the most intense reactions to a transition and experience strong forces for maintaining the status quo. They adapt to change and mourn their losses through what is typically a private process but one that nonetheless consumes personal attention and time. Significantly, however, their adaptation process is accelerated by the high degree of control they enjoy relative to others in the organization. Senior executives are the architects of the transition; they understand why change is needed and where it is headed. The other members of the organization have much less influence and a lot more uncertainty when it comes to adaptation.

By the time executives at the top of the organization are looking ahead to new realities, people lower in the hierarchy are only beginning or somewhere in the middle of their adaptation process. In large organizations, transition implementation may not ripple down to the lowest levels for quite some time. Many employees do not experience their first wave of transition-related change—and thus do

FIGURE 4.4. Adaptation to Transition by Hierarchical Level.

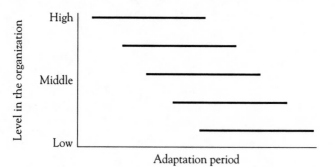

not *begin* their adaptation process—until senior executives have put the old behind them and are well on their way to accepting the new. Just as lower-level employees are beginning to contend with holding on and letting go, senior executives frequently repress memories of the pain and confusion of leaving the old behind. Consequently, they are unsympathetic to others' needs for holding on. Having let go of the past, they are concerned with the future. Either because they are impatient to move on or because they refuse to consciously accept the pain of their own personal transition, executives sometimes forget that beginning the new starts with ending the old.

When executives deny or ignore the reality of letting go of the old before accepting the new, they are attempting to circumvent the essential nature of transition. The result is all too clear: the best talent jumps ship to another company, customer commitments are missed, and as noted, over three-fourths of all transitions are financial failures. We can do better than a 25 percent success rate, and the next chapter tells how to accept the realities of organizational transition and individual adaptation in designing workplace recovery.

5

The Realities
and Requirements
of Workplace Recovery

Given that all transitions—even relatively well managed ones—have unintended negative consequences and that adaptation to transition is a natural and deliberate process that cannot be circumvented, what can be done to generate the desire and ability among employees to charge back up the hill when new opportunities emerge? *Workplace recovery* helps survivors of mergers, acquisitions, downsizings, and other major transitions by accelerating ending the old and accepting the new, in terms of both the transition's emotional realities and business imperatives:

- Recovery recognizes the need to drive business success by minimizing the unintended effects of transition, gearing people up for their new roles and responsibilities and renewing motivation for making a run at business challenges and opportunities.

- Recovery happens when all members of an organization have a shared idea of the direction in which they are headed and are tolerant of the pain involved in getting from the old organizational order to the new.

- Recovery involves managers in helping their work team members rebound from the psychological trauma of transition, clarify work roles and responsibilities, and secure the organizational capability and individual motivation needed for success.

- Recovery engages people in understanding how and why their workplace is changing and how and where they can exert control during and after the transition. And it helps them let go of frustrations and anger over things beyond their control.

The design of workplace recovery is based on the realities of organizational transition and individual adaptation that have been presented to this point in this book. This chapter summarizes those realities, along with the two requirements and two levels of workplace recovery—the product of which yields four elements that make up a comprehensive approach to workplace recovery. The chapter concludes with principles drawn from lessons learned that give a practical sense of how to implement workplace recovery following transition.

A Dozen Realities About Workplace Recovery

Twelve realities of organizational transition and how people adapt to transition form the basis for workplace recovery.

1. *Transitions are difficult events to manage; the very way they are executed runs counter to common tools of organizational change management.* The secretive nature of mergers and acquisitions and the thorny process of downsizing restrict opportunities to clarify a vision of a new and better organization, communicate in a timely manner, and provide opportunities for employee involvement. The inevitable result is lessened employee morale, team productivity, and organizational effectiveness. Even if current leadership did not manage the transition itself, it inherits a posttransition organization with a workforce still carrying a lot of emotional baggage from the transition.

2. *Transitions are difficult events for people to cope with—and employees in many firms are saturated after years of stress from organiza-*

tional MADness. A transition is a very complex event—a journey to an unknown state resulting in many simultaneous and interactive changes. Transition poses a break from the past. Existing practices and routines must be abandoned and new ones discovered and developed. Adapting to transition is much more psychologically taxing than adapting to change. And after years of mergers, acquisitions, downsizings, and other major transitions, people's ability to cope with transition has become saturated. Even when they themselves have not gone through a difficult transition, people learn vicariously from the experience of their friends, relatives, neighbors, and counterparts in other organizations.

3. *Mismanaged transitions have a negative, not a neutral, impact on people and organizations.* Even the best-planned and most carefully executed transitions produce unintended personal and business consequences. Employee morale, trust, and confidence in themselves and their leaders suffer as a result of living through a difficult transition, as do productivity, quality, and customer service. People become pessimistic about their own ability—and that of their leadership—to steer out of the chaos and confusion.

4. *The way transitions are mismanaged weakens motivational forces.* The uncertainty and stress of organizational life during and after major transitions reduces employees' perceptions of their ability to get the job done, the attractiveness of rewards, and the expectation that organizations will deliver on those rewards. These vital components of employee motivation are weakened as a result of the way most transitions are managed. As a result, when urged to charge back up the hill to capture new business opportunities following transition, employees shrug and ask, "Why bother?"

5. *People regress to primitive forms of behavior during and after transition but also crave direction and control.* When their coping mechanisms are saturated, people regress to politicking, withholding communication, and clinging to old perceptions and behaviors. Looking for a way out of the darkness, they seek direction and some sense of being able to control their fate—a definition of the new organizational order and involvement in bringing it to life. Yet in

almost every transition, that direction has not been fully articulated, and people assume that they have lost control over their immediate work lives and longer-term fate in the organization.

6. *Executives adopt crisis management orientations and rely on the tried and tested rather than risk innovative solutions.* With a self-imposed sense of crisis and urgency, executives and middle managers "go with what they know" rather than take the time or appropriate risks to look for innovative solutions. This strengthens forces for the status quo, including cynicism toward leadership's promises of a new and better organization emerging after the transition.

7. *Transitions have the potential to unfreeze people and organizations.* If well managed, transitions shake up organizations and their employees. Transition disturbs the status quo: it jars people, changes relationships, redefines work team composition and goals, and disrupts accustomed ways of doing things. Inherent in this disruption are opportunities to think proactively about what life after the transition could be like and enhance employees' receptivity to a new organizational order. This is the first step in getting people to develop new expectations, perceptions, behavior, and mental models that are consistent with the desired new organization.

8. *People need to let go of the old before they can accept the new, and in between they struggle with the neutral zone.* Before people can accept the new organizational order, however, they have to end the old. Employees have to vent their anger, deal with their stress, let go of outmoded perceptions and behaviors, and realize that the status quo is insufficient for achieving desired business objectives and personal development. Then they have to struggle with the dark, confusing time when the old organizational order no longer exists but the new organizational order is not yet firmly in place. This neutral zone is an essential but uncomfortable way station on the journey from old to new.

9. *Executives typically ignore or deny the need to let go of the old before accepting the new.* Executives are human, too, and they spend time ending the old before accepting the new. Yet their discomfort in dealing with intangible people issues and their impatience with

the adaptation process prompt them to deny or ignore its reality. As a result, they come up with unrealistic transition objectives, timetables, and expectations. When these are not met, the sense of crisis and the lack of perceived confidence in leadership grow.

10. *The more consistent the forces for the new organizational order, the more readily people will accept it.* The forces for maintaining the old and for accepting the new are always ebbing and flowing. Eliminating excuses and opportunities to continue to hold on to the old will help people accept the new. So will consistency in the posttransition systems, procedures, and behaviors that employees experience.

11. *People want to identify with their workplace and want a fair chance at succeeding in the new organizational order.* Despite years of mismanaged transitions, the vast majority of employees still care about their workplace. They want it to succeed and are willing to do their part for the organizational good. But they want to share in the success. And they want to be treated like adults in the journey from the old organizational order to the new, not like children who should be seen and not heard. Employees want opportunities to control their fate by contributing to the transition and recovery and by having the direction and resources needed to get the job done.

12. *A posttransition culture will emerge—either the status quo or a modified one by design or by default.* Transition is a petri dish in which a culture grows. It may be the same culture that predominated prior to the transition, or it may change— either by design or by accident—as a result of how the transition is managed. The more that leadership proactively manages the transition process, the more likely it is that the posttransition culture will reflect and support leadership's desired end state for the new organization.

Two Requirements and Two Levels of Workplace Recovery

Workplace recovery accepts and works with the realities of organizational transition and individual adaptation, rather than denying these natural processes or futilely attempting to work around them.

One of these realities is that people have to end the old before they accept the new. Look back at Figure 4.2, and you will see that this adaptation occurs more as a fading out and in than a quick cut. In each phase of holding on, letting go, and accepting the new, every person encounters forces for the maintenance of the status quo and forces for change. These forces operate counter to each other, with a constantly shifting balance. Thus there are two requirements for recovery after transition: weaken the forces for maintaining the old organizational order and strengthen the forces for developing the new organizational order.

The forces for the old and for the new are varied and cover both personal and organizational matters. To sufficiently weaken forces for the old and strengthen forces for the new, workplace recovery must address both the emotional realities and the business imperatives associated with a transition or a series of transitions. *Emotional realities* are the ways in which people experience transition in the workplace. In the ending-the-old phase, these emotional realities are the perceptions, experiences, mental models, beliefs, and viewpoints that individuals carry over with them from before and during the transition that must be weakened if the new organizational order is to be embraced. In the accepting-the-new phase, they are the characteristics of the new organizational order that motivate employees and attract their attention. These forces need to be strengthened for people to let go of the old and accept the new.

Importantly, these emotional realities are in the eye of the beholder, that is, reality as perceived from the employee perspective. This confounded the business unit leadership of a large pharmaceutical company when it purchased a small biotech company. The acquisition target had a series of nice products in the development pipeline, including two that were on the verge of FDA approval. At the same time, it suffered from a lack of muscle in marketing drugs. The target's CEO believed that selling to a major pharmaceutical company was the best way for the drugs to reach their full potential in the marketplace. He also felt that the combination would benefit employees' long-term job security. During due diligence, the buyers did not dig deep into the target to identify employee perspectives on the deal. As a result, they assumed that the entire workforce was as rosy about the combination as the CEO. In reality, employees perceived the deal as a sellout by their CEO, who was suspected of "cashing in so he could retire to Aspen." Having endured the ups and downs of years of product testing, employees saw "the rug pulled out from under us just as we are about to turn a profit." To their surprise, the buyers acquired a bitter workforce, looking back in anger, rather than one looking ahead to new opportunities.

Business imperatives are the things that need to get done for business success to occur. These include everything from setting strategies to selecting work procedures, from patterns of communicating with people to ways of rewarding them. To facilitate ending the old, certain aspects of the business imperatives that predominated in the old organizational order must be abandoned or made less prominent— that is, the forces for their maintenance must be weakened. To strengthen forces for accepting the new, employees must understand not only what is changing but also why the changes are being made and how those changes will contribute to both business and personal success. In the acquired biotech firm, employees had to forgo some of the looseness of their operating style and adopt more detailed financial reporting practices (required of a larger entity) and more rigorous product marketing procedures (required to bring the strategic synergy at the core of the deal to life).

By addressing the two levels of emotional realities and business imperatives, employees let go of the unintentional pain and consequences they experience during and after transitions while simultaneously contributing to using transitions as opportunities to build new and better workplaces. This is how to take shell-shocked troops, rebuild their confidence in themselves and their leaders, and prepare them to triumph in charging enthusiastically up the hill, committed to capturing the prize.

The Elements of Workplace Recovery

The two requirements of workplace recovery (weakening forces for the old and strengthening forces for the new) and the two levels of workplace recovery (emotional realities and business imperatives) produce four elements of workplace recovery after transition: empathy, engagement, energy, and enforcement (see Figure 5.1):

> *Empathy:* Letting people know leadership acknowledges that things have been difficult and will continue to be difficult for a while longer

> *Engagement:* Creating understanding of and support for the need to end the old and accept the new organizational order

> *Energy:* Getting people excited about the new organizational order and supporting them in realizing it

> *Enforcement:* Solidifying new mental models that are congruent with the desired new organizational order

FIGURE 5.1. The Process of Workplace Recovery.

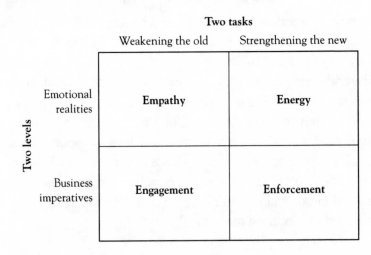

	Two tasks	
	Weakening the old	Strengthening the new
Emotional realities	**Empathy**	**Energy**
Business imperatives	**Engagement**	**Enforcement**

Two levels

Empathy

The first element of workplace recovery is to express empathy to employees (see Exhibit 5.1). This means making it *clear* that leadership is cognizant of the needs, feelings, problems, and views of employees who have lived through a merger, acquisition, or downsizing. It does not matter if leadership thinks these employee perspectives are legitimate. What does matter is that workers get a sense that leadership knows what they have been through and what they are currently thinking and feeling about the workplace, their role in it, and the future of both.

Expressing empathy contributes to unfreezing employees. They are not accustomed to hearing their superiors admit that times have been tough and that transition has taken a toll on people. In most organizations, employees are surprised when they hear leadership admit awareness of the difficulty people have been through. Seeing

EXHIBIT 5.1. Empathy.	
Theme:	Empathy
Overriding objective:	Let people know leadership acknowledges that it has been difficult, currently is difficult, and will continue to be difficult for a while.
Key tasks:	• Acknowledge realities and difficulties of transition and recovery. • Offer workshops to raise awareness of the transition process and help people understand where they do and do not have control. • Use symbols, ceremonies, and forums to end the old.

their superiors talk and act in new ways gets employees to think about their own responsibility in letting go of the old and accepting the new. They think to themselves, "If leadership is owning up to—rather than denying or ignoring—the problems stemming from the transition, then maybe I should do the same." When empathy is expressed and received in an organization following a transition, it is like pressing a reset button to help eliminate the lingering negativity of the past and enhance receptivity to the positive potential of the future.

Executives convey empathy through a combination of activities. They acknowledge the realities and difficulties of living through a transition and recovering from its unintended consequences. Part of this acknowledgment is to own up to one's own role in contributing to the pain of the past. Leaders back up their words by sponsoring workshops that help employees understand the complexity and intricacies of the transition and adaptation processes. An important function of these programs is to help individuals understand where they do and do not have control and to guide them in letting go of what is beyond their control and focusing on what is within it. And leaders weaken the forces for the status quo by getting the word out to all executives, managers, and supervisors that the recovery effort is genuine and that time and resources must be freed up to allow employees to participate in these activities.

Engagement

You've owned up to the pain of transition and acknowledged the need for employees to end the old before they can begin the new. In an ideal world, pressing the reset button would start you off with a clean slate. But life during and after a merger, acquisition, or downsizing is anything but ideal. Forces for holding on to the comfortable status quo continue to dominate those for accepting the new. So the second element of workplace recovery weakens forces against desired change by engaging people in understanding the business imperatives of recovery and eliminating roadblocks to achieving them (see Exhibit 5.2).

You engage people by helping them accomplish their immediate work objectives. Clarifying priorities and providing resources to get the job done weaken the characteristics of posttransition life that commonly demotivate people. When people know what is expected of them and have the information, tools, and time they need to get it done, the feeling of "Why bother?" seems less and less warranted.

You also engage people by stepping up communication and employee involvement. This is Organizational Behavior 101: the more people understand about what is going on and the more involved they feel in the process, the less resistant they are to organizational change. If this makes little or no sense to you, you should probably close this book right now. Even if it does make gut sense, don't shrug off this requirement of recovery as a no-brainer. Communication here does not mean the cursory or infrequent sharing of information. Rather, it implies a genuine effort to keep people in the know through frequent and thorough communication. This is no easy task when executives are stretched thin between running

EXHIBIT 5.2. Engagement.	
Theme:	Engagement
Overriding objective:	Create understanding of and support for the need to end the old and accept the new organizational order.
Key tasks:	• Help people get their work done. • Communicate and provide opportunities for involvement. • Diagnose and eliminate barriers to adaptation.

the business and managing the transition and when support staff have been let go in a reduction in force. And involvement means taking people off-line from their jobs and giving them the time to problem-solve and recommend ways of working smarter—a truly tough call when the employee ranks have been downsized and external stakeholders are impatient for a short-term turnaround in operational results.

Increasing communication and involvement following transition have a symbolic as well as a substantive value—it demonstrates that leadership is aware of the need to stay in touch with employees and is genuinely interested in their viewpoint. This leads to a third way to engage people in the recovery process: identifying and eliminating barriers to adaptation. If you do not know—*from an employee perspective*—what the barriers to letting go of the old are, you cannot expect to take the appropriate action to weaken people's grip. The best way to understand what is inhibiting people from ending the old is to ask them. This highlights obstacles to the letting-go process and provides leadership with specific opportunities to weaken forces against desired change. But as always, this is easier said than done. What should a CEO do if a key senior vice president bad-mouths the recovery process as "touchy-feely garbage" but has tremendous contacts with current and potential new customers? The CEO's choice of whether to eliminate or tolerate this barrier sends a clear message to employees.

Energy

While the first two elements weaken forces for the status quo, the next two strengthen forces for the desired posttransition organization. The third element of workplace recovery is to generate employee energy for charging up the hill to capture new opportunities (see Exhibit 5.3). This occurs when employees know what is in it for them to accept the new organizational order and feel they can succeed in it. This link between organizational success and personal impact generates energy. Understanding where the organization is headed—and having the confidence that they can play a role in

---

EXHIBIT 5.3. Energy.

Theme:	Energy
Overriding objective:	Get people excited about the new organizational order and support them in realizing it.
Key tasks:	• Clarify a vision of a new and better organization.
	• Create a learning environment that motivates people to experiment and open up to new ways of doing things and create opportunities for short-term wins.
	• Connect with people and provide support; accept confusion and backsliding; give people time to move through adaptation.

---

getting there—is what helps people latch on to the new after weakening their hold on the old.

The starting point for creating energy for recovery is a clearly articulated vision of a new and better organization. This conveys the business case for why change is essential and provides details regarding the new organizational order—the changes in the organization's direction, mission, culture, and architecture that will contribute to an enhanced workplace. Importantly, this vision is brought down to a human level—what is in it for people to contribute to achieving it. As distinct from merely being "communicated," the vision of a new and better organization is *clarified* to the point of providing sufficient precision in conveying why change is essential, what changes will occur, and how they affect employees personally.

Forces for the old and the new organizational order continue to work opposite each other, however, and people will have setbacks in their adaptation. Sometimes these setbacks are due to frustration as people encounter gaps between actions and words in achieving the new organizational order. Other times people slip back because they fear moving away from the comfort of accustomed behaviors and perceptions. To sustain the energy for moving forward, a learning environment needs to be created in which employees can experiment with identifying new and better methods for achieving personal and organizational success. Trial-and-error learning abounds in the neutral zone between the old and the new. It is a powerful way to learn but also a painful way to learn—employees have probably not been rewarded for raising up and discussing their errors in the old organizational order. For recovery to occur, not only do employees have to be cognitively aware that leadership understands that mistakes will occur, but they also need incentives to turn those mistakes into learning opportunities for the overall organization.

Energizing employees also requires the "human touch." To help people swing to the new ring, leadership continues to connect with employees on a human level and provides support—both practical and emotional—to encourage people to move forward. In any recovery, confusion, cynicism, and concern will conspire to put the value of the new organizational order in question. They will tug at people and prompt them to backslide to the comfort zone of the old organizational order. So part of leadership's being supportive is being patient and accepting that people take time to move through the adaptation process.

Enforcement

According to the dictionary, *enforcement* means giving force to or strengthening something and also carrying it out effectively. That is precisely what needs to happen to create a new organizational order (see Exhibit 5.4). Enforcement brings the momentum for desired change to the level of consistency required for true cultural and cognitive change. Senior leadership aligns all of the obvious and subtle components of the organization—systems, procedures, actions, im-

EXHIBIT 5.4. Enforcement.	
Theme:	Enforcement
Overriding objective:	Solidify new mental models that are congruent with the desired new organizational order.
Key tasks:	• Align systems and operating standards with the new organizational order. • Involve people in bringing the vision to life. • Track the development of the new organizational order.

pressions, innuendos, and so on—to send as clear a message as possible to strengthen the forces for the desired new organizational order. There is no way around the fact that the less consistent these messages are, the less quickly the organization will arrive at its desired posttransition state.

Consistency compels people to accept the new organizational order and abandon the old. To enforce acceptance of the new business imperatives, organizational systems and operating standards may need to be revised to fit the new organizational order. This is one reason it takes time for people to let go of the old and accept the new—systems and procedures often lag behind leadership's espoused messages. A compensation system that punishes team leaders for short-term declines in productivity when they experiment with new ways of approaching work will not sustain a CEO's vision of "innovation." Boring staff meetings plagued by dysfunctional group dynamics will not contribute to a desired culture of "teamwork and respect."

With macro-level systems and standards in place, enforcement of the new organizational order continues by aligning individual on-the-job behaviors with the desired vision. The best way to do this—both because they know the work and because involving them in problem analysis generates ownership of solutions—is to involve employees in bringing the new organizational order to life. Working within the context of the new organizational order, employees "translate" generalities and operating standards into specific work procedures.

Finally, the work of workplace recovery needs to be monitored. Collecting valid data and tracking the extent to which the new organizational order is truly being realized—that is, the extent to which forces for maintaining the old are being weakened and forces for developing the new are being strengthened—provides feedback to every level in the hierarchy regarding the success of workplace recovery. Some methods for tracking the development of the new organizational order are objective (for example, measures like productivity, quality, and voluntary turnover); others, like attitude surveys and focus group interviews, have the added benefits of involving people and enhancing upward and downward communication. This is especially important when the new organizational order includes intentions to increase involvement and communication. In this way, workplace recovery "walks the talk" in the truest sense.

Timing Workplace Recovery

The elements of workplace recovery are not necessarily sequential. This is because the phases of individual adaptation to transition do not have discrete boundaries—the forces for maintaining the status quo and the forces for growth continually operate counter to each other, with a constantly shifting balance. You don't abruptly stop weakening the forces for the old and then turn your attention to strengthening the forces for the new. Rather, you continue to weaken the resisting forces even as you strengthen the desired forces. The model of workplace recovery clarifies the four elements— empathy, energy, engagement, and enforcement—that enable people to let go of the old and accept the new but does dictate a specific order.

Some activities sensibly occur at specific points in the recovery process. Expressing empathy for what people have been through during a difficult transition should occur early in the recovery process so that employees can let go of their psychological baggage and be more receptive to engagement in the process. Some actions may seemingly occur "out of order." Take the articulation of the new organizational order. Discussing it with people engages them in understanding the desired new organizational order, an activity that strengthens forces for accepting the new. A well-articulated statement of the new organizational order is also likely to weaken forces for maintaining the status quo by confronting employees' concerns that leadership is unclear about where the organization is headed. So it is not unusual to begin communicating it early in the recovery process.

Some activities may span all four elements. Communication and involvement are obvious examples, as well as diagnosing barriers to the adaptation process. Diagnosis is an excellent way to engage people in the recovery process—when guided by a skillful interviewer and confident that "heads will not roll" for being candid, employees love to talk about what is on their minds and are curious about what others are thinking. Although diagnosis is an engagement activity, it makes good sense to conduct some form of diagnosis when designing activities throughout the process—the more accurately you know what is interfering with ending the old, the more precisely you can focus your efforts to weaken them; conversely, the more clearly you understand the opportunities to strengthen acceptance of the new, the better you can appropriate resources to those areas.

Think of the elements like ingredients in a recipe. What ingredients you use and how you use them in a recipe depends on what you are making and who you are making it for. In workplace recovery, the order and timing of the activities will vary from one situation to another. You conduct a diagnosis, consider your resources, and customize your efforts accordingly. Each element contributes in its own way to the recipe, however: expressing empathy helps you gain employee attention and convey to people you are aware of the difficulty of transition, engaging people helps them understand and support why the old must be abandoned and what the new has to offer, energy helps motivate people to contribute to the creation of the new organizational order, and enforcement helps lock in desired new behaviors, perceptions, and expectations.

Leading Workplace Recovery

Workplace recovery can be orchestrated by anyone with authority over employees. Obviously, the higher one is in the hierarchy, the more resources and control are available to conduct workplace recovery. While CEOs, business unit leaders, and department heads typically sanction workplace recovery programs, I have seen middle managers and front-line supervisors do an excellent job of leading recovery in their work teams. In some instances, they are building on recovery efforts initiated by senior executives. But even when senior executives have not embraced the need for recovery or provided resources to facilitate it, team leaders have stepped up and taken personal responsibility for reviving their employees following difficult transitions.

In one of the most inspiring cases of workplace recovery I have witnessed, a manufacturing supervisor in a high-tech firm in Silicon Valley led a recovery program on her own initiative. Prompted by an erosion of its margins and the high cost of manufacturing in the region, this company acquired a firm in a rural area with expertise in low-cost manufacturing. Soon after, it announced its first ever involuntary reduction in force. About 75 percent of the manufacturing employees and supervisors were let go; the remainder were needed to produce prototypes for new products and to customize special orders for key customers. Despite retaining their position and receiving assurances from the CEO that their jobs were secure, the surviving manufacturing employees were in shock. With the bursting of the high-tech bubble, the continued high costs of doing business in Silicon Valley, and the company newsletter applauding the successful move of operations to the acquired company, surviving employees feared the worst, and productivity plummeted.

For three months, the manufacturing supervisor pleaded with senior executives to do something about the situation, but the consistent reply was "Give it time, and they will get over it." Seeing no movement in her people, the supervisor scraped together some funds from her budget and engaged a consultant to conduct a series of workshops with employees. Although they did not constitute a full-blown recovery program, these sessions accomplished some key objectives, including educating employees on the adaptation process, letting them vent some of their anger and concern, and identifying ways to improve efficiency and reduce costs in manufacturing.

With the company grapevine buzzing about how well the sessions were going, senior leadership agreed to attend the final one to hear a presentation on proposed methods for enhancing productivity in the manufacturing area. The CEO was so impressed with the creativity evident in the recommendations, he gave a spontaneous from-the-heart talk admitting that he had been unaware of the depth of employee angst in the manufacturing group but also acknowledging that the initiative shown by the group was exactly what was needed to help the company get through the difficult market conditions. He subsequently provided funds for similar workshops to be held in all other company functions.

This case shows that workplace recovery can spread from the bottom up. Obviously, it is preferable to have the resources and guidance from senior leadership—not just dollars, but also a clear sense of leadership's vision and intentions for the new organizational order. Yet this case should breed confidence in supervisors, managers, and executives that they can lead recovery from their position. In huge corporations, it is not unusual for recovery to begin as a pilot program—say, in a plant, an office, a region, a department, or a business unit—and then spread, after perhaps a little fine tuning, throughout the overall organization. This provides the opportunity to learn from mistakes and enhance the process as it is expanded companywide.

Principles of Workplace Recovery

Designing and implementing workplace recovery always involves trade-offs. You may have to choose between sending people to a focus group to diagnose deep-seated organizational issues and having them focus on meeting short-term operational goals, between spending money on a ceremony to help people mourn the loss of their organization and spending it on a marketing survey, or even between admitting your own miscalculations in a poorly executed merger and retaining your image as a no-nonsense get-the-job-done executive. And there is no one-size-fits-all prescription for workplace recovery—every situation is different. How recovery is approached depends on the situation, culture, personalities, technology, and other internal and external dynamics influencing your workplace.

The next four chapters, constituting Part Three, present methods for conducting the tasks of each of the four elements of workplace recovery. These are but a sample of the myriad interventions available to achieve empathy, energy, engagement, and enforcement. The key is not to copy these interventions directly but to apply them in a manner that works in your situation. Nonetheless, my observations from dozens of transitions have yielded some timeless truisms of workplace recovery. Keep these principles in mind when designing your approach to workplace recovery.

1. *Desired change happens by unfreezing-changing-refreezing.* You have to thaw out the old organizational order before you can change its mold and refreeze in a new, more desirable one. If well managed, a merger or downsizing can be an unfreezing event. This is your opportunity to make meaningful change, as people are going to settle down into the mold you desire, the mold you inadvertently create, or back in your status quo mold. The longer you delay workplace recovery, the more you will have to work backward to unfreeze the organization and its people. *Implication for action: strike while the iron is hot, and make your changes now.*

2. *People regard transition as a half-empty glass.* People initially think of the many potential ways in which a transition might be detrimental rather than beneficial to them personally. This obstructs an "objective" assessment of the new organizational order and what it will take to get there. People are going to envision the downside of the transition in their own fertile imaginations and hear about it through the company rumor mill. They also carry baggage from previously mismanaged transitions they have lived through, and they learn vicariously from the pain suffered by relatives, neighbors, and friends in other organizations. This is why leadership must go out of its way to overcommunicate the upside of the transition—taking the time to repeat communications and to ensure that what was communicated was heard, understood, and inspiring enough to get people to accept the new. *Implication for action: provide straight talk about the recovery process, and keep employees involved in it.*

3. *Workplace recovery is a nonlinear process.* The path from the old organizational order to the new is not a straight line. The constant give-and-take between ending the old and accepting the new means that the best you can hope for is a course of two steps forward and one step back. Every time a force for desired change is articulated, resisting forces will be unleashed. When the new organizational order is announced, for example, cynics will contest its value or leadership's sincerity about it. In any event, you will make mistakes in designing and implementing recovery. These and other resisting forces can never be completely eliminated in complex work organizations—there will always be some pressure toward staying with the status quo. Preparing people for this realistic journey (as opposed to claiming that "everything is under control" or "all we need to do is steer the course") will help people take the setbacks in stride. When mistakes or disappointments occur, taking a step back to learn from them—and sharing the lessons with all involved—propels the entire process two steps forward. *Implication for action: track the recovery process, learn from the mistakes, and disseminate the knowledge throughout the organization.*

4. *People have difficulty driving in two lanes at once.* Even when leadership is fully committed to recovery, the company's current obligations to customers, shareholders, people in the community, and other stakeholders remain. Despite the need for efforts to plan and implement recovery, there is still a business to run. Someone has to mind the store. Yet recovery does not happen without the investment of financial, human, and other resources. The cost of fixating on current business demands often means a delay in recovery or even its doom. *Implication for action: Give recovery high-priority status, and help managers determine how to prioritize it within the context of current business requirements.*

5. *You pay now, or you pay later.* You pay now by giving people time to vent and mourn the loss of the old, or you pay later by having a workforce that continues to hold on to the past rather than look ahead to the future. You pay now by taking the time to diagnose the true forces that are enabling or inhibiting the realization of the new organizational order, or you pay later by missing the key forces that need to be weakened or strengthened. You pay now by pushing back some production deadlines so that employees can have time to analyze and recommend new approaches to getting work done with fewer resources, or you pay later by having a burnt-out, demotivated, and uninspired workforce. *Implication for action: do it now.*

Turn to Part Three, and start designing your workplace recovery.

PART THREE

The Four Elements of Workplace Recovery

6

Empathy

The 1990s began in a fairly typical manner for the people of the Seagram Spirits and Wine Group (SSWG). With 28 percent of Seagram shares controlled by the wealthy and powerful Bronfman family, employees were accustomed to the continuity of family ownership over multiple generations. A patriarchical culture predominated—inwardly focused, with formal, top-down communication and many hierarchical levels, but also a disciplined, dedicated, and committed workforce. The family business mentality had been particularly prevalent in the spirits business, Seagram's original focus. SSWG employees were mightily proud, even arrogant, regarding the prestige and performance of well-known brands like Chivas Regal, Crown Royal, Seagram VO, Martell, Glenlivet, Captain Morgan, Absolut, and Sandeman.

Then in 1994, CEO Edgar Bronfman Jr. began a major transformation of the liquor company founded by his grandfather in the late 1920s into a world-class entertainment company. This was the start of organizational MADness for SSWG employees. Over a five-year span, Seagram people went through a massive reengineering effort, a culture change process, the acquisition of two major entertainment assets, and the divestiture of the core beverage business. In the reengineering, more than forty cross-functional teams examined and redesigned every single process in the areas of finance, consumer marketing, customer development, order fulfillment, manufacturing, purchasing, IT, and business planning. These efforts resulted in a more process-oriented company, significant cost reductions, a number of layoffs, and enhanced business performance. Concurrently, CEO Bronfman initiated a companywide culture change process in which the "Seagram Values" were formulated, cascaded, and integrated in the way the company did business and managed people. The six values guided the implementation of redesigned processes with more customer and consumer focus, quality, innovation, teamwork, respect, and integrity.

But two blockbuster deals—Bronfman's 1995 acquisition of MCA (owner of Universal Studios) for $5.7 billion and the 1998 purchase of Polygram music for $10.4 billion—signaled that the transformation of Seagram was going to be more fundamental than simply reorganizing the firm in a drive for enhanced performance and effectiveness. The subsequent sale of the profitable Tropicana juice business to PepsiCo in 1998 raised $3.3 billion to put toward the forays into entertainment and firmly indicated the direction in which Bronfman was taking the company.

For years, many SSWG employees felt that they were the "masters of the universe" in the Seagram empire. However, by 1998, they increasingly saw themselves as reduced to the position of "cash cows" subsidizing the junior Bronfman's newly acquired entertainment assets, some of which were clear money losers. Nevertheless, employees remained loyal to the Bronfmans for the next few years, largely because they were convinced that Bronfman would never sell the core spirits and wine business.

SSWG's transformation from a complacent family business to a high-performance company came to an abrupt end when Edgar Bronfman Jr. sold his entire company for $23 billion to the French media and utilities company Vivendi in June 2000. The combination vaulted the newly named Vivendi Universal into the top ranks of media and entertainment companies, with 2001 revenues of $65 billion.

Vivendi wanted Seagram for its entertainment assets and put the now "nonstrategic" spirits and wine business up for sale. An intriguing auction process ensued, involving the world's top six spirit and wine producers as well as SSWG's own management team. On December 19, 2000, SSWG was sold to a coalition between Diageo, from the United Kingdom, and Pernod-Ricard, from France, two of SSWG's fiercest competitors. The two companies split up the brands—Pernod-Ricard acquired six Scotch whiskies, including Chivas Regal and Glenlivet, as well as Martel cognac and Seagram's gin. Diageo, already the industry leader, strengthened its position by taking Crown Royal and VO Canadian whiskies, as well as Captain Morgan rum.

The irony was that all this happened at a time when SSWG had posted record earnings of $5.1 billion for the fiscal year ending June 2000. It accounted for 35 percent of Seagram's total revenues but contributed over 60 percent of the parent company's operating income for the 2000 fiscal year. Further, SSWG had recorded double-digit growth in ten of the last eleven quarters. Thus from an earnings perspective, SSWG was leading the spirits industry. These great profits boosted the morale of employees, who only now were realizing the positive results of five years of reengineering and culture change. People felt part of a highly streamlined and winning organization with a growing performance discipline.

The split-up of SSWG into what were regarded as two "lesser" enterprises rippled like a shockwave through the organization. Six months had passed since the sale of Seagram to Vivendi, and many employees throughout the SSWG ranks were angry and resentful over what they perceived as being sold out by the Bronfmans as well as the manner in which they felt Vivendi was treating them. Despite efforts to excite employees about the future through regular communications, the idea that something great was coming to an end was very difficult for people to accept.

To make matters worse for SSWG, the date for the close of the deal kept getting pushed back. When the deal was announced in December 2000, all parties involved were adamant that they would get regulatory approval in the United States, Canada, and Europe by the end of March 2001. In the "hot merger and acquisitions summer" of 2001, General Electric saw its deal with Honeywell blocked by the European Union Commission in Brussels, and United Airlines got a no for its takeover bid for USAirways in the United States. Diageo and Pernod-Ricard, in turn, had clearly underestimated the difficulty and the complexity of the transaction and the scrutiny of the Federal Trade Commission in the United States. Although the European Union gave its approval in May 2001, the closing date in the United States had slipped to the end of June, then to July, then to August, and so on. The deal that was expected to close in four months was finally approved in December 2001, a year after the sale date. Add in the six months that Vivendi had SSWG on the auction block, and it makes eighteen agonizing months in which SSWG employees were in limbo about their careers and their lives.

Not Change as Usual

The people who plan and implement organizational change—be they external consultants, internal training and development professionals, or executives acting on their own—traditionally use a "future orientation" approach. They diagnose the present situation, state the goals of the change effort, and develop and implement a plan for moving from the present to the desired future. They assume that the organization and its people are at a starting point of acceptance—an assumption that is dead wrong on the heels of a transition.

Not recognizing or addressing the need for holding on is a primary reason why so many change programs have difficulty generating or maintaining momentum. Little or no attention is given to working through the potent need to hold on to the old organizational order. The deeply felt experience of frustration, loss, grief, anger, helplessness, and depression is almost completely ignored, except possibly at a relatively superficial level called, almost dismissively, "resistance to change."

Consider the plight of SSWG employees. While their year-and-a-half ordeal of being auctioned off and waiting for regulatory approval—on top of the five years of reengineering, culture change, acquisitions, and divestiture—may be more extenuated than other cases of organizational MADness, it is representative of the emotional roller-coaster ride taken by people in many organizations today. Confident and comfortable in a prestigious family-run business, SSWG employees closely identified with the Seagram organization and were proud of working for what they considered to be the premier spirits business in the world. Then a CEO who was serious about reengineering and culture change pulled the rug out from under them. It may be that Edgar Bronfman Jr. was pursuing a sinister plan to rob the SSWG division to pay for his indulgences in the entertainment industry. Or perhaps he was doing the right thing by shaking up his complacent organization and instilling a more cost-conscious and customer-sensitive culture.

Whatever their leader's motivation, SSWG employees went through the pain of five years of cultural transition and successfully adapted to it. They let go of the attitudes and behaviors consistent with a family-run industry leader and adopted mental models and business practices more congruent with a customer-focused and prudent organization. After a persistent multiyear effort, SSWG employees intellectually understood the need for change and emotionally came around to support it. But just as they were buoyed by the overwhelmingly financial positive results of the reengineering and culture change initiatives, they were put on the auction block. Rather than share in the fruits of their labor, SSWG employees saw themselves taken advantage of and cast aside.

SSWG employees were stunned by their fate and thoroughly upset by it. Rather than look ahead to new opportunities, they were stuck looking backward and asking why they were abandoned after going so brilliantly through the difficult culture change, why they did not receive a payout from their hard work during five years of transition, and why they should bother to exert any more effort to adapt to a new regime. More than anything, however, SSWG employees were angry, and the anger that was initially directed at the Bronfman family carried over to their new owners.

Empathy as an Element of Recovery

Let people know leadership acknowledges that it has been difficult, currently is difficult, and will continue to be difficult for a while.

The march toward workplace recovery begins by empathizing with the plight of employees who have been through a major transition and are currently adapting to its emotional and business implications. Empathy is expressed by acknowledging that employees have experienced a difficult transition, understanding that employees still feel they are in a difficult situation, and indicating awareness that the difficult times are not over as people still have to let go of the old and adapt to the new. Importantly, executives must indicate they are aware of and sensitive to the impact of transition *as experienced by employees*. In other words, let people know that leadership acknowledges that it has been, currently is, and will continue to be difficult for a while.

Expressing empathy enables workplace recovery in a few key ways. First, it contributes to unfreezing people. Employees are not accustomed to hearing their superiors admit that times have been tough and that transition has taken a toll on people psychologically and behaviorally. In most organizations, they are literally shocked when they hear leaders admit awareness of the difficulty people have been through. Second, witnessing their superiors talk and act in new ways gets employees to think about their own responsibility in letting go of the old and accepting the new. They think to themselves, "If the big guns are owning up to—rather than denying or ignoring—the problems stemming from the transition, maybe I should, too." Third, the enhanced sensitivity to the plight of people in transition creates a context within which people cut one another some slack in moving through transition and recovery. All involved recognize that just about everyone in the organization is or has been stressed out, overworked, anxious, or upset. Empathy does not eliminate these symptoms of living through a transition, but it does weaken the lingering negativity of the past and enhances receptivity to the positive potential of the future.

As Exhibit 6.1 shows, actions that demonstrate awareness of and sensitivity to the emotional realities of living through a transition are based on the first three realities of workplace recovery. *Acknowledge the realities and difficulties of transition and recovery* to employees. Mergers, acquisitions, and downsizings are very difficult events to manage. So own up to this fact. Talk to people about it. Explain to them why transitions are frequently mismanaged, and admit your own missteps. Transitions also are very difficult events for individuals to deal with. To show your understanding of this, *offer workshops that educate employees on the process of individual adaptation to organizational transition.* These programs validate what people are going through, alert them to the tendency to hold on to the old, and prepare them for the chaos and confusion of adopting the new. Many of these workshops I have designed and facilitated provide attendees with strategies and tactics for dealing with the adaptation process, which in turn raises their confidence that they can successfully change with the organization.

A third way to demonstrate empathy for what employees have experienced during transition is to *use symbols, ceremonies, and forums to help people loosen their grip on the old.* By sanctioning these formal activities, you signal that you recognize that there have been unintended consequences stemming from the transition, but you also give people support in actively ending the old. Knowing that the emotional realities they experience during and after transition are legitimate and recognized, employees move more quickly through the process of ending the old.

You can expect pushback from executives who regard this work as a step backward rather than accelerating the natural and normal process of adaptation. "Why spend time looking back on what is past," they ask "when we can be putting resources into making this quarter's numbers?" Expressing empathy is counterintuitive to most executives. Although the transition event may have already occurred, the residual

---

EXHIBIT 6.1. Transition Realities and
Recovery Activities to Create Empathy.

Reality	*Activity*
1. Transitions are difficult events to manage; the very way they are executed runs counter to common tools of organizational change management.	Acknowledge the realities and difficulties of transition and recovery.
2. Transitions are difficult events for people to cope with—and employees in many firms are saturated after years of stress from organizational MADness.	Offer workshops to raise awareness of the transition process and help people understand where they do and do not have control.
3. Mismanaged transitions have a negative, not a neutral, impact on people and organizations.	Use symbols, ceremonies, and forums to end the old.

---

impact on employees and other unintended consequences are very much in the present, blocking the path to the desired future.

Acknowledging the Realities and Difficulties of Transition

The need for holding on to the known and familiar is powerful. Not to be aware of this, or to ignore or try to circumvent it, guarantees failure for those charged with changing workplaces or motivating individuals after a transition. An organization's employees will be so saturated with change, filled with anger, stuck in denial, or demotivated to the point of "Why bother?" that they will not accept even the most carefully designed program for moving on to the desired new organizational order. Furthermore, cynicism and distrust toward management will only grow when employees are confronted by yet another program or initiative that appears insensitive to their current psychological frame of reference, no matter how sincere the intentions.

As a step in helping people end the old, leaders need to do something that shakes people out of their current state. This is accomplished by conveying messages to people that they have probably not heard from their leaders:

The transition has been, is, and continues to be difficult.

We at the helm have contributed to the difficulty.

You need—and will be allowed—time to recovery from the difficulty.

Empathy does not occur through the cursory communications practices typical of workplaces today. Organizations regularly hand out little pamphlets paying brief attention to employee concerns on the heels of a merger, acquisition, or downsizing. Usually, this token effort is sandwiched between a promise of "business as usual" and a call for "getting focused back on work." There isn't much meat between the bread, and the meal is neither satisfying nor fulfilling for employees stuck in the emotional realities of organizational MADness.

Empathy is expressed and received by conveying to employees—in clear and consistent terms—that leadership understands the difficulty of transition, shoulders some responsibility for contributing to organizational MADness, and recognizes that individual adaptation must be calculated into business plans going forward. In very few work organizations has this kind of awareness of and sensitivity to the plight of people following transition been expressed with any depth or sincerity. As a result, when empathy is conveyed in a truly genuine manner, employees take note and start loosening their grip on the old.

Acknowledgment Through Words: Mea Culpa

One step in overcoming the unintended consequences of mergers, acquisitions, and downsizings is for leaders to acknowledge their own role in creating the MADness. A mea culpa dramatically signifies to employees that what they have experienced are legitimate and natural responses to living through an organizational transition. In most organizations, hearing leaders express their responsibility for contributing to the pain is anything but "business as usual" and clears the way for individual employees to let go of their own outmoded beliefs and actions and move ahead to adopting new ones.

I have seen a senior executive's mea culpa command employee attention and begin a process of rebuilding faith and trust between employer and employee in organizations ranging from a public utility in the Southwest to a New York–based financial services powerhouse. The case of one CEO is representative of how the admission of responsibility aids the process of workplace recovery after transition.

Joe Douglas took over as CEO of a medium-sized high-technology firm in 1999. The first two years of his tenure were a great run, but then the economic downturn and bursting of the technology bubble brought down the company's profits, stock price, and morale. In March 2001, Douglas announced the first downsizing in the company's history. About 10 percent of employees lost their jobs, mostly in lower-level support functions. A month later, Douglas announced another first for the company—the acquisition of a struggling competitor. The timing of the announcement confused employees—how could the company pay a premium price for an acquisition target when it had just laid off scores of well-performing employees? What employees did not know was that Douglas had been working on the deal for months, decided to abandon it when the economy softened, but abruptly reversed himself when he heard that a third party was expressing interest in the target. Douglas rushed to close the deal before a bidding war ensued. He announced the deal to employees but had few answers to their questions of what the combined organizational would be like and what the merger would mean for them personally.

The next few months paralyzed the workforce. Everyone knew that the merger created several redundant positions, but no one in leadership discussed how they would be handled. Worried about their own security, employees read reports in the local newspaper about how several executives from the acquired firm had structured a generous buyout provision for themselves as part of getting the deal done. These golden parachutes totaled millions of dollars in severance for the senior team. Meanwhile, the company grapevine buzzed with reports of how integration planning was bogged down due to friction between the two sides. Finally, in October 2001, the postmerger organization structure was announced—but so was the year's second reduction in force. Rumors of politicking in the integration task forces had been overblown, and the resulting structure appeared to leverage the strengths of the two partner organizations. But the damage had been done: rather than look ahead to how the new structure could propel the firm toward business success, employees were stuck looking backward and concluding that "we have to suffer through a downsizing and do more work with fewer resources to pay for those fat cats' golden parachutes."

In early 2002, Douglas's company scored some big wins in the marketplace. He felt that the worst was behind him and his company, and he looked forward to improved financial results. But the view from the employee perspective was different. Managers regularly complained to Douglas that employees seemed dispirited and not giving their all on the job. An employee attitude survey revealed very low morale. Voluntary turnover spiked up as many top performers jumped ship. Rather than deny or ignore the data he was receiving, Douglas summoned his business unit leaders and department heads for a special senior staff off-site meeting to discuss the situation. After a day of reviewing employee research data and doing some soul searching regarding his stewardship of the firm, Douglas realized that he had to make a dedicated effort to revive employee spirit and get his people into a more positive frame of reference. The second day of the off-site meeting was used to plan an approach to workplace recovery and to secure the full support of his senior team in implementing it. But Douglas knew he had to personally lead the effort and, moreover, do so in a manner that made clear to employees that he knew they had legitimate concerns but also that the company had turned the corner and was poised for success.

A few days after returning from the off-site meeting, Douglas called a special all-hands meeting. Typically, when he wanted to communicate with the entire workforce in person, Douglas would hold a series of town hall meetings in the company cafeteria—at least four sessions were needed to accommodate all employees in the cramped quarters. To signify the importance and distinctiveness of this event, Douglas held the all-hands meeting in the company parking lot so that all employees could attend at one time. The speaking points Douglas used were designed to express empathy for what people in the company had been through:

- *Personal responsibility.* Douglas opened the meeting by personally taking responsibility for the MADness he had put his employees through. He owned up to the fact that in his rush to close the deal, he compromised integration planning and communication.
- *Insight into the transition process.* Douglas confided in employees why he took the actions he did and spoke earnestly about how the secrecy that shrouded the acquisition prevented him from communicating as openly and fully as he would have liked with employees. Importantly, his tone was not to make an excuse for his lack of communication but to give employees some insight into the difficulty of managing the transition.
- *Awareness of the difficulty of coping with transition.* Douglas acknowledged the difficulty of going through two downsizings within a six-month period, as well as the disruptiveness of the acquisition integration. He noted that everyone in the company had experienced some form of loss in recent months—acquired employees had lost their premerger company identity, and employees from his firm had lost coworkers and the security of believing they were immune from

involuntary layoffs. He even used his own experience—losing his self-image as a CEO who treated each and every employee well—to illustrate how loss comes in many varieties during a transition.

- *Understanding of the employee viewpoint.* Douglas indicated he had heard that employees felt they were paying the price for acquired executives' severance packages. He did not debate whether this was an accurate perception, but he did express his understanding of how that perception could be derived from the recent course of events. He also cited findings from the recent employee attitude survey and other indicators of employee perceptions. Again, he did not contest the viewpoints but accepted them as a result of the turbulent year the company and its employees had gone through and as the starting point for moving forward.

Douglas closed his comments with a brief review of the recent executive off-site meeting. He described how the full senior team had digested the employee research data and discussed employee viewpoints. He joked about how some of his team members became defensive when hearing of the unintended consequences of the company's series of transitions but underscored that the full team took the data seriously and committed to a formal workplace recovery program. Douglas then committed to individual follow-up meetings with the members of the senior team in the coming week to discuss how the transitions affected their particular area of the company and what was needed to help adapt to life after the downsizings and acquisition.

Acknowledgment Through Actions

Of course, words need to be backed up with actions if the forces against desired change are to be weakened. A leader who talks a good game about the need for people to have time to adapt to transition and then hands out stretch targets with short time frames only contributes to employee confusion and distrust. Keep in mind that adaptation is a natural and normal process—employees require time to let go of the old and latch onto the new whether or not leaders factor this into their plans. So leaders might as well gain some goodwill with employees and accelerate the letting-go process by acknowledging it and accounting for it in their actions:

• *Set realistic timetables.* A look back at Figure 4.4 shows that people higher up in the organization have already begun their adaptation process well before most employees learn their fate in a transition. People need time to come to terms with how transition affects them, to accept what is being lost and to understand what is and is not changing. People simply cannot respond quickly to business demands when they are unsure of themselves and of how to get things done in the posttransition organization. At the computer company, initial integration planning recommended the instillation of a new IT system by end of June 2002. To ensure that people had time to cope with another major disruption to their work situation, CEO Douglas delayed the integration for six months. He figured that people would need time to learn the new system and wanted to ensure that employees felt well trained in and comfortable with the system before the full conversion.

• *Set attainable targets.* People who feel overwhelmed and underresourced following transition will become even more demotivated when confronted with goals or objectives they regard as beyond their ability to accomplish. The workforce is not firing on all cylinders following transition, so this is not the time to expect peak performance. Giving them significant but attainable targets will build motivation and confidence by allowing people to score some early wins in the posttransition organization. At the computer company, business plans were evaluated to determine the performance pressures being put on people through the ranks. While Douglas and his leadership team obviously wanted to achieve the greatest business results possible, they recognized that by letting go of some short-term targets, they could regain employee motivation and performance over the long haul.

• *Coach managers and supervisors*. Certainly, senior executives can set a tone of acknowledging and understanding employee realities following a transition, but it is employees' immediate superiors who have the most immediate influence on people. These are the representatives of management people see on a daily basis. At the computer company, senior executives met with all managers and supervisors in their departments to set expectations and engage them in the process of expressing empathy. This began with senior executives' acknowledging the difficulty middle managers themselves had during the transition. It then moved on to specific instructions for managers and supervisors to revise timelines and performance expectations in their work teams. And middle managers were coached on the need to demonstrate their understanding of the emotional realities their direct reports had experienced during and after the downsizings and acquisitions.

Raising Awareness of the Transition Process

The second reality of workplace recovery is that transitions are difficult events for people to cope with—and employees in many firms are saturated after years of stress from organizational MADness. The words and actions of executives and managers who express empathy following transition certainly demonstrate an understanding of the difficulty of moving through mergers, acquisitions, and downsizings. A complementary—and usually more explicit—way to convey understanding of the transition process is to offer workshops that raise people's awareness of what they are experiencing.

These workshops have two objectives. One is to educate people on the complexities of transition—specifically, the need to let go of the old before accepting the new. Explaining the phases of adaptation helps people understand why they may be holding on to the old, why they feel confused in the neutral zone, and why they will require time to align their perceptions, expectations, and behaviors with the new organizational order. Part of the job here is to validate for people that what they are going through is normal and to be expected—they are not weak or weird for feeling concerned or disoriented. In addition to raising awareness of individual adaptation, these workshops educate employees on organizational transition. They explain why transitions are such difficult events for all involved and why so many transitions are mismanaged. The point here is to let employees know that their leadership team, while not absolved of its responsibility for mismanaging the transition, is not necessarily inept because of the difficulties involved in managing a merger, acquisition, or downsizing.

The second objective of transition awareness-raising workshops is to help people understand where they do and do not have control over their situation. Employees who have just been through a merger, acquisition, or downsizing tend to fixate on areas over which they have little or no control. They lament, "Leadership doesn't give us sufficient direction," "Leadership doesn't communicate well with us," or "Leadership doesn't understand what it is like to work on the front lines." Employees cannot control leadership. Employees can only control themselves. So these workshops help employees create action plans where they do have control and move beyond what they don't have control over. Letting go of areas outside of their control is a major contributor to weakening forces against desired change.

"Adaptation After Transition" workshops typically last from a half-day to a full day, depending on the amount of time dedicated to employee discussion. Many organizations I have worked with offer special versions of the workshops for managers and supervisors who lead work teams, often called "Leading Teams out of Transition." In addition to educating attendees on the complexities and processes of individual adaptation and organizational transition, they provide tactics for maintaining productivity during chaotic times.

These "Adaptation After Transition" workshops should not be confused with stress management programs. Although strategies and tactics for managing one's stress may find their way into workshops, the programs I am describing aim primarily to raise employees' awareness of the transition process and help them focus their efforts on areas where they have control. Certainly, practicing effective stress management is one way employees can take control of their situation, but generic stress management programs do not come close to meeting the objectives of raising awareness of the transition process and focusing people on areas under their control.

As with most actions associated with workplace recovery, these workshops have symbolic as well as substantive value. The mere fact that leadership sanctions these sessions tells employees that their superiors understand what they are going through and legitimizes the feelings that people experience during and after transition. And dedicating the time and money to allow people to attend these sessions lets people know that leadership is sincere about helping people move through the adaptation process of letting go of the old and embracing the new.

Workshops at SSWG

The Seagram Spirits and Wine Group's human resource staff knew that transitions were very negative experiences for employees, their families, and the communities they live in. They reasoned that they should be proactive and help employees through the transition with respect and integrity. Doing this, however, required that SSWG's HR professionals learn more about transitions in short order. Under the guidance of Ronny Vansteenkiste, vice president of organization development and learning, a two-day workshop was designed to prepare HR staff for helping employees deal with the aftermath of their divestiture. A key design principle of the conference was to influence the reigning mind-set of being "victims of transition" and to help the participants see that there could be a different way of approaching a transition. Even though not in charge, they could work with new business partners and envision an inclusive win-win scenario for the new venture.

The meeting agenda was highly interactive and participative (see Exhibit 6.2). A welcome dinner featured a senior SSWG executive

---

EXHIBIT 6.2. SSWG "Adaptation After
Transition" Workshop Agenda.

Welcome Dinner
- News update on latest transition events
- Dinner speech from senior executive on "how this process feels from my perspective"

Day One
- Icebreaking activity
- Personal expressions of living through transition
- Presentation on "the future of work"
- Case examples from other organizations

Day Two
- Presentation on "the adaptation process after integration"
- Regional teams' discussion of the question "What can we do to help our business partners succeed?"
- Full group meeting to review regional plans
- Presentation to business partners on the adaptation and recovery process

---

talking about how the transition to new owners affected him personally. This set the tone for people to use the meeting to convey their individual concerns, hopes, and fears. The next morning, after an icebreaking activity, the meeting began with personal expressions of what people had been through during the years of reengineering, culture change, abandonment by the Bronfman family, and finally, sale to the new owners. After lunch, an outside expert made a presentation on "the future of work." His point to this group was that transition was affecting all workplaces and that former Seagram employees should wake up to the fact that the paternalistic culture they enjoyed for so many years would have ended sooner or later. He also made it clear that SSWG employees were not just victims singled out by a ruthless corporate leader. Rather, they were like millions of others who were experiencing the realities of organizational MADness. Day one closed with two presentations from executives from other companies that had gone through transitions and recovery. This ended the first day on a positive note, promising that there was indeed "life after transition" and informing attendees of practical methods for leading recovery in the workplace.

Another presentation from an external expert opened day two of the meeting. This educated attendees on "the adaptation process after integration." Specifically, it presented the phases of adaptation and of organizational transition. It also reviewed various methods for facilitating the recovery process. With this information in hand, attendees broke out into regional groups to discuss how to work with new business partners to promote workplace recovery. After lunch, the full group reconvened and shared and learned from each other's proposals. The meeting concluded with presentations to line managers on the adaptation and recovery processes and commitments to next steps for helping SSWG employees let go of their current anger and fears and more readily accept their new workplace realities.

The HR workshop served as a model for similar sessions with employees in each geographic region. A one-day version educating employees on the adaptation process was offered. And the basic discipline of extensive Q&A sessions within the HR group became the model for communication sessions for line managers. Such sessions would be repeated very regularly across the globe in the months that followed whenever management or employee meetings were taking place.

By the end of the conference, members of the HR function had not only enhanced their capabilities but also unified themselves in understanding what their function was expected to do and how to go about their work in the context of new workplace realities. This event proved to be a major catalyst for the entire transition process. It built strong confidence and created cohesion within the HR function and between HR and line executives. HR people who had worried that their function might not be well regarded by their new owners ended up playing a lead role in the dialogue with the buyers. The HR function quickly became the best-prepared function and an example for the other functions in the transition from the old SSWG to the new owners.

Symbols, Ceremonies, and Forums to Help End the Old

It is one thing to intellectually know that the "good old days" are over; it is another to emotionally accept that fact. Similarly, it is one thing to be aware that transitions are difficult events—both for the leaders who plan and implement them and for the employees who have to live through them—and quite another to let go of the unintended psychological and behavioral consequences of living through a transition. As the third reality of workplace recovery indicates, mismanaged transitions have a negative, not merely a neutral, impact on people and organizations. To speed up recovery after transition, empathy needs to be conveyed at the emotional level as well as at the intellectual level.

Many organizations use symbols, ceremonies, and forums to help people come to terms with the loss of the old organization and recuperate from the unintended consequences of transition. These are effective tools for bonding together people who are adapting to life after a transition and for accelerating their acceptance of the inevitable changes confronting them. Symbols abound in work-places. The CEO of a historically paternalistic financial services firm tore up the company's catalogue of service awards for five-, ten-, and twenty-five-year employees to denote the end of expectations for long-term employment after the firm went through its first major downsizing.

Ceremonies are symbolic events that dramatically mark the transition from old to new. Many ceremonies in organizations in transition build on the theme of death and involve burials and wakes. Others celebrate the good old days left behind in ways like placing items in a time capsule. One utility I worked with used a downsizing as an opportunity to promote a culture change toward more entrepreneurial and risk-taking behaviors than had prevailed historically in the organization. An internal HR manager created a display that featured the grim reaper taking away "deceased" behaviors and a diapered baby delivering the new behaviors.

Ceremonies are sometimes rejected out of hand by executives who regard them as too exotic or, much to my chagrin, too "Californialike." (Interestingly, many of my midwestern clients have been more receptive to these events than those on the two coasts.) Though a ceremony is not a surrogate for direct acknowledgment of the difficulty of transition, many executives appreciate their metaphorical ability to convey that the old must be abandoned and the new embraced.

The Venting Meeting

A powerful event to help people loosen their grip on the old is the venting meeting. By raising awareness and accelerating learning, this meeting heightens people's understanding of how they are dealing with adaptation to transition. The objective of the venting meeting is to facilitate the letting-go phase of the adaptation process. It accomplishes this by helping people move through the three steps of the letting-go process identified in the mid-1980s by UCLA professors Robert Tannenbaum and Robert Hanna:

1. *Consciousness raising.* The venting meeting alerts employees to common patterns of organizational and individual reaction to transition and, in particular, the personal adaptation process. This shows that reactions to loss are to be expected following a transition and acquaints employees with the sequence of letting go of the old, dealing with the neutral zone, and accepting the new. The goal is to help employees acknowledge intellectually what they are personally holding on to and to help them become aware of their reasons for doing so.

2. *Reexperiencing.* The reasons for and implications of holding on become truly understood only when they are expressed experientially. Talking through where they have been and what they are

currently experiencing as a result of the transition helps employees bring their feelings to a conscious level. This is typically an emotional and highly charged process, in contrast to the more intellectual level at which initial consciousness raising occurs.

3. *Mourning.* The psychological process of letting go is completed through an active mourning of what is being left behind—old ways of seeing and doing things, lost hopes and expectations, and the loss of what was once satisfying, meaningful, or simply familiar. Sometimes this mourning is accompanied by remorse—a sense of guilt for time wasted or about the work situation that could have been but may never be. Yet it also instills a sense of renewal and rebirth and an acceptance of what lies ahead.

Benefits of a Venting Meeting

A venting meeting provides many benefits to a workforce recovering from a transition. First, it validates the experiences of employees who are coping with loss in their personal situation and adapting to the death of the old organizational reality. The mere acknowledgment from the organization that there is a *need* to mourn legitimizes the emotions and feelings experienced by employees as they cope with loss and change. Second, the venting meeting gives people guidance for dealing with and moving through an uncomfortable experience. It is a visible forum in which a group of people comes to see that holding on to the old, though normal and natural, is a maladaptive response to the new organizational realities. The venting meeting is a turning point at which people let go of anger and blame and take personal responsibility for accepting their situation in the resized organization.

Third, bringing people together to share in the venting meeting establishes a bond among members of the group. The tendencies to turn inward during times of crisis, to constrict communication, and to restrict involvement are replaced by a reaching out to each other as members of a community. Fourth, the venting meeting accelerates the pace at which people let go. Group members are at once providers and receivers of support and coping strategies. Finally, the venting meeting clarifies and confirms to those who may be stuck in denial that something is being lost. The dramatic scene of watching others acknowledge that the old order has ended weakens enduring forces for maintaining the status quo.

Venting is distinct from bitching. Bitching is blaming, whereas venting raises up, legitimizes, and works through feelings. Employees who actively work through the stages of consciousness raising, reexperiencing, and mourning are better prepared to accept new realities and move forward. For a workforce that is banged up and burned out after a transition, a venting meeting is a forum for healing and renewal. In organizations that have experienced repeated waves of transition, whose workers' threshold for dealing with stress, uncertainty, and disorientation has been reached or surpassed, a venting meeting helps people wring away the built-up consequences of dealing with ongoing change.

The meeting also helps people come to terms with ambiguous organizational endings. If the organization flat out ceased to exist, the individual members could begin a process of mourning and letting go. When aspects of an organization's culture or identity are lost but its basic structure lingers through a transition, this is a less obvious ending. The mourning component of the venting meeting transforms what might be perceived as a lingering hope for survival of the status quo into a finite experience of death—an event that can be dealt with, adapted to, and eventually moved on from.

A venting meeting by itself does not complete the letting-go process, but it can be a powerful facilitator to accelerate workplace recovery. If an atmosphere of safety and openness can be established in the venting meeting, people will jump at the opportunity to express their feelings. The internal pressure built up over months of uncertainty and stress, combined with the acknowledgment that these reactions are legitimate, creates a tremendous need for people to talk about what they have been and are currently going through.

Venting Meeting Agenda

Venting meetings range in length from a few hours to a few days and can be scheduled on an ongoing basis or as a one-time-only event. After an airline downsized, lunchtime brown bag venting meetings were sponsored for employees on a weekly basis. Following an internal restructuring that included a reduction in force in a telecom giant, a single three-day off-site meeting was designed to help people let go of the old and begin accepting the new.

Exhibit 6.3 presents a typical venting meeting agenda. Not all components are intended for use in all meetings, either because of their poor fit with the organization's culture or owing to time constraints. The full agenda typically requires two days of work but can be expanded to three days if strong holding-on forces are anticipated. Alternatively, the meeting can be condensed to one day or less if components like the mourning ceremony or the feedback session with senior management are dropped.

The tone and atmosphere of the venting meeting gets set early on by clarifying the meeting's purpose and objectives, establishing the facilitator's credibility, and loosening up people through an ice-breaking activity. Then awareness raising begins through a presentation that educates attendees on organizational transitions and their impact on employees. This kind of presentation validates what employees have been experiencing during and after the transition, which in turn gives the session and facilitator credibility and brings people's energy and interest into the process.

The presentation is typically met with considerable head nodding and verbal confirmations that the discussion reflects the attendees' situation. In some cases, the attendees may be bursting at the seams to let out their feelings in an emotional and energetic catharsis. In others, however, a more conservative approach is taken by conducting a breakout group activity that serves as a segue between the consciousness raising and reexperiencing components of the meeting. This increases employees' comfort level with the venting process—people typically feel more at ease in a small group and feel

---

EXHIBIT 6.3.   Venting Meeting Agenda.

   I. Introduction
- Meeting objectives
- Facilitator's background
- Icebreaking activity

  II. Presentation on organizational and individual responses to transition

 III. Breakout group assignment: Identify key issues affecting this transition and prioritize them for discussion

 IV. Full group meeting
- Breakout group reports on high-priority issues
- Consensus on key issues for discussion

  V. Discussion of key issues

 VI. Mourning ceremony

VII. Presentation on guidelines for managing oneself and others during the recovery period after transition

VIII. Individual assignment
- "What can I do to facilitate recovery?"
- "What does the company need to do to facilitate recovery?"

 IX. Breakout group assignment: Consolidate lists from item VII

  X. Full group meeting
- Presentation of lists by breakout groups
- Preparation of final consolidated lists

 XI. Feedback session with senior management

---

more responsible for contributing to the group discussion. Consequently, attendees move into small groups to identify and prioritize the issues from the presentation that are the most pertinent to their personal situation. A lively exchange usually ensues and continues until the facilitator persuades the members to return to the full group.

In the full group, each breakout group reports its list of high-priority issues. The full group achieves consensus regarding the key issues in this particular transition and organizes them into a set of discussion items to guide the reexperiencing portion of the meeting. Now comes the emotional highlight of the venting meeting as the facilitator leads a discussion that addresses salient issues weighing on the minds of employees. Precisely following the consensus list of items is less important than letting the group go where it wants with the discussion. Invariably, discussion of one issue will bleed into discussion of another. The depth of the discussion will vary according to the skill of the facilitator and the openness of the group. The full reexperiencing step rarely occurs at one meeting. Still, the facilitator may take advantage of the presence of the group and conduct a mourning ceremony to facilitate bonding, supportiveness, and acceptance of the end of the old organizational realities among the attendees.

In addition to covering the three steps of the letting-go process, the venting meeting may include a module that readies people for their responsibilities in the posttransition organization. This forward-looking preparation typically addresses a common request by senior leadership to finish the meeting on a positive note. Although the mourning process itself may end in a celebratory fashion, much like a traditional Irish wake, the notion of grieving retains a negative stigma in most organizational cultures.

To help people look forward and feel optimistic about their chances for success, the venting meeting can close with a segment on preparing for life in the new organization. In meetings involving nonsupervisory employees, this could be in the form of suggestions for managing oneself. Typically, these guidelines include some mix of tactics for continuing the work of letting go and adapting to the new organizational realities. When the meeting involves participants who manage other people, guidelines for managing subordinates during the revitalization period are presented along with those for managing oneself. An individually focused exercise to get people to distinguish between areas they can and cannot control prevents attendees from fixating on matters beyond their influence. Finally, the full group makes summary lists of individual and organization's actions that can be taken as part of revitalization.

These lists should be reported to senior leadership as a first step in using the data collected in the meeting to aid the recovery process. If time permits and the climate is appropriate, the venting meeting can conclude with members of senior leadership making a scheduled appearance to hear the findings firsthand from participants. This symbolizes leadership's genuine interest in what people have to say about what they have gone through and where they are headed, and it also lets executives hear the issues in employees' own words and with their emotions attached. Prepare executives for this portion of the meeting by reminding them that this is the attendees' meeting and not theirs. Their role is to be active listeners during the reporting session—first showing empathy for what the attendees have been through and the emotions they are experiencing and then acknowledging that they have heard the employees' ideas about how the company could help manage revitalization after transition. Alternatively, summaries of the work produced in the venting meeting can be presented to senior leadership in a written report following the meeting.

Venting in the High-Tech Sector

The strategy that guided the internal merger of the communications and information systems divisions of a telecommunications company was straightforward: give customers "one-stop shopping" for their computer and communications needs and realize cost savings from resulting economies of scale. Bringing this strategy to life, however, hinged on making one team out of people who "grew up" in two very different business climates.

The communications group, composed of veterans of the telephone industry, enjoyed years of market leadership and customer loyalty and had a track record of high-quality products and services. Its management, however, was somewhat complacent and, at least in the eyes of some executives, not responding quickly or appropriately to competitors. By contrast, the information systems (IS) group was a relatively new venture that had yet to achieve profitability. IS managers were seen as risk takers but had a reputation for being in-sensitive to both people and bottom-line concerns.

Through the months of merger implementation, the head of the western region of the merged operation ran into continual "peo-ple problems." Three factors in particular frustrated him and his efforts at realizing a new organizational order. First, strong we-they dynamics persisted between the two sides. Both groups continued to feel that the other's management style was inadequate to the needs of combined operations. Second, business unit leaders were not reinforcing the regional president's direction within their work areas. They had little experience in managing change of this sort and even less confidence that they could mold a new way of doing things. Finally, there was a strong orientation toward holding on to past identities and practices rather than developing new ones. The regional president, appointed in part because of his ability to lead change, knew that his only hope of building a new organizational order depended on speeding up his team's adaptation process. So he commissioned an off-site meeting to weaken forces for maintaining the status quo.

As a first step, each of the eighty managers in the combined divi-sion was interviewed, individually or in focus groups, and completed a questionnaire assessing his or her feelings about the transition. It did not take much prodding in the interviews to get managers to talk about differences between the two sides. Communications people regarded themselves as the winners in the internal merger and their counterparts as losers, based on the two sides' financial perfor-mance. Communications people also believed they were led by "professionals," whereas IS executives were "mavericks." By com-parison, managers from the IS side felt that they were performing as well as could be expected given their relatively recent entry into the market. Moreover, they attributed the success of the communica-tions group to traditional customer loyalty and not to the ability of its management.

Both sides acknowledged an upside to the combination, includ-ing increased benefits to customers and more opportunities to advance in the company. Yet they also saw the downside. Nearly two-thirds of the surveyed managers expected that the combination would lead to a substantial downsizing, one-half reported less job security, and only one-third felt that people from the two sides would have equal opportunities to advance in the merged unit.

Still, most managers expressed a wait-and-see attitude in response to questions about whether the integration would capitalize on the strengths of both organizations. The survey also revealed a major deterrent to joining together: only 23 percent of the communications managers said they trusted IS people, and just 17 percent of IS managers trusted their counterparts.

A three-day retreat was scheduled and designed around the three steps of the letting-go process. The first day was devoted to consciousness raising about the adaptation process and started the reexperiencing step, the second day continued with the reexperiencing step and a mourning ceremony, and the third day focused on the future with a series of presentations on the structure, policies, procedures, and expectations of the new organizational order.

Day one began with a presentation on common patterns found in organizations and people engaged in transition. Then key findings from the survey and interviews were presented. This put the concerns on the table, using the words and responses of the people in the room. No one at the meting could deny that the issues raised in the presentation were applicable to his or her own situation. The various concerns sorted into five factors central to the success of this internal merger:

- The degree to which the merged division managers managed the integration process well (in terms of communicating, providing chances for people to participate in decisions affecting them, and building ownership of the new organization)

- The level of energy and enthusiasm the managers had and developed in their people (for example, minimizing burnout, and addressing concerns about limited growth opportunities and worries about whether the ax would fall again)

- The quality of direction provided (such as developing a sound business strategy and a workable implementation plan)

- The degree to which managers educated one another about their businesses (including developing knowledge regarding each side's products and services, the new boss's expectations, and criteria for success)

- The degree to which the managers addressed the clash of cultures and developed trust with their counterparts

The eighty managers were divided into ten groups, two addressing each issue. Each group was asked to recommend (1) what, as individual managers, they could do about that issue to foster recovery in the combined unit and (2) what they needed from senior management in the way of leadership, structure, and support. The full group reassembled, and each small group reported its recommendations. The first day concluded with each manager preparing a personal action plan for leading recovery in his or her work area, based on the roster of recommended actions for individual managers. The regional president took on the responsibility of reviewing the group's feedback to senior management with his direct reports as part of his own action plan.

The highlight of the second day was a "graduation" ceremony. After the managers presented their action plans in front of their peers in small groups, they came back together as a full group and were asked to write down "the three worst ways in which the integration could affect me personally." Each one also received a sheet of his preintegration letterhead and an old business card. Managers were then led outside, where a wooden coffin awaited. Off to the side, a band played a somber funeral march.

One by one, each of the eighty managers stepped up to the coffin, crumpled his or her worst-case list, letterhead, and business card, and tossed them in. As the last manager stepped back from the coffin, the group was startled to hear a low, grumbling noise. Slowly, a hundred-ton paver rolled around the corner and headed straight for the group. At first, the managers stood paralyzed, unsure of what was going to happen. The band broke into a rousing rendition of "On, Wisconsin," and the paver veered toward the wooden casket, flattening it and its contents. Spontaneous cheering broke out among the executives as the paver rolled back and forth over the coffin.

Abuzz with excitement, the managers were asked to return inside. As they entered the building, they received academic caps and gowns and instructions to put them on. Ushers assembled the managers into two orderly lines and led them into an auditorium where a banner proclaiming "Congratulations, Graduates!" awaited them. Once all were seated, the regional president welcomed them and embarked on the classic graduation speech: "The day has come for which we all have worked so hard to prepare you. It is now your turn: our destiny lies in your generation's hands!" The managers sat quietly, absorbed in the speech, understanding its relevance to them. Then the ushers brought one row of "graduates" at a time to their feet and marched them up to the stage. There the president presented each one with a diploma, conferring a "master's of merger management," and a graduation gift—a share of company stock. After all had proceeded across the stage and back to their seats, the group moved the tassels on their caps from the left to the right side and proclaimed that they had graduated into their positions as leaders of the workplace recovery process.

7

Engagement

"The entire mind-set of the *Examiner* is to hate the *Chronicle*."
This was just one of many stinging employee comments I quoted in
a report prepared for Matthew Wilson, executive editor of the *San
Francisco Chronicle* newspaper. Wilson had asked me to assess
employee sentiment regarding the acquisition of their morning
paper (circulation 500,000) by the Hearst Corporation, owners of
the afternoon rival *San Francisco Examiner* (circulation 100,000).
Hearst's plan was to close the *Examiner*, combine its staff with that
of the *Chronicle*, and produce one paper.

Wilson contacted me because he knew his staff had strong feelings about their new owners and colleagues. More than this, however, Wilson recognized that *Chronicle* employees had been through
a difficult transition in the sale of their firm. They needed to let go
of their old workplace realities—a family-owned business with a
solid paternalistic culture—but did not like what they perceived to
be the new realities—being owned by a corporation with a track
record of not investing in making the *Examiner* a great newspaper
and joining forces with newspeople perceived as "lower-quality" and
led by a management team with "negative human skills." Indeed,
many of the current employees had fled to the *Chronicle* from the
"oppressive" management regime at the *Examiner*.

Since the *Chronicle* was founded by two brothers in 1865, ownership of the paper passed down through generations of San Fran-

cisco's de Young family. Over the years, ownership had fragmented among a few dozen relatives, some of whom wanted to unload their stake. However, a family shareholder agreement specified that no one could sell any portion of the holdings because it would trigger significant tax consequences. When the agreement expired in the 1990s, the family did not establish a new one.

There was some dissension in the family over what to do with the *Chronicle* and their other holdings, including San Francisco's NBC-affiliate television station. Nan McEvoy, the largest shareholder, made her intentions clear when she declared that her shares would be sold "over my dead body." But issues within the family and the advantageous tax structure of a full sale prevailed, and in May 1999, the family announced it was engaging investment bankers Donaldson Lufkin & Jenrette to explore the sale of its assets. Thus began an eighteen-month odyssey for *Chronicle* employees (see Exhibit 7.1).

At first, there was some hope in the *Chronicle* newsroom that Nan McEvoy herself would lead a buyout of the newspaper. Optimistic scenarios filled the company grapevine. One had McEvoy taking over and lifting the constraints of the *Chronicle's* joint operating agreement (JOA) with the afternoon *Examiner*. (To keep the existence of multiple newspapers in a single community an economic possibility, Congress provided exemptions from antitrust regulations. Under the terms of their JOA established in 1965, the *Examiner* and the *Chronicle* jointly owned all of the assets used to produce and distribute their newspapers. They also created the San Francisco Newspaper Agency to perform all business functions for the newspapers, including circulation, advertising sales, printing, and distribution. The news and editorial departments of both newspapers remained entirely separate and independently operated.)

The terms of the San Francisco JOA called for Hearst and the *Chronicle* to share all noneditorial costs but also all revenues. So both sides were hesitant to make significant investments in their respective newspapers—they would have to shoulder the entire investment on their own but share half of the profits that resulted from any

EXHIBIT 7.1. Timetable for the Sale of the *San Francisco Chronicle*.

May 10, 1999	Family engages Donaldson Lufkin & Jenrette
June 16, 1999	Family puts company up for sale
August 9, 1999	Hearst Corporation announces purchase of *Chronicle*
February 2000	Justice Department withdraws objections, allowing deal to go forward
February 2000	Clint Riley gets restraining order to delay closing
May 2000	Clint Riley trial commences
July 27, 2000	Judge says deal can go forward following four-month waiting period so that the Fangs can get ready
November 26, 2000	Transition day

improvements with the competition! So any enhancements to the *Chronicle*, such as more in-depth reporting or new features, were difficult to realize under the JOA. Enthusiasm grew in the *Chronicle* newsroom that McEvoy would not just purchase the paper but also negotiate the end of the JOA and free up the *Chronicle* for economic investments and editorial improvements.

But the McEvoy buyout never materialized, and on August 9, 1999, the Hearst Corporation announced it was acquiring the *Chronicle*, terminating the JOA, and putting the afternoon *Examiner* up for sale. If no buyer came forward, Hearst would combine the *Examiner* staff with that of the *Chronicle* and close down the afternoon edition. This announcement riled politicians in the San Francisco Bay Area. If the *Examiner* was losing money under a JOA that covered half of its operating expenses, how could any new owner turn a profit outside the JOA? The politicians cried foul and claimed that Hearst had no serious intention of finding a buyer for the *Examiner* but was instead planning to shut it down and eliminate the competition for its new morning *Chronicle*.

The approval process for Hearst's purchase of the *Chronicle* was one of the most bizarre and most highly politicized in business history. Many local and some national politicians, some of whom had been on the receiving end of critical *Chronicle* or *Examiner* editorials, used the approval process as their chance to jab back at the papers. Some made public statements, while others influenced the back rooms. Many observers questioned whether Hearst would prevail, adding to the emotional mix experienced in the *Chronicle* newsroom—while *Chronicle* employees held out hope that Hearst would be blocked from acquiring them, that meant that the fate of their paper would be unsettled for even longer. Then, in an eleventh-hour move that only added to the wackiness of the deal, Hearst agreed to *give* the *Examiner*—and a $66 million subsidy—to the Fang family, owners of the *Independent*, a newspaper delivered for free to many San Francisco neighborhoods. Soon after, in February 2000, the U.S. Justice Department dropped its antitrust investigation of the purchase of the *Chronicle*.

But the story didn't stop there. Former San Francisco mayoral candidate Clint Riley filed a lawsuit to resurrect claims of antitrust against the deal. Riley truly had a personal vendetta against Hearst—after some unfavorable coverage in the *Examiner*, Riley came to visit executive editor Phil Bronstein and left with a broken leg. The court case produced more angst for the *Chronicle* workforce as some of the testimony reinforced their perceptions that their new owners were less ethical journalists than themselves. In one stunning admission, the new publisher Hearst had selected for the *Chronicle* testified that he met with and offered preferential treatment in the paper to San Francisco Mayor Willie Brown in return for supporting the acquisition.

Finally, on July 27, 2000, U.S. District Judge Vaughn Walker said that Hearst's acquisition of the *Chronicle* could go forward following a four-month waiting period so that the Fangs could get ready to run the *Examiner*. Not until November 26, 2000, the day before

Thanksgiving and a full eighteen months after the family announced it was exploring the sale of the *Chronicle*, did Hearst take over.

Throughout this period, Matthew Wilson knew that the transition was psychologically confounding for *Chronicle* employees. Their paper was the larger, more prestigious of the two, but the owners of the *Examiner* would be in control of the combined operation. There was relief that the transaction was completed, appreciation that the stifling JOA was now ended, and even some guarded optimism that perhaps Hearst would use its resources to make improvements in the paper. But the perceived downside of the deal filled the minds of the *Chronicle* staff. Although the *Chronicle* name was surviving, employees were being taken over by Hearst. They would have to work alongside a staff regarded as inferior to their own and for editors from the *Examiner* who were viewed as being in the "dark ages" of management. Add to this the fact that Hearst was giving $66 million to the Fang family to run the *Examiner*. "That's money that they could have invested in us," one reporter commented to me. "Heck, give me $66 million and I could run a newspaper" was my reply.

Engagement as an Element of Recovery

Create understanding of and support for the need to end the old and accept the new organizational order.

The second element of workplace recovery is to engage people at the level of business imperatives so that they understand and support the need to let go of the old organizational order and, as a result, be more receptive to the new organizational order. The first element of expressing empathy acknowledges and validates what people are experiencing on an emotional level. The second element literally engages people in understanding and supporting the need to end the old and accept the new at the business level. This accelerates the rate at which people conduct their work in a manner more consistent with the desired new organizational order and at which they abandon work practices and expectations that may have been appropriate for the old organizational order but not for life after the transition.

Engagement contributes to weakening forces for the old in a number of ways. First and foremost, it brings potentially cryptic or ambiguous statements of business imperatives down to the specific level of on-the-job behaviors. People cannot be expected to end the old if they do not have a good understanding of why that is necessary and how it applies to their personal work situation. Second, engagement increases confidence in both oneself and one's leadership at a time when people are feeling insecure about short-term work requirements and long-term direction and viability. Understanding what is expected of them and eliminating hindrances to getting it done raises employees' sense that they can accomplish work tasks in the posttransition context. Third, the increased communication—in addition to clarifying expectations—counters the tendency for employees involved in transition to fill information voids with worst-case scenarios. Fourth, engaging people focuses energy and attention on the business needs of workplace recovery.

Three streams of activity engage people in the workplace recovery process and weaken forces against the new organizational order (see Exhibit 7.2). The first is to *help people accomplish their immediate work objectives.* Clarifying priorities and providing resources to get the job done abate the characteristics of posttransition life that commonly demotivate people. When people know what is expected of them and have the information, tools, and time they need to get it done, the "Why bother?" attitude is weakened.

The second stream involves the basic activities of *enhanced communication and employee involvement.* It is difficult to imagine workplace recovery without these components, but their role in the process is often taken for granted. Communication here means the ongoing sharing of information in a full and timely manner up, down, and across the organization. And involvement happens by giving people sufficient time to problem-solve and recommend ways of working smarter as the organization moves from the old to the new order.

EXHIBIT 7.2. Transition Realities and
Recovery Activities to Create Engagement.

Reality	Activity
4. The way transitions are mismanaged weakens motivational forces.	Help people get their work done.
5. People regress to primitive forms of behavior during and after transition but also crave direction and control.	Communicate and provide opportunities for involvement.
6. Executives adopt crisis management orientations and rely on the tried and tested rather than risk innovative solutions.	Diagnose and eliminate barriers to adaptation.

One way to involve people and enhance communication is to engage people in *identifying and eliminating barriers to moving through the adaptation process*, the third stream of activity. The best way to understand what is inhibiting people from ending the old is to ask them. This involves them in the recovery process and enhances upward communication. It also gives senior leadership the opportunity to address obstructions to the letting-go process. The more these barriers can be eliminated, the more likely it is that the forces against desired change will weaken and those for desired change will prevail.

Helping People Get Their Work Done

The fourth reality of workplace recovery addresses one of the most harmful unintended consequences of mergers, acquisitions, and downsizings—their adverse impact on employee motivation. Transition weakens employees' expectations that they can accomplish work requirements and receive desired rewards for doing so. After a merger or an acquisition, employees typically have questions about the new entity's direction and priorities. They want to make a good impression on new owners but may not be aware of what is expected of them in the postmerger organization. Frequently, employees do not know who to turn to for support or assistance in getting their regular work activities accomplished—the postmerger structure is unclear to them, as are the "rules of the road" for when and how to get assistance. And they may also face competing demands between getting work done and contributing to the transition. After a downsizing, of course, many former coworkers are gone. Among those who exited the company may be support staff and contacts in other departments who were instrumental in helping people accomplish their work. Thus employees find themselves having to get more work done with fewer resources.

The result in the posttransition organization is that employees feel less able to meet their performance expectations. Even if they felt confident in their ability, odds are that rewards for doing their jobs well (ranging from pay to opportunities for promotion) are either severely limited following a downsizing or unclear after a merger or acquisition. And leadership is nowhere to be seen in the chaotic posttransition period, so the many small intrinsic rewards, like a pat on the back for a job well done, are lacking as well.

Focus on Short-Term Objectives

The starting point for rebuilding employee motivation is to increase people's perception that they are able to accomplish what is expected of them on the job. This, in turn, begins by making sure that employees know what is expected of them on the job. If employees have any degree of uncertainty regarding work objectives or priorities, they cannot feel confident about their ability to "do the right thing."

The way out of this uncertainty is quite simple: meet with employees and clarify their short-term work objectives. Senior leadership may be talking at a high level about market conditions, organizational vision, and the broader context for recovery, but individual contributors have an immediate need to know what they should be doing right now. Following two waves of downsizing at a consulting firm, every team leader met individually with each subordinate to conduct a work expectation meeting. Exhibit 7.3 shows the outline used for conducting these meetings.

The work expectation meeting begins by stating the purpose of the session—to clarify the immediate work expectations for the employee. The superior gives specific, short-term objectives to the employee. The consulting firm had a corporate priority to generate more revenue, so one consultant's objectives included "Set up three cross-selling opportunities with current clients each month." Next, the employee reviews the various ways in which he or she spends time on the job, and the superior gives feedback on any activities that should be stopped or delayed. In this consultant's case, she was asked to delay working on new marketing materials and instead focus on immediate selling opportunities. The superior and subordinate then brainstorm any activities that are currently not being conducted but should be. In this case, the consultant and her superior agreed that rather than work on glossy marketing materials, the consultant should take some time to prepare a simple PowerPoint presentation showing how the firm's various services relate to one another. This would help in the immediate task of cross-selling services. After this, the superior and subordinate review the various work activities and come to a mutual agreement on their prioritization. In this consultant's case, contacting clients to make introductions for cross-selling was job number one. The meeting concludes with the identification of a specific date to meet and review work activities again.

Repetition counts here. Even if you think you have set expectations with employees, do it again. At the consulting firm, several consultants were clamoring for collateral materials to assist their cross-selling opportunities. At a follow-up work expectation meeting, the team leader asked the consultant to make a top priority of

---

EXHIBIT 7.3. Outline for Employee Work Expectation Meeting.

   I. State the purpose of the meeting.

  II. Clarify short-term work objectives—what is expected of the employee right now.

 III. Identify any work activities the employee is doing that should be outright stopped or put on the back burner.

 IV. Identify any work activities the employee is not doing that need to be initiated.

  V. Prioritize the employee's work activities.

 VI. Set a time for the next work expectation meeting.

---

the presentation. Without a scheduled follow-up meeting, this would have stayed on the back burner far longer than it did. Another reason to have regularly scheduled meetings is that there are considerable uncertainty and insecurity following transition, and employees may misinterpret signals about what matters now. At the consulting firm, the office head resigned from his position on the board of directors of the local chapter of a professional group. Employees interpreted this to mean that they should stop attending these networking meetings. Communication conducted in the course of the work expectation meetings clarified that the office head withdrew for personal reasons—his wife was returning to work after a hiatus, and he wanted to spend more time at home with their teenage children. In the meetings, leaders encouraged people to keep networking at these meetings.

Even when individuals have no major disruptions to their personal work objectives—and this is the case for many employees who survive transitions—it helps to review short-term objectives. People will want to know that they are doing the right things and appreciate the opportunity to raise any issues. And activities like work expectation meetings are opportunities to bring the recovery process down to the level of each individual contributor.

Focusing on Short-Term Objectives at the Chronicle. Matthew Wilson had a particularly difficult challenge in keeping his newsroom staff focused on short-term objectives after the *San Francisco Chronicle's* acquisition by the Hearst Corporation. This was the height of the dot-com boom in early 2000, with journalists being cherry-picked by start-ups to provide content for their Web sites. San Francisco journalists were especially desired, given their proximity to Silicon Valley and San Francisco's own new "media gulch" in its South of Market district. Moreover, the *San Jose Mercury News,* owned by rival newspaper conglomerate Knight-Ridder, was expanding into the *Chronicle's* turf by adding a San Francisco edition.

Chronicle newspeople had a host of distractions: When would the court challenges to the acquisition be settled? What were Hearst's true intentions for the combined paper? What would life be like under the "repressive" management style of former *Examiner* executives? What would it mean to leave the security of the *Chronicle* for the stock options of a start-up? A dozen top-notch reporters left the *Chronicle,* and Wilson could not replace them due to a hiring freeze (the assumption being that the combined news staffs would create redundancies). Paralysis afflicted the newsroom, as the new owners could not invest in their acquisition until all the court challenges were settled. Morale suffered, and Wilson feared more fallout from the aftereffects of the transition.

Wilson responded first by enlisting the aid of his lieutenants in the organization—the section editors who oversaw the day-to-day publication of the paper. He asked them to meet with their troops to clarify immediate opportunities for enhancing the quality of the newspaper. Wilson set two conditions for this short-term focus: the recommendations could not require major capital investments or the addition of new people. This was an important move by Wilson— he focused people on what was within their control and got them to let go of what was beyond their control. Working in their regular section teams, staffers recommended ideas for new features and enhancements to current offerings. Seeing improvements in their daily product gave employees immediate feedback that in a broader context of uncertainty and insecurity, they were doing the best they could to perform their work. Although this did not offset all of the employees' many valid postacquisition concerns, it did provide a bridge from the previous sense of paralysis to the eventual adoption of new ways of doing things in the posttransition organization.

Working Smarter

Whether the disruption to their personal work routine is large or small, the situation in which all employees conduct their work has changed. Recovery presents an opportunity to stop and think about how work is approached and, potentially, find new and smarter ways of getting the job done. While clarifying work expectations tells people the extent to which they are doing the right things, enhancing the methods through which those expectations are met gives people a sense that they are doing things the right way.

Searching for enhanced work methods is essential for work teams dealing with lower staffing levels and other significant changes yet benefits all work areas following a transition. But a common complaint in posttransition organizations is that there is little or no time available to assess work methods and approaches. So formal mechanisms need to be set up to help employees identify ways to get things done in a more effective manner. At the consulting firm, weekly brown bag lunches brought employees together to brainstorm cross-selling ideas, share success stories, and discuss failures. On occasion, outside experts on selling professional services came in to add their observations.

At a manufacturing firm that had experienced a 15 percent reduction in force, employee work groups met for an hour twice a week to identify unnecessary work that could be eliminated and propose simple steps to take to conduct work more efficiently. These sessions were run like classic quality circles in which employees could make recommendations to core management but did not have the authority to make decisions. After receiving and reviewing the recommendations, managers met with the work groups and declared whether the recommendations were accepted or rejected. If rejected, the manager gave specific reasons why so that the work groups, if they desired, could revise the recommendations. One side benefit of this process was that it enhanced cross-functional communication in the organization. If a recommendation involved, say, procurement, then the manager from that department would receive and react to the recommendation.

Working Smarter at the Chronicle. At the *San Francisco Chronicle*, employees had plenty of ideas for enhancing their sections of the newspaper but not the financial or human resources to implement all of them. Executive editor Wilson had to find some ways to get people to work smarter with fewer resources. He ended up taking a step back to help himself, his paper, and his people move forward. After a bitter strike in 1994, Wilson embarked on a culture change project to enhance upward, downward, and lateral communication and build better relations with employees and their union. In 1997, he initiated a program simply called "The Change Project"—ad hoc working groups in which people from across the newsroom came together to discuss aspects of putting out the newspaper.

The Change Project yielded thirty-nine recommendations in three broad areas: content, quality, and process. (Admirers of Alfred Hitchcock in the group affectionately referred to the set of recommendations as "The Thirty-Nine Steps.") Several months after the announced sale to Hearst, Wilson went back to the Thirty-Nine Steps and asked work groups to recommend actions that could be taken to help people work smarter in the postacquisition context. Again, as he did with his effort to get people in each section to focus on short-term objectives, Wilson asked participants in these cross-section groups to extract from the Thirty-Nine Steps actions that were within people's control and did not need significant infusions of manpower or money.

One recommendation for working smarter in the posttransition world was to accelerate the adoption of digital photography throughout the newsroom. Digital photography was just coming into its own at this time, and early adopters praised its quality, convenience, and cost-effectiveness for news reporting. Replacing conventional cameras with digital photography affected nearly everyone in the newsroom—just about every reporter worked with photographers, and every one saw the resulting pictures in the newspapers. It was a small financial investment but one that paid a big dividend in two important ways. First, it showed *Chronicle* people that their efforts could have an impact on the newspaper. This created some encouragement and excitement among the troops. Second, the enhancements to getting work accomplished helped people understand that there could be tangible business benefits in the new organizational order. As a result, this lessened the forces for holding on to the old.

Training

Of course, employees do not just show up at meetings to identify ways to work smarter in the posttransition organization and spontaneously act on their best behaviors. All the things that can go wrong in a work team meeting do—multiple conversations, hidden agendas, poor listening, and the like. Especially if participants have not had opportunities to let off some anger and express some concerns, the odds are these types of meetings will be unproductive.

Employees need training in group dynamics and team processes, as well as in creative problem-solving skills. An acquired, downsized, and restructured telecom firm asked me to design a straightforward, no-nonsense training program to enhance group dynamics and process skills in work teams (see Exhibit 7.4). The workshop, attended by people in their regular work groups, began with a warmup activity that asked participants to make two lists—one of characteristics of teams they have been on that have worked well and one of characteristics of teams that have been poor experiences. Following a presentation on group dynamics and running effective team meetings, the work groups set their own guidelines for team effectiveness. These included standards for how to set the agenda, how decisions will be made, and how the team will evaluate its

---

EXHIBIT 7.4. Work Team Training Agenda.

I. Warmup activity: List characteristics of effective and ineffective teams you have been on

II. Presentation on group process dynamics

III. Group activity: Ground rules for our team

IV. Presentation on creative problem solving

V. Group activity: Selecting an approach to problem solving for this team

VI. Close: Evaluation of group process and scheduling of first team meeting

---

effectiveness. Another presentation covered creative problem-solving approaches. From the menu of alternatives presented, each group selected the tactics it wanted to use in its problem-solving meetings. The way in which the work team made its selection was then debriefed—this provided a real-time test case that provided the group with feedback on the extent to which it abided by its own ground rules. The meeting closed with the scheduling of the first full-blown problem-solving meeting.

The idea behind this approach is to prepare the work group as fully as possible so it can hit the ground running at its first meeting. Early successes—in this case, coming to a consensus on ways to work more effectively together—are important motivators for work teams recovering from transition. By separating the training from the actual team meeting—and by preparing the team with both problem-solving and process skills—the work team comes to regard the meetings as creative, productive forums. This approach also allows for any lingering cynicism or resentment to be voiced at the training session and not contaminate the actual problem-solving sessions.

***Training for Managers at the* Chronicle.** Also beneficial is training to prepare managers and supervisors to lead their work teams through the transition from the old organizational order to the new.

At the *Chronicle*, Matthew Wilson relied on the strong contribution of his section editors and other leaders to get people focused on short-term objectives and work enhancements. At first, these editors were quite anxious about their personal fate in the combination. Hearst was folding the *Examiner* staff into the *Chronicle*, so despite a promise from Hearst that no one would be involuntarily terminated, everyone knew there could be only one sports editor, one photography editor, one entertainment editor, and so on. Wilson asked me to craft a training program for the members of his leadership team to help them get their subordinates focused on controllable, short-term objectives and recommending ways to enhance how work was getting done. In addition to covering content in these areas, the training sessions became another opportunity for senior people to vent with and support one another. Neither the section editors nor Wilson wanted displays of concerns to demotivate employees further. So the training sessions became an important forum for the leaders. These journalists never received much in the way of leadership development, so the workshops significantly raised their confidence that they could lead their troops through this difficult transition. Wilson also sponsored training in areas like meeting management and time management to support team leaders.

Communication and Involvement

I've played softball since my college days, and the aspect I most love about the game is base running. When I am sprinting toward third base and the coach gives me the signal to keep running home to score, it is a great feeling. First of all, I am focused. I don't have to think, "What should I do?" or "What's right or wrong?" All I have to do is perform—and since I am so focused, my performance will most likely be better than if I slowed down, sized up fielders, and gave thought to whether I should try to make it home to score or not. Second, I am following a direction. I don't have to worry about the repercussions of doing the wrong thing because I am simply following the coach's orders. I have less stress to wear on my performance and don't get distracted by things beyond my control. If I am safe, we both rejoice. If I am tagged out at the plate, my coach takes responsibility. (Note here that my coach is not a dysfunctional leader—he accepts responsibility for his actions.) It is a wonderful feeling to be out on the field and just do and not think.

During and after mergers, acquisitions, and downsizings, people regress to primitive forms of behavior in ways like becoming very political and distrusting, holding on to information rather than sharing it, and avoiding taking appropriate risks on the job. This fifth reality of workplace recovery occurs because of the perceived repercussions of doing something wrong. If my company just went through a downsizing, making a mistake could be used as a strike against me in the event of another wave of layoffs. Any signs I show of even just feeling anxious may get me cast as vulnerable and be used against me when the next list of victims is being drawn up. So I turn inward, keep my feelings bottled up, withdraw, and regress. (Some people may respond by causing a ruckus or even sabotaging the workplace, but they are few and far between.)

In this primitive mode, people crave direction. They want to know what the right thing to do is. They want to know what to avoid. And they want the peace of mind of knowing that they are following orders. They want their third-base coach to tell them whether to run home or stay at third.

During and after a transition, people also want a sense of control over things that matter to them. It feels good to take action, especially when one's security and well-being are on the line. On September 11, 2001, I was in Chicago for a meeting. That afternoon, the airports were shut down, and no one knew when they would reopen. I made a decision to rent a car and drive back to San Francisco rather than stay in my hotel room and stare at the television. I second-guessed myself numerous times as I waited my turn in line at the car rental counter. But once I got behind the steering wheel of my rental car, I knew I had made the right decision. It simply felt good to be in control and driving down the road.

When going through a transition, people feel that their sense of control is considerably lessened. Consider reporters at the *Chronicle*—the Hearst Corporation publicly stated that no one would be involuntarily terminated after it merged the staffs of the two newspapers, but employees figured there could not be duplicate television critics, restaurant reviewers, copyeditors, and so on. They did not know who would be put in place to lead the combined newsroom or what criteria would be used to fill positions, so they felt helpless to influence their likelihood of receiving a desirable position. Psychological researchers have uncovered a fascinating phenomenon of control in stressful situations: when individuals feel their control is lessened, they assume they have lost all control. This all-or-none reaction is why so many good people jump ship following transitions—they figure that the only control they have is to leave the company for seemingly greener pastures elsewhere. (Odds are, however, that they will be landing at another firm that is going to merge, acquire, or downsize.)

It may seem like a contradiction that people crave both direction and control following a transition—they want the peace of mind that comes from knowing they are doing the right things but also want to influence their work and personal situations. The two needs actually play off of one another. *Direction* gives people a context for influencing their posttransition activities, and *control* allows them to take action to follow that direction.

Communication

Workplace recovery requires the exchange of accurate, timely, and complete information. Employees will not know how to align their tasks with where leadership wants to take the organization unless they understand what that vision is and what the guidelines are for their expected behavior on the job. Teams will not be able to coordinate and convey knowledge within and across their boundaries unless information flows freely in multiple directions. And organizations will not receive valid and reliable feedback about critical internal and external matters unless a climate is established that invites upward communication in a relatively uninhibited and uncensored manner.

Communicating to revitalize after transition is much more than conveying information, however. It is a yardstick by which the predominating values and behaviors of the posttransition organization are measured. The content and frequency of communications, for example, indicate the degree of trust and concern between parties that prevails in the new organizational order. The accuracy and genuineness of communications reflect the extent to which teamwork and organizational effectiveness have developed. And the proactiveness and multidirectional nature of communications demonstrate commitment to and consideration from employees in the organization.

Communication contributes to workplace recovery by conveying facts about the organization, its actions, and its points of view. This includes problems and controversies as well as attributes and achievements. Open and honest communication contributes to individuals' sense of involvement and control. One major multinational corporation installed a toll-free telephone hot line so that the business press could have daily recorded updates of company news. Much to their surprise, company executives discovered that most of the calls were from their own managers, who wanted to know what was going on in the corporation.

Communication that promotes recovery requires more than simply committing to telling the same story in more and different ways. Rather, it takes a commitment to assessing and understanding the fundamental role of communication in the organization. This, in turn, requires an understanding of the communication needs of the intended audience. Certainly, organizational communications must identify, define, and articulate issues from management's own perspective. But those issues must be tempered with and couched in terms that are important to the employee audience.

In most organizations, it is not difficult to find out *what* happened but very difficult to find out *why* something happened. This leaves people to speculate on the event's cause and significance. This reactive communication process depends on people's ability to figure out reasons and management motivations by starting at the event itself and reasoning backward. This is difficult to do because employees do not have access to all the facts and because business events generally have complex causes. The company grapevine spreads an overly simplistic portrayal that may fit the incomplete data at hand but is likely not to reflect the true underlying causes or management's intentions.

The antidote to the reactive communication process is a proactive process of issues communication: identifying, defining, and articulating the major issues that the organization must address if it is to be successful. Such an issue is any major concern that is likely to have a significant effect on the organization's ability to achieve its goals and whose outcome is in doubt. Employees want to know early in the life of the issue, not when it has tightened its grip on the organization and is threatening to do serious harm.

The proactive communication process offers some important advantages over the reactive process during recovery. First, it tends to identify the organization's concerns and priorities and to indicate what management intends to do about them. This is reassuring to employees, who would otherwise become even more anxious if they do not hear the organization's problems—which they experience on a daily basis—discussed and possible solutions considered. Second, it focuses on the significance of events and not their mere occurrence. Third, the proactive communication process provides a frame of reference within which particular events may be placed and explained ("Yes, this may be a setback, but it is no disaster. Remember, we told you that we anticipated one of the toughest issues confronting us this year would be . . ."). A fourth advantage of the process is that it can be used to foreshadow subsequent change and provide justification for the change. Organizations in recovery following transition may have to take actions that look poorly conceived when viewed in isolation. But when explained in the broader context of where the organization is headed and why, they can begin to make very good sense. Finally, proactive communication encourages hope and optimism among employees who understand and see more clearly where their organization is headed, why it is going in that direction, and how it will get there.

Guidelines for Communicating for Recovery

General rules of effective organizational communication apply during recovery: explain the why underlying the what, repeat messages through multiple media, recognize that people prefer face-to-face communication from their immediate superiors, check to ensure that the message sent was the message received, and accept that not communicating has negative rather than neutral effects. Communicating to facilitate recovery, however, does pose some special needs and opportunities.

• *Provide a compelling rationale for why the status quo is no good.* Even if there have been adverse conditions that led the firm to downsize, merge, or be acquired, many employees (especially those with power bases, perks, or positions to protect) will still be holding tightly on to the old. They may rationalize that uncontrollable external factors are the culprit, not internal strategies, decisions, or dynamics. Others will hold on simply because the new organizational order has yet to be fully articulated—they prefer the known to the unknown, even if the known has proved unsuccessful. The new organizational order does not materialize overnight, and neither does support for it. In the meantime, leadership needs to convey to people—in clear and convincing terms—that the status quo cannot produce desired organizational and personal success.

• *Assure people of what is not changing.* Concurrently, leadership can ease employee fears and worst-case scenarios that the sky is falling. The reality is that many characteristics of the pretransition organization are likely to be retained in the new organizational order. Knowing this helps employees cope with the stress of transition. At the *Chronicle*, Matt Wilson's reaching back to the Thirty-Nine Steps signaled that the commitment to improving the newspaper's quality was being retained from before to after its acquisition.

• *Use language carefully.* It is common for executives to make comments like "It's business as usual" or "The transition is behind us." Executives many times are just trying to soothe their troops, but the sloppy use of language sends mixed signals to employees and reinforces holding on to the old. When executives say things like "It's business as usual," they often mean "Just stay focused on your work." If that is the case, then that is what they should say and make certain that people know what objectives and priorities to focus on.

• *Share information again and again.* The need to overcommunicate during and after transition has been, well, overcommunicated! The fact remains, however, that most executives and team leaders do a poor job of repeating and reinforcing their messages. The forces against desired change are strong, and communicators have got to share information over and over again. You can be sure that the grapevine, rumor mill, and individuals' fertile imaginations are creating and conveying messages that are far more dire than reality.

• *Use low production standards.* I have had clients delay the release of a simple employee newsletter or memo for several weeks because it has to fit the company's templates and production standards. This is not the time for slick, glossy communications. It is the time to get the word out to people as quickly as possible. Using production standards that differ from those used in the old organizational order reinforces the message to employees that times are changing. They will appreciate leadership's efforts to forgo style in order to get substance out to people as soon as possible.

• *Be comfortable saying, "I don't know."* You don't have all the answers, and employees don't expect that you do. But they do want to know what you know when you know it. Most executives and team leaders are uncomfortable going in front of a group unless they have the full story to tell. Well, even if the full story is not yet available, that does not excuse you from communicating. Keep in mind that how you communicate matters along with what you communicate—changes in your communication style signal a break from the past to employees. At the *Chronicle*, Matt Wilson held regular town hall meetings with all shifts of employees. At many sessions, his opening presentation was simple: "There is no new news to report this week." But then employees responded with many questions about rumors they had heard or clarifications about points previously communicated. After several rounds of these meetings, I assessed employee reactions to them. They were universally appreciated (remember, this employee group was made up of typically cynical journalists) with comments like "I go to the town hall meetings expecting to hear no news, but I am amazed how much information gets conveyed just by answering employee questions" and "It's a great forum in which to compare and dispel the latest rumors."

• *Set communications expectations.* After the acquisition and integration of a slightly larger competitor, the CEO of an electronics company went on a global road show to announce a major culture change initiative to employees. He put this question directly to the groups: "I can communicate to you during this process in one of two ways. I can wait until I know that every thing is a done deal and can report things to you then, or I can tell you what I know as I know it, with the caveat that what I tell you initially may change later. Which do you prefer?" Unanimously, employees said they wanted information as it was known, even if it might change. The very act of setting expectations is an opportunity to communicate with employees and once again model a change from the old.

The lessons learned from communicating with employees during recovery are straightforward: level with people; let them know what you do and do not know, what is and is not changing, and what is and is not within their control. How can employees be expected to charge up the hill if they don't know what the opportunities are, what matters in achieving them, and how they can help realize them?

Involvement

People are more apt to let go of the old when they feel like architects of change rather than victims of change. The more people feel involved in the recovery process, the more they are going to support it. Just about everything mentioned in this chapter involves people in some way. Engaging people in setting work expectations and objectives, having them participate in task forces to identify smarter ways of getting work done, putting them through training programs, and communicating with them all create opportunities for involvement.

There are both symbolic and substantive ways to involve people in recovery. After it purchased Qualcomm's telephone business, local managers at Kyocera launched a "design the new company T-shirt" contest. This paid homage to the acquired workforce's tradition of creating T-shirts displaying their work group identity. A more substantive and more common form of involvement is to get people to participate in ad hoc task forces to plan or implement aspects of recovery. Employees who perform the work are abundant sources of ideas for how to integrate operations, reduce non-value-added work, or revise work procedures in line with the new organizational order. Whenever possible, it is helpful to "stack the deck" with employees who are relatively forward-looking and whose viewpoints influence those around them. Employees not on a task force can be involved by having the task force present work in progress to them for review. Too often, planning groups conduct their work in a vacuum, shut off from the overall organization. This only breeds resistance to subsequent implementation because people like to feel that they have at least some input. Open up the process by securing involvement, and implementation will proceed much more smoothly.

Diagnosing and Eliminating Barriers to Adaptation

Just as employees regress into primitive behaviors, another reality of workplace recovery is that executives conduct their own defensive retreat during and following mergers, acquisitions, and downsizings.

Merging executives circle their wagons and lurch into crisis management mode. This feels heady and invigorating, as those in senior positions believe they are taking decisive action to protect their interests. But a crisis mentality blocks the collection and processing of valid information. As a result, executives' gambits typically miss their intended mark.

Leaders who fall into crisis mode following a merger, acquisition, or downsizing centralize decision making. Centralization is very useful to an executive team following a transition. It ensures that information flows to the top so that executives are able, in concert with trusted associates, to sort out possible losses and gains and map strategy for moves and countermoves. But this crisis orientation has its costs. Centralized decision making can shut the top team off from important information that would otherwise be developed in an open exchange with subordinates or, in the case of a merger, with executives from the partner organization. It can also insulate the top leaders and promote a "groupthink" mentality as strategies as considered. A crisis mentality mode hinders recovery by reducing decision quality after the transition.

The way to counter these crisis management tendencies is for leadership to open up to, solicit, and deal with employee input on the dynamics of the posttransition organization. The task at hand is to ask, "What is preventing employees from ending the old so that they can move forward and embrace the new?" Engaging employees in answering this question is one of the fullest ways to involve employees in the recovery process.

There will be resistance to diagnosing inhibitors to adaptation. Many executives will argue for reinforcing the attraction of the new rather than weakening the attraction of the old—it feels like the more action-oriented and time-efficient approach. However, it is a less effective strategy—people have to end the old before they accept the new. And it is common following a merger or acquisition for months to go by before the new organizational order is fully articulated. So the sequencing of diagnosing inhibitors to facilitate the letting-go process while the new is still being developed is quite practical. There will be plenty of opportunity to strengthen the appeal of the new down the road. Now is the time to start at the beginning—finding and attending to impediments to ending the old.

You can also expect resistance from executives and managers who claim that "we know what people are thinking" and ask, "So why bother spending the time and money?" Even if you have a good sense of what your people view as the impediments to moving forward, the process of collecting and discussing the content is of value. But do you know for sure what employees consider to be barriers to adaptation *from their perspective?* People put on their poker faces following a transition. Managers are too busy driving in two lanes at one time to relay information up and down the hierarchy. Teams, departments, and business units are so caught up in getting their own acts together that they don't cooperate and communicate laterally. You need to diagnose, if for no other reason than to confirm your sense of what is going on.

Diagnosing Barriers to Adaptation

The tools most commonly used to diagnose inhibitors to adaptation include individual interviews, focus group interviews, and employee attitude surveys. Individual and focus group interviews provide tremendous color and insight into how employees are conceptualizing the posttransition organization. Surveys are cost-effective means to involve large numbers of employees or even the entire workforce. The methods can be combined—interviewing a sample of employees to identify issues to ask about on a survey that will go to the broader population.

What to Look For. Basically, you want to find out what is standing in the way of people's ability to end the old and accept the new. Employees tend to cite three types of inhibitors:

- *Demotivating forces.* These are forces that weaken people's perceptions that they can perform their jobs, have desirable rewards for performing, and will indeed receive those rewards if they perform adequately. We have discussed these three components of employee motivation and how they get damaged in a transition. The job now is to diagnose specifically what is lowering employee motivation. *What do people need to feel that they are able to perform their work? What rewards do people regard as attractive? To what extent do employees believe management will pay out for a job well done?*

- *Transition impact forces.* All transitions have unintended consequences. The task here is to diagnose the ways in which the merger, acquisition, or downsizing has affected people, psychologically and behaviorally. *What are people's prevailing mental models? Do people see a posttransition organization that is by design (congruent with expectations set by leadership), by default (incongruent with promises made about the transition), or the status quo (the same old organization)?*

- *Uncertainty forces.* Although the pretransition organization may no longer exist, the posttransition organization has yet to be refrozen. The requirement here is to find out what employees need to know to get their jobs done and embrace the new organizational order. *What is uncertain or unclear to employees regarding the organizational vision and strategy, their team's mission and performance requirements, and their own role and expectations?*

I find that employees appreciate the opportunity to participate in the recovery process and readily offer their views. Straightforward questions asking people about inhibitors usually suffice. Sometimes employees need or want prompts to get them responding, and the questions just presented in italics are quite helpful. For the vast majority of individual and focus group interviews, however, I use a core set of general questions that get slightly altered to fit the specific situation of the client organization (see Exhibit 7.5). After briefing participants on why the data are being collected and how they will be used and after assuring participants that their identity will be kept anonymous, I ask people a warmup question—for example, about their career history—to get them talking. The interview begins in earnest by asking people their take on the rationale underlying the merger, acquisition, or downsizing they just experienced and the ex-

---

EXHIBIT 7.5. Core Diagnostic Interview Questions.

0. Introduction: Why the data are being collected, how they will be used, assurance of anonymity, warmup questions (for example, "Please give a thumbnail sketch of your career history")
1. Why did the (merger, acquisition, or downsizing) occur?
2. To what extent do the people you work with understand and support this rationale?
3. What makes you feel good or optimistic about the transition?
4. What concerns you or makes you feel pessimistic about the transition?
5. What current dynamics will enable a successful transition?
6. What current dynamics will inhibit a successful transition?
7. What needs to happen to manage the transition well?
8. What is your advice to (the senior executive) at this time?
9. What else should I know about your experience of the transition?

---

tent to which the people they work with understand and support the rationale. If people don't have a sense of why the transition occurred, that is an obvious inhibitor to employees' ending the old and accepting the new. Then I assess employees' general views of the transition by asking what makes them feel good or pessimistic about it and what concerns them or makes them feel pessimistic about it. For the next two questions, I ask employees to limit their responses to actual dynamics and conditions in the organization and to avoid hypothetical responses (for example, "If we had good communication, I would . . ."). Either the firm has good communication or it doesn't. These two questions are the core of the diagnosis: What current conditions will enable a successful transition from the old to the new? And what current conditions will inhibit a successful transition? Finally, I ask the interviewees their thoughts on what needs to happen to make the transition a success and what advice they have to the senior executive at this time.

Who to Ask. A questionnaire can be administered to the overall workforce in a cost-effective manner, but individual and focus group interviews generate much greater depth and detail regarding employee perspectives, and that usually means that only a sample of the employee population needs to be invited to participate. Because the political realities of the organization need to be considered, I often end up interviewing a disproportionate number of senior-level people. That's OK, because they are undeniably members of the workforce and are more likely to support the diagnosis if they are involved in it.

My basic rule of thumb is to get people who are likely to speak up—why waste time with individuals who are unlikely to voice their views? I ask for a range of supporters of the transition and naysayers, opinion leaders whom other employees look to for interpretation of company events, and of course, a good mix of people from various functions, levels, and demographic groups. It is also helpful to get a mix of relative newcomers and veteran employees to determine their viewpoints.

If only a portion of the organization has been directly affected by the transition, it's a good idea to overpoll that area. But don't ignore employees from other areas of the organization—they may have experienced some indirect impact. A professional services firm I consulted to made an acquisition that was integrated into its smallest of three practice areas. The CEO was careful to communicate to employees from all business units why he was taking on debt and making the most significant acquisition in the firm's history: "This is the practice area that our future will be built on, and we are investing in it to ensure our continued success for years to come." After the integration, the CEO asked me to assess employee viewpoints on what they had been through. I spoke mainly to individuals in the integrated business unit but also met with a fair number of individuals from the two other practice areas. In one, the acquisition truly was regarded as a nonevent. People in this area really didn't interact much with the other practice areas, were busy making their numbers, and, for better or worse, just didn't care all that much about the acquisition. In the other practice area, employees acted like three-year-olds when Mommy and Daddy bring a bouncy new baby home from the hospital. "If they are the practice area of the future, then what are we—chopped liver?" asked one interviewee. "Excuse me, but wasn't it our hard work and profitability that put us in a position to acquire them? Give *us* those millions of dollars to invest in our business, and I am sure we can get some handsome returns," begged another. This sibling rivalry is very common in mergers and acquisitions and is a prime example of how good intentions in managing a transition often produce unintended consequences: the CEO thought he was doing the right thing by "selling" veteran employees on the merits of the acquisition.

When to Diagnose Inhibitors. Managers come up with excellent reasons for when *not* to conduct employee research after a transition. Early on, they will say that things haven't settled down yet, so employees won't have enough to comment on. A few months down the road, managers will plead that they are too busy adapting to the new organization and now just isn't the right time to take people off-line for interviews or surveys. A year later, well, by then the transition is old news.

There is no right or wrong time to diagnose inhibitors to letting go of the old. Obviously, the earlier you ask, the sooner you will uncover and be able to address them. In cases of posttransition organizations by default, early diagnosis can help identify undesired dynamics. Early diagnosis also provides a baseline for subsequent tracking of the extent to which people are ending the old and accepting the new. As will be discussed in Chapter Nine, the desired posttransition organization is more likely to be realized when its development is monitored through systematic data collection.

Eliminating Inhibitors: What to Do with the Data

Many executives avoid employee research during and after a transition because they falsely assume that soliciting employee viewpoints creates an expectation that changes will be made. What employees expect is to know that their leaders have heard their issues, whether the issues will be addressed, and, if not, why not. Leadership can respond in a variety of ways:

- *Correct misperceptions.* At the professional services firm afflicted by posttransition sibling rivalry, rumors floated around the lead company that acquired staff were earning salaries 25 to 50 percent higher than their own. This issue was raised in some focus groups I conducted. Leadership responded by presenting pay data from the two companies showing that the differences were much slighter than the grapevine made them out to be.

- *Explain why the issue cannot be addressed.* Employees at the acquired firm complained that their health care benefit options were being reduced as a result of the merger. Yes, they were, admitted senior leadership, but the firm had decided to restrict the number of options for health care insurers so that it could save administrative costs. "We know that some of you will have to change your current coverage and that this will be inconvenient," acknowledged the CEO in one of his periodic integration update memos to employees, "but we made a decision to keep administrative costs in hand by offering fewer options. Please note that you do have a choice of eight plans, including HMOs and Preferred Provider options, a number that I understand is still above the number of choices typically made available by a company of our size."

- *Put a task force on the case.* In a major midwestern city, one merger partner had its office downtown and the other in the suburbs. Both sides had signed three-year leases for their offices just prior to the acquisition announcement, and the costs of getting out of either of the leases were prohibitive. But one impediment to getting work done in the posttransition organization cited by employees in that city was the distance between the offices. Local leadership set up two task forces—one of senior practitioners and the other of administrative support staff—to propose recommendations for facilitating teamwork despite the separate offices.

• *Put the issue on the back burner.* You can let employees know you heard an issue but explain to them why it is just not of high enough priority to deal with now. In the professional services acquisition, consultants from the two sides expressed some concerns about membership in professional organizations. Senior leadership had communicated that it wanted to cut costs by avoiding duplicate memberships and reducing the overall number of associations with which consultants affiliated. But this was not a big-ticket item, and leadership had other matters more critical to its core business strategy to attend to. So leadership acknowledged that it heard the issue but also told the consultants that it was being tabled until the next calendar year. In the meantime, consultants were advised to stay the course with their current memberships.

• *Weaken or eliminate the inhibitor.* My interviews with employees from the practice area with sibling rivalry indicated that their business unit leader regularly bad-mouthed the acquisition and the CEO's efforts to diversify the company. The CEO's first response to hearing this was to launch a communications campaign to convey to veteran employees why diversification was good for the company and, in turn, for them individually. Yet their business unit leader continued to tell them otherwise. So the CEO demoted the business unit leader, who eventually left to seek opportunities outside the firm. Not only did this eliminate an inhibitor to letting go of the old, but it also contributed to unfreezing the veteran practice group so that new attitudes more consistent with the new organizational order could take hold.

Engagement Don'ts and Dos

There is a real gap between the lip service executives and managers give to engaging employees and how little care they put into doing it. Exhibit 7.6 summarizes this gap in some engagement don'ts and dos. Most leaders take for granted that they know what is on their employees' minds. *Don't assume that you know what your people are*

EXHIBIT 7.6. Engagement Don'ts and Dos.

Don't		*Do*
Don't assume that you know what people are thinking.	→	Do assume that people are afraid to tell the emperor he has no clothes.
Don't assume that people hear you the first time.	→	Do assume that you have to repeat yourself more and check for understanding.

---

thinking. As noted earlier, people put on their poker faces during and after transition. Even if you are an ace at reading people's moods and sentiments, you have to be conservative and assume that you do not know for sure what they are thinking or what is motivating their behavior on the job. *Do assume that people are afraid to tell the emperor he has no clothes.* Digging deeply to understand what people need to get their work done and what is inhibiting them from moving through the natural adaptation process thoroughly engages the workforce.

Similarly, most leaders do not do a careful and thorough job of conveying information to assist people in getting work done and accelerating adaptation. *Don't assume that people hear you the first time you say something.* Transition-related stress produces a sense of crisis that impairs perception. You have to overcommunicate using a variety of media. *Do assume that you have to repeat yourself more and check for understanding.* Yes, it is boring to repeat yourself, and yes, it takes time to stop in your tracks to make sure that people hear and truly understand your messages. But that is what it takes to fully engage people in the march up the hill. You pay now by identifying and removing or minimizing those roadblocks, or you pay later by having a workforce that is unable or unwilling to dedicate itself to achieving the new organizational order.

8

Energy

Transitions do not have to be hellish to be disruptive. Even transitions that are perceived by employees to have a sound business rationale, be reasonably well managed, and contribute to employee well-being and organizational capacity involve a change from the status quo.

The 2000 acquisition of Warner-Lambert by pharmaceutical giant Pfizer is about as positive an organizational transition as you'll find. Ironically, Pfizer's initial overture to Warner-Lambert was a hostile bid to preempt the target from merging with American Home Products. The cholesterol-reducing drug Lipitor was about to come to market, and Pfizer, which had co-developed it with Warner-Lambert, did not want to share the potential billions of dollars in revenues with a competitor. Most rank-and-file Warner-Lambert employees welcomed Pfizer's preemptive bid after American Home Products put their company in play. They recognized that there was considerably more overlap between their firm and AHP than with Pfizer and consequently anticipated that many fewer jobs would be at risk due to redundancy in a combination with Pfizer. Certainly, being acquired disrupted the status quo and relegated them to the status of being taken over, but Warner-Lambert's people figured that in an era of organizational MADness, they could do worse than combining with Pfizer, the perennial leader among pharmaceutical companies in *Fortune* magazine's rankings of most admired companies and best places to work.

Prior to this deal, mergers and acquisitions had not been a part of Pfizer's growth story. For Pfizer employees, then, the Warner-Lambert acquisition was a dramatic departure from their firm's strategy of going it alone in the consolidating pharmaceutical industry. They also had the fire turned up under them when Pfizer CEO William Steers coupled the announcement of his intent to acquire Warner-Lambert with a bold promise to Wall Street that the combined company would grow at an annual rate of 15 percent over the next several years. Wall Street liked what it heard, but many employees wondered how a firm that already seemed to be running at full throttle could achieve such growth.

To its credit, Pfizer leadership had a very clear idea of the desired end state of its posttransition organization. A model of postcombination change developed by Philip Mirvis and myself illustrates the new organizational order for the combined Pfizer/Warner-Lambert (see Figure 8.1). Prior to the combination, Warner-Lambert had acquired Agouron, a biotech firm located in La Jolla, California. Known for its white-shirt-and-tie conservative culture, Warner-Lambert recognized that if it imposed its ways on the acquired company, it would lose valued personnel, who were accustomed to coming to work in jeans or shorts and sandals. After Pfizer acquired Warner-Lambert, it listened to the target and adopted a hands-off stance with Agouron. Pfizer imposed its financial reporting systems and other infrastructure components on its acquisition target in a clear absorption but, in contrast, folded its smaller consumer products business into the larger one of Warner-Lambert, which featured such prominent brands as Listerine mouthwash, Trident gum, and Certs mints. Even though Pfizer had a world-class human resource function, it was not so arrogant as to assume that it could not learn anything from its acquisition. A "best of both" approach was employed, and while Pfizer ways predominated, the company nevertheless did adopt Warner-Lambert practices in areas like college recruiting.

FIGURE 8.1. Postcombination Change in Pfizer/Warner-Lambert.

Finance Acquired company conforms to acquirer—cultural assimilation (**Absorption**)		**Research and Development** Both companies find new ways of operating—cultural transformation (**Transformation**)
	Human Resources Additive from both sides—cultural integration (**Best of Both**)	
Agouron Acquired company retains its independence—cultural autonomy (**Preservation**)		**Consumer Products** Unusual case of acquired company dictating term—cultural assimilation (**Reverse Merger**)

High / Low — Degree of change in Warner-Lambert

Low / High — Degree of change in Pfizer

Source: Adapted from M. L. Marks and P. M. Mirvis, *Joining Forces: Making One Plus One Equal Three in Mergers, Acquisitions, and Alliances* (San Francisco: Jossey-Bass, 1998), fig. 3.4.

Then there was R&D. If you are familiar with the pharmaceutical industry, you know that what Wall Street analysts care about is a firm's pipeline of future drugs: "It's nice that Viagra brings in billions of dollars a year," concede the analysts, "but," they want to know, "what is your next blockbuster drug?" Following the companywide growth commitment made to Wall Street, John Niblack, president of Pfizer's Central Research function, announced to his troops that the company had to transform how it conducted research and development—neither Pfizer's nor Warner-Lambert's approach to R&D would suffice in generating the discovery and development of new drugs that would feed the desired growth. His vision: a transformed R&D function that abandoned the status quo of both Pfizer and Warner-Lambert.

As a first step, Niblack put a structural stake in the ground for the new organizational order: he leveraged the scale of the combined Pfizer and Warner-Lambert R&D organizations into a global matrixed organization. There were three dimensions to the matrix: location, line function, and therapeutic area. Local line leaders operated in a decentralized manner but coupled with line leadership (in areas like discovery and development) to achieve global alignment and direction setting. R&D work was also coordinated across major therapeutic areas including cancer, pain, and respiratory illness. As part of the structural transformation, the number of worldwide R&D sites was reduced from eleven to nine (including the closing of one heritage Pfizer site).

Making the structural transformation work required cultural transformation. Prior to the acquisition, Pfizer R&D laboratories in places like Groton, Connecticut; Sandwich, England; and Nagoya, Japan, operated like fiefdoms. Literally, scientists in one part of the world could be doing drug discovery work that was being replicated elsewhere in an uncoordinated manner. Work on discovering pain medication, for example, was going on at six sites. Although multiple programs could still exist in the new operating model, they had to be coordinated. Expectations and behaviors congruent with teaming were needed to replace old models of autonomy. People, many of whom had worked in the old Pfizer their entire careers, had to learn how to partner and how to work in a complex matrix.

Concurrently, Pfizer and Warner-Lambert employees experienced their own version of integration MADness. Changes abounded, in everything ranging from systems and policies to pay and titles. Things as basic as vacation time (some sites closed Christmas week while others let employees select their own vacation days) and funeral leave (three hours at some sites, half a day at others) had to be aligned across the organization, further indicating that the old order of every location doing its own thing was being replaced by a new order of partnership.

Energy as an Element of Organizational Recovery

Get people excited about the new organizational order and support them in realizing it.

With empathy for their emotional experience and engagement in the business imperatives of recovery, people's grip on the old is loosened. Now comes the time to energize people to charge up the hill and capture new workplace opportunities, both personal and organizational. Energy is created when leadership addresses the emotional realities of accepting the new organizational order by letting employees know what is in it for them to bring the new order to life and how they can succeed in it (see Exhibit 8.1). This begins with a clearly articulated *vision of a new and better organization* that provides details regarding the changes in the organization's direction, mission, culture, and architecture that will contribute to an enhanced workplace. Importantly, this vision has to be brought down to a human level—what is in it for people to contribute to achieving it.

The struggle between forces for the old and the new continues, however, and people will experience setbacks as they try to adapt to the new organizational order. To help them move forward, a *learning environment* allows people to experiment with new and better methods for achieving personal and organizational success. It also strengthens employee perceptions that their efforts will be rewarded, which in turn generates motivation for moving forward.

The energy required for recovery after transition is sustained by maintaining the *human touch*. It is all too easy for leaders to act like the transition is "over." Whether reflective of leadership's true intentions or not, inaction that is interpreted by employees as leadership inattentiveness or indifference to employee needs and motivation will weaken forces for accepting the new organizational order. To help people swing to the new rung, leadership needs to continue to connect with employees on a human level and provide support—both practical and emotional—to encourage people to

---

EXHIBIT 8.1. Transition Realities and
Recovery Activities to Create Energy.

Reality	Activity
7. Transitions have the potential to unfreeze people and organizations.	Clarify a vision of a new and better organization.
8. People need to let go of the old before they can accept the new, and in between they struggle with the neutral zone.	Create a learning environment that encourages people to experiment and open up to new ways of doing things and creates opportunities for short-term wins.
9. Executives typically ignore or deny the need to let go of the old before accepting the new.	Connect with people and provide support; accept confusion and backsliding; give people time to move through adaptation.

---

move forward. The human touch also counters the tendency for people to want to retreat to the comfort zone of the old, familiar workplace realities rather than move forward. Part of being supportive is being patient and recognizing that people take time to move through the adaptation process.

Hang Time

Even as people move forward in their adaptation process, forces for maintaining the status quo are sustained and even temporarily strengthened by confusion about and lack of confidence in the new organizational order. This does not imply that employees find fault in the new organizational order, but they are not yet fully convinced that this is indeed the path up the hill to capture the prize. Employees may not have liked everything about the old organizational order or have confidence in its ability to generate business and personal success, but at least people knew what it entailed. To move forward, they must risk letting go of the old and struggle with accepting the new. This period of slow internal psychological transition is the inevitable *hang time* that occurs when one has let go of the old ring but has not yet grabbed the new ring.

This is a difficult time for many people adapting to organizational transition— earlier I noted that William Bridges terms it the "neutral zone" but my clients dub it the "twilight zone" due to its dark and scary nature. Unless prepared emotionally for hang time through empathy and prepared for it practically through engagement, people in the process of adapting to transition will mistakenly conclude that the lack of stability they feel means that something is wrong with them personally. Some will panic, tighten up, and brace themselves for a fall. Others will lurch back toward the old ring and hold on tighter than ever. Some, however, will recognize the fluidity of hang time and see it as a chance for creativity, renewal, and development. They will try to accept the awkwardness and uncertainty as an opportunity to remold themselves with the new organizational order.

During hang time, if the inhibiting forces have been sufficiently weakened, people become increasingly aware of their patterns carried from the old organizational order and recognize that they are responding in what now is a maladaptive manner. The only way to learn this is through trial and error, either by oneself or by watching others being rewarded or punished for certain behaviors. Eventually, if the forces for desired change are sustained and strengthened, employees will develop new mental models of life in the new organizational order. When people are assisted through a clear understanding of that new organizational order, encouraged to experiment with how to contribute to it, and supported through the two-steps-forward, one-step-back realities of adaptation, they become energized to move through hang time and make the effort to advance forward.

A Vision of a New and Better Organization

In my parlance, *vision* is not just a statement of organizational aspirations but rather a broad portrayal of the desired posttransition end state. The classic vision statement may be a component, but it is not the entire explanation of the new organizational order. As defined in Chapter Three, the contents of the new organizational order contribute to a vision of what employees can expect in the posttransition organization and what is expected of them. It may include descriptions of desired direction, mission, strategy, culture, architecture, psychological work contract, and core competencies.

Vision tells people about the new organizational order—where the organization is headed, what will matter in getting there, and how people can play a role in making it happen. To clarify the vision of a new and better organization means to make sure that people understand the *why* and the *how* underlying the *what*—that is, not just what the new organizational order is about but also why it should lead to organizational success and how the individual plays a role in it. And as distinct from merely "communicating" the vision of a new and better organization, clarifying it provides people with sufficient *precision* in understanding why change is essential, what changes will occur, and how these changes affect them personally. It is this connection between personal impact and organizational success that is the foundation for creating the energy required for recovery after transition.

Why Vision Is Essential to Recovery

One of the benefits of organizational transition, if well managed, is its potential to unfreeze work organizations and their employees. If people have become relatively unfrozen, a clear statement of the new organizational order can cast the mold within which people will refreeze. Alternatively, if the transition has been mismanaged, people will retreat to the comfort zone of their accustomed norms, attitudes, and behaviors (the status quo) or, worse yet, will adopt undesirable mental models that inadvertently become refrozen (transition by default). The longer you wait to articulate your desired vision, the more likely employees will create inadvertent mental models that are not necessarily aligned with the desired direction of the posttransition organization. Then, to realize the desired new order, you have to go back to square one and unfreeze employee perceptions and behaviors.

Vision matters considerably in workplace recovery. And the manner in which the vision is introduced matters as well. Think of it: the point here is to create energy. If you are going to energize your troops, you need a vision to point them in the right direction when that energy takes off. The content of the vision provides that direction. But it is the manner through which the vision is developed and disseminated that gets people to take the first step in developing new expectations, perceptions, behavior, and mental models in that desired direction.

Articulating Vision

A good vision reaches people at an emotional as well as a practical level. Leaders who use vision well inspire and excite their employees, in addition to providing direction and insight. To be motivating, a vision has to have four characteristics. First, the vision needs to be seen by employees as being *important* through its ability to make a difference in organizational and personal success. It needs to be *credible* by relating to the aspects of the work situation that matter to people. The vision has to be *attractive*; people have to find it desirable. And the vision must be viewed as *attainable* so that people feel they have a realistic chance of doing what needs to be done.

Vision statements need not be elegant. In fact, the simpler they are, the easier they are to communicate and to relate to on-the-job behaviors. One of the best statements of corporate vision came from a 1993 front-page *Wall Street Journal* article that dubbed vision as "overrated" and cited "no-nonsense" Chrysler Corporation CEO Robert J. Eaton as an example of an executive who disdained the process of articulating where the organization is headed and what matters in getting there. Yet the article went on to describe how Eaton had clarified his desire for the company to "stay healthy" along with his personal ambition to be "the first chairman never to lead a Chrysler comeback." This *was* Eaton's vision—not especially uplifting but nevertheless clear. And he gave equally clear orders on how Chrysler would achieve this vision, by concentrating on "nuts-and-bolts" management.

Humanizing the Vision

As inspiring as a clear vision of organizational direction can be, people following transition will still ask, "What's in it for me to make it worth charging back up the hill?" Whereas contributing to the greater good will suffice for some employees, most will want to know what personal benefits will come along with the organizational gains before they commit to the new. Thus the vision needs to be brought down to a human level.

Articulating the personal benefits in the new organizational order is a fairly straightforward process. Literally, it is the answer to "What's in it for me?" Here are some examples of the ways leaders have cited the human benefits of a new organizational order:

• After an entertainment firm was sold to Japanese owners, female employees worried about how they would be treated by what they regarded as "sexist" owners. The buyers touted "respect for diversity" as a component of the new order. They backed up their words by taking a mentoring program for female executives that had been very popular in one unit of the acquired company and expanding it throughout the organization.

• When a firm known for "businesspeople who happen to be engineers" acquired a smaller competitor that prided itself on being "engineers who happen to be businesspeople" (read that to mean that the buyer made a profit and the seller didn't), the lead company made it clear that it was going to address issues like the backlog in accounts receivables. Simultaneously, however, the buyer also touted its in-house "university" as a tangible commitment to developing engineers' leadership and managerial skills. The smaller firm had no such program, and its people looked forward to this investment in their development.

- A computer hardware firm that downsized introduced a commitment to professional performance review as part of its new organizational order. Prior to the waves of downsizings, performance reviews had been a joke at the firm—some employees had never had a formal review in three years, and those who did regarded the process as a charade. In fact, the downsizing itself was hindered by the lack of valid data on employee performance, and there was considerable suspicion regarding how decisions were made regarding who to let go. As part of the new organizational order, senior leadership set expectations that performance reviews would be taken seriously—all managers and supervisors would receive training in conducting performance reviews, and their own reviews would be influenced by the extent to which they upgraded their skills in this area.

Vision at Pfizer

The transformation of research and development at Pfizer following the Warner-Lambert acquisition shows how, to truly energize employees to charge up the hill, a vision of a new and better organization is much more than a statement. To symbolize that he was ending the old and building a new operating model, John Niblack changed the name of his function from Pfizer Central Research to Pfizer Global Research and Development (PGRD). This underscored the movement from individualized locations to a global network of partnered operations.

But Niblack's challenges were much more than symbolic. One immediate need was to retain senior Warner-Lambert leaders. Warner-Lambert had a tight-knit R&D organization, and Pfizer executives recognized that scientists there would look to their leaders to determine if they themselves should stay on board. But the acquisition triggered Warner-Lambert's change of control agreements, common in most major organizations in this era of golden parachutes. Warner-Lambert executives qualified for enormous payouts through the company's Enhance Severance Plan. In addition, the market for scientists and laboratory professionals was robust—R&D people had many options outside of Pfizer. The Warner-Lambert grapevine was asking, "Could anything be worth turning down this kind of money to stay?"

Niblack literally had to sell people on staying. His sales pitch was the vision of the new organizational order for PGRD, expressed at both the business and personal levels (see Exhibit 8.2). To bring energy to these words, Niblack and other executives touted Pfizer's $4 billion commitment to R&D. "This was a growth story," recalled Kym Goddu, senior vice president of human resources at PGRD. "Our message was 'Where else are you going to go in the pharmaceutical industry today, when many firms are in a survival mode, where senior leadership is ready to commit billions of dollars to investing in R&D?'" The vision portrayed a compelling advantage over the competition as a place to work and to discover the next generation of drugs. Importantly, the vision was aligned with line leadership's commitment to Wall Street—this was not a set of words on a plaque; this was a commitment to produce the premier R&D organization in the world to meet the need for high-quality drugs to fuel company growth projections.

This led to a very human aspect of the vision: the opportunity to be part of the world's largest pharmaceutical R&D organization. How exciting it was, personally, to be in on the ground floor in shaping a new approach to doing R&D in this industry. Conversely, where else at this moment in the industry could there be a similar opportunity and possibility for personal and organizational growth? Through formal and informal channels, using line executives and human resource specialists, PGRD got out the word that this was a great place to work and offered as data to these scrutinizing scientists both hard evidence (enhancements in the benefits package) and some "intangibles" (like Pfizer's commitment to respect for all individuals).

EXHIBIT 8.2. The New Organization Order at Pfizer Global Research and Development.

Our Purpose
Our work at Pfizer Global Research & Development has but one purpose: We restore health and hope through innovation.

It's that simple. The fundamental reason for our existence is to innovate and to help others. Our business decisions are governed by this purpose, and Pfizer's corporate decisions are based on our commitment to health care as well.

Our Mission: A Broad Future
- We will develop an unmatched number of new products that are recognized worldwide as significantly enhancing health and quality of life.
- We will sustain unparalleled vitality in all our product pipelines.
- We will attract and retain world-class researchers and product developers who will utilize ever-expanding scientific knowledge to discover lifesaving and life-enhancing medicines and health care products.

Our Values
These are not just words. The seven core values below form the foundation upon which we do business every day.

- *Contribution:* We contribute to humanity and work to improve the quality of life around the world. We energetically support the communities in which we live and work.
- *Creativity and innovation:* We are driven to continually seek new ideas and novel approaches. We are willing to accept and try new ideas. We think outside normal processes and take risks in seeking the new and the best. We are driven to continually learn and find ways to apply new knowledge.
- *Integrity:* We expect the highest possible standards of ethical conduct and honesty in all our behavior, our science, and our business practices.

EXHIBIT 8.2. *Continued.*

- *People:* We strive to create a supportive environment for all our people and to build a sense of community held together by trust and mutual respect. We invest in people, encouraging individuals to reach their full potential.
- *Personal leadership:* We express the courage to take initiative and assume responsibility. We step forward to seize opportunities and set the example in achieving goals.
- *Quality and excellence:* We seek to be the best in all we do and stick to a job until it is done. We are not content with the status quo but continually search for ways to improve our science and deliver better services and products to our customers.
- *Teamwork:* We recognize the importance of diversity in opinions and approaches. We foster a sense of unified purpose and interdependence in reaching common goals.

Source: Pfizer Global Research and Development.

The vision also reiterated what was not changing in the new organizational order. At the highest level, this was the mission of helping people live better lives. More specifically, it included the intent to keep decentralization alive even while moving toward being a global organization.

With a confident vision of a new and better organization to share, PGRD used both conventional and novel approaches to convey the vision. Senior executives made presentations to entire sites, local managers received tool kits to help them follow up with their employees, and communications professionals renamed and recast the division newsletter as a record of the transition from old to new. Meanwhile, all employees had access to the PGRD Web page—with updates on progress and acknowledgments that transformation does not happen without pain—and to chat rooms where managers would answer employee questions in real time.

A vision of a new and better posttransition organization was used to energize employees in other Pfizer business units. Exhibit 8.3 shows a statement of the new organizational order at Pfizer Global Manufacturing. Note how it describes the same Pfizer values (quality, integrity, innovation, teamwork, and so on) cited in the PGRD's new organizational order in a manner specific to its own situation. To add detail to the vision and to display leadership's passion for it, a "vivid description" of the posttransition Pfizer Global Manufacturing was developed as well (see Exhibit 8.4). It sets clear expectations for employee attitudes and actions in the new organizational order. Together these documents were disseminated and discussed with employees throughout the organization and used as a foundation for bringing the new organizational order to life.

Helping People Deal with the Hang Time Between Old and New

The hang time between ending the old and accepting the new can be a dark, uncomfortable, and scary time for individuals, or it can be a time marked by *learning* and *encouragement*—learning about how to succeed in the new organizational order and encouragement to move away from the comfort zone of the status quo and toward the desired new organizational order. Adaptation occurs in a nonlinear manner, the process of two steps forward and one step back I have described. Part of leading people through hang time is making it known that everyone involved will make mistakes and will be tempted, when they occur, to fall back into the old comfort zone; but also that these mistakes are the basis for learning and that now is the time to experiment with new ways of doing things within the bounds of the new organizational order. Combined with a vision of the new organizational order, this sets a context within which to guide employees' movement from the old to the new.

There are no clear-cut paths to success. Only by trying different approaches and learning from these efforts will an organization and its work teams and employees find their way. One reason why

EXHIBIT 8.3. The New Organizational Order
at Pfizer Global Manufacturing.

Purpose
We improve the quality of people's lives by assuring the supply of
Pfizer's high-quality human and animal health products.

Mission
We will be the #1 supply organization in our industry and a strategic asset to Pfizer.

Mission Elements
- We will have the #1 quality performance in the industry.
- We will satisfy our customers 100% of the time.
- We will have the best environmental, health, and safety per-
  formance in the industry.
- We will bring new products to market faster than our
  competition.
- We will continually improve product cost.
- We will be a globally integrated organization.

Values
- *Quality:* Our customers and regulators hold us in the
  highest regard for the quality of our products, operations,
  and people.
- *Integrity:* As an organization and as individuals, we make decisions and take actions that are consistent with the highest
  standards of business and personal ethics.
- *Innovation:* We are a learning organization. We embrace
  change and are dedicated to continuous improvement
  and technical excellence. We value ingenuity and original
  thinking.
- *Respect for people:* We value our diversity as a source of
  strength. We trust and respect each other. We maintain an
  open and candid work environment that encourages personal
  growth, individual contribution, and participation in the
  business.

EXHIBIT 8.3. *Continued.*

- *Customer focus:* We understand the needs of all of our customers. We meet or exceed their expectations 100% of the time.
- *Teamwork:* We work together as individuals, teams, and operating units. We support each other and share knowledge and responsibility. We hold ourselves accountable for the achievement of our common goals.
- *Leadership:* We are all responsible for achieving our mission. We make decisions in the best interests of our stakeholders. All of us lead by striving to be the best in all aspects of our jobs. We live our Values in all that we do.
- *Performance:* We set and meet challenging goals and establish metrics to assess our progress. We recognize and reward the accomplishments of individuals and teams. We are committed to develop and operate reliable processes.
- *Community:* We are responsible corporate citizens. We play an active role, as an organization and individuals, in making every country and community in which we operate a better place in which to live and work.

Source: Pfizer Global Manufacturing.

---

workplace recovery is so difficult is that it implies real-time, on-the-job learning and training. Employees have not had the benefit of being at boot camp for six weeks, training for various contingencies and preparing for action. They have to learn as they make the march up the hill, and the organization, in turn, has to create opportunities and incentives for that learning to occur.

Creating a Learning Environment

How did you learn to do your job? I learned mine by making mistakes. Fortunately, I learned from these mistakes. Mistakes are powerful learning opportunities, but they are also painful—employees

EXHIBIT 8.4. Pfizer Global Manufacturing's "Vivid Description."

We are a worldwide network of manufacturing and supply organizations that is integral to Pfizer achieving its mission of becoming the premier research-based health care company.

We are proud of being part of Pfizer and PGM. We understand the PGM business and its goals, know what is expected of us, and work hard to accomplish it. Our performance is characterized by a strong work ethic, a constant desire to learn and grow, a sense of responsibility, and the willingness to take well-conceived risks and hold ourselves accountable for the results. As an organization, we are constantly learning and continuously looking for improvement opportunities.

We are driven to meet or exceed our customers' expectations. Our customers know they can rely on us to manufacture and supply high-quality products with the necessary speed and flexibility to respond to an ever-changing marketplace. We pursue cost improvement in all aspects of our operations, but never at the expense of product quality or service. Our processes are robust and in control at all times.

Teamwork is ingrained in our culture. We communicate openly and candidly with each other, sharing across functions and sites. We view problems as challenges; finding solutions through a combination of individual effort, teamwork, diverse ideas, rigorous analysis, technical expertise, and creative thinking. We are mutually accountable for each other's success. We openly and actively celebrate our successes and review our failures to learn from them.

Our work environment is based on mutual respect, with an attitude of "we're all in this together." Diverse people from a variety of countries, cultures, and technical backgrounds work well together. Our relationships are characterized by respect for one another and commitment to our shared values. The best people want to work with us.

We are fervent about our environmental responsibility and the health and safety of our colleagues. We are proud to con-

---

EXHIBIT 8.4. *Continued.*

tribute to making the countries and communities in which we operate better places in which to live and work.

Integrity is fundamental to our day-to-day decision making and is never compromised in pursuit of business goals. We do the right thing because it is the right thing to do—for the business and for the people who use Pfizer products.

We are passionate about the PGM Vision: our Purpose, Mission, and Values. These statements focus the integrated global organization that is PGM.

We are a strategic asset and major contributor to Pfizer's success.

Source: Pfizer Global Manufacturing.

---

in traditional organizations tend not to be rewarded for discussing their errors. To recover from transition, employees need to know, first, that their leaders understand that mistakes will occur and, second, that there are incentives for turning mistakes into learning opportunities. At both the individual and organizational levels, this is a dedicated process of continually monitoring behaviors and outcomes, gaining insight from personal experiences and those of others, and adjusting the way people and groups operate. In short, this is developing the capacity to learn.

Experimentation and Learning. Learning through experimentation is a tangible sign that a different and better way of doing things is indeed emerging from the aftermath of the transition. It reinforces the concept that change to the new organizational order is for real and that to gain the best chances for personal success, individuals had better be prepared to change also.

Learning through experimentation became an integral component of the recovery process at a consumer products firm that was attempting to rebound following a difficult acquisition. The acquisition was opportunistic—the firm was not looking for an acquisition, but a major competitor was teetering on the brink of bankruptcy, and a business broker shopped it around. While executives in the lead company had not planned for making an acquisition, they jumped at what seemed like a "bargain basement" price. Poorly prepared, leadership woefully mismanaged the integration, and employees from the lead company were upset that the leaders squandered money on another firm rather than investing in their own operations. One positive aspect of the deal was that it gave the lead firm its first ever international presence. After the painful integration, the CEO used this as the platform for defining a new strategic intent—going global and growing the business more aggressively than before the acquisition.

To help people link their job activities with the new strategic intent, as well as to enhance the capabilities of middle and upper managers to lead in the new context, the CEO commissioned a program that embraced and reinforced the process of learning by experimentation. The program began with an assessment of the extent to which each manager's current work activities were contributing to the new organizational order by generating results consistent with its direction. Managers identified specific activities that were not producing desired outcomes and over which they had some control to alter. This became their "personal challenge." Managers then attended a workshop to review learning and experimentation techniques and met in follow-up groups with four to six peers to discuss their personal challenge and experiment with implementation alternatives before committing to follow-up action. The managers also received 360-degree feedback from their superiors, peers, and subordinates regarding their own ability to encourage and nurture a learning orientation in their work teams. The basic message of the program was that the company that succeeds is not the one that avoids mistakes; it is the one that makes mistakes and learns from them.

Learning Forums. For learning to occur to a degree sufficient for contributing to building a new organizational order, it needs to be supported through formal learning forums. These are events in which individuals come together to learn from experts or from each other regarding how to adapt to the new organizational order. In this way, learning is accelerated and disseminated in a systematic manner rather than expected to occur through good intentions or by accident.

Learning forums are most effective when not stand-alone events and when they occur on company time rather than after hours. This demonstrates to employees that learning via experimentation is a true component of the new organizational order as well a vehicle for helping people let go of old ways and adopt new ones. Attendance at learning forums is usually at the peer level—supervisors with supervisors, managers with managers, and so on. Bringing peers together from various parts of the organization helps spread learning across traditional boundaries. It also minimizes the likelihood that individuals will feel "on the spot" if their superiors are in the room. There will be other opportunities, like staff meetings or department off-site gatherings, for learning to be disseminated within teams and functions.

Learning that opens people up to new ways of doing things covers both content and process matters. At the company making the renewed commitment to performance evaluations as part of its new organizational order, all managers and supervisors went through a program to learn how to conduct effective performance reviews. The program featured an outside trainer describing the process and expectations for using it but also provided time for each participant to role-play and receive feedback on his or her use of the practices. Then, after the first wave of performance reviews occurred in the organization, all managers and supervisors came together for a second learning event. This time, they learned from each other—real case examples from their peers applying the new process were presented and discussed. These included both successes and failures. Managers and supervisors openly discussed topics ranging from how to differentiate rankings across subordinates to how to deal with employees who contested their reviews.

Learning Versus Copying.   An important distinction exists between true learning and mere copying. Popular best practices studies help educate people in an organization on the variety of procedures and activities that have proved successful elsewhere. Reflection on what works elsewhere, however, does not satisfy the need for organizational experimentation and learning. What works well in one setting—with its particular strategy, culture, personalities, and competitive pressures—may not necessarily be the best way forward in another. At most, copying can lead an organization to yesterday's best practices. Moreover, it will not build the internal learning capacity to help the organization and its people adopt a continual learning mode to help contend with ongoing change.

This also holds true for the dissemination and copying of best practices within organizations. Experimentation and learning in one part of the organization can reap additional dividends through application elsewhere. Realistically, however, time has to be spent on considering how to apply a practice developed in one area to another with differing dynamics.

Encouraging People to Experiment and Open Up to the New

People have yet to refreeze mental models regarding the cause-and-effect relationships that will prevail in the new organization order. They will look around for clues about what really matters in the posttransition organization. Actions speak louder than words, and even the most carefully crafted vision statement takes a back seat to people's perceptions of who and what gets rewarded. So if you want people to experiment with new ways of doing things in the new organizational order, give them some incentives for doing so.

The annual performance review is a helpful tool in molding behaviors and perceptions consistent with the new organizational order. But it takes a couple of cycles to make a true impact on people. You don't have two or three years to wait to send signals about desired actions and attitudes. You want to take advantage of immediate opportunities to open people up to learning new approaches.

Opportunities for Short-Term Wins. Certainly, giving people short-term objectives and recognizing when they are met strengthens motivation in the posttransition organization. But keeping people's nose to the grindstone is not going to result in an enhanced organization. Identifying and adopting new and better ways of doing things will. Odds are you will need to redefine what a "win" means in your organization—identifying ways to do things more in line with the new organizational order is as much a win as landing a new account. In fact, the more broadly a win is defined, the more people in the organization have a chance at accomplishing it. Everybody contributes to the new organization, not just rainmakers.

As always, process counts right along with content. *How* you go about rewarding learning will make an impression about the new organizational order in addition to what is learned. In its old organizational order, a software development company was notorious for its highly politicized culture. The founding CEO regularly played favorites, as did most other executives and managers in the firm. After it was acquired and merged into one of the buyer's established business units, a business unit leader (BUL) from the lead company replaced the CEO. From his diagnosis of barriers to adaptation, the BUL learned of the highly political nature of the acquired organization. The BUL wanted to reward people for experimenting with new ways of doing things and considered a program in which anyone could submit a recent lesson learned and a panel of supervisors would select the "learning of the month." But in discussing the diagnostic results with employees, they warned that no matter whose lesson was selected, someone would cry foul and claim politics had seeped into the selection process. So the BUL amended the plan to have the winning lesson learned be selected at random among those nominated. This reinforced the desired cultural end state of "limiting politically motivated decisions" along with encouraging people to experiment with new practices.

Symbolic Rewards in Addition to Substantive Ones. Your objective is to get people to embrace learning, not to vie for a prize. As a result, less extravagant and more symbolic rewards are fine to complement more formal and substantive rewards. The reward for being selected as the "lesson learned of the month" at the software company was not large—a $100 gift certificate to a local restaurant. At a call center for a financial services firm, a similar program offered winners their choice of tickets to a rock concert, a sports event, a fine art performance, or a "mystery event." To add a little fun, winners could select only a category and did not know which specific event that month's tickets were for. Each month the troops would assemble over pizza, and the department head would pull the winning nomination out of a jar, the winner would select a category, and all attending would get a kick out of learning what event the tickets were for. To increase the likelihood that the winner received tickets to a desirable event, the department head took suggestions.

Intrinsic as Well as Extrinsic Rewards. Not all incentives to embrace learning through experimentation need to be fancy or formal programs. A superior talking up the importance of experimentation and speaking admiringly of such efforts can be a powerful motivator. Such talk can occur informally on the job; there's no need to wait for a formal learning event. Success stories about people experimenting can be promoted through newsletters, Web sites, and mentions at meetings and events. They are especially powerful in organizations where the old order had meetings and events that focused on numbers and operational results. The act of giving learning a status worthy of mention at these meetings sends a strong message to employees that it is no longer business as usual.

Learning from Mistakes the Right Way. Recovery is not a time for indiscriminate trial and error. The vision of the new organizational order should set a context for experimentation, and guidance from superiors on priorities should give a sense of what is in and out of bounds for experimentation.

Creating a Learning Environment at Pfizer

The matrixed Pfizer Global R&D organization was a sharp departure from the preacquisition Pfizer and Warner-Lambert approaches to pharmaceutical research and development. For the new organization to succeed—and for individuals to succeed in it—people had to learn new skills and approaches, from how to partner to how to assess R&D productivity. One of the biggest lessons to be learned for people from both pretransition organizations was how to define roles appropriate to the matrix organization.

Line executives drove the process of learning how to operate in the new PGRD organization, with support from educators at Pfizer Research University. To identify and reinforce how to do things in the new organization, executives integrated opportunities for learning into their daily activities. Executives explained how they made decisions, used a common language, and discussed effective approaches for getting work done throughout the organization. The process started with the desire of senior executives who ran PGRD to measure productivity through quantitative analysis. Before they could measure, however, they had to agree on definitions and approaches to assess R&D productivity. In addition, norms and expectations were established as part of PGRD's new organizational order that encouraged open debate and challenge as employees felt out the new organizational order during hang time.

PGRD employees also had to learn how to operate in a matrix organization. New approaches, attitudes, and actions were required for partnering, making decisions, resolving conflict, and forging compromises or novel solutions. Line leadership and staff specialists worked together to drive experimentation and learning through the organization, from broad concepts to specific activities. An example of the comprehensiveness of this approach to learning is presented in Exhibit 8.5. The expectation of managers in the new organizational order to "create an inclusive environment" was expressed along with specific attitudes and behaviors appropriate to the new organizational order. The concept was even conveyed in

---

EXHIBIT 8.5 Learning the New PGRD Way.

Concept	Create an inclusive environment
Attitudes	Everyone can make a difference if they are given a chance to contribute.
Behaviors	1. Be open to new ideas.
	2. Seek different ways to do things, and use good ideas wherever they come from.
	3. Include colleagues; work hard at excluding no one; pull in both new and veteran people.
	4. Ensure that managers do the same, and hold them accountable.
Applications	Conducting meetings

Source: Pfizer Global Research and Development.

---

very practical ways, such as how to conduct meetings in the new order. To strengthen the learning, these concepts, attitudes, and behaviors became integrated into leadership development activities and the performance evaluations process.

Supporting and Reassuring People

I had this notion after September 11, 2001, that businesspeople would chill out a bit—maybe broaden their tunnel vision on meeting short-term financial results, look around, reassess priorities, and smell the roses. Some did just that, ranging from Gerald Levin of AOL Time Warner to less renowned individuals who chose to give up responsibility and compensation to strike a better balance between work and the rest of life. But it seems that most businesspeople have gotten, well, back to business. They can't wait to turn their cell phones on the moment they debark from a plane, they stuff their calendars with back-to-back-to-back meetings, and above all, they fixate on making the numbers. Call it aspiration, greed, or whatever; the bottom line is that it did not take long for most businesspeople to regress to business as usual following a tragedy that had tremendous potential as an unfreezing event.

Similarly, it doesn't take long for most executives to regress to business as usual following a transition. They deny or ignore the emotional realities of ending the old, moving through hang time, and adapting to the new. Perhaps they are not to be blamed for this, as they themselves had to cope with adaptation from the old to the new and no one was there to support them. Yet senior executives have more control over their situation and organizational resources than employees through the ranks. The large majority of the workforce needs emotional support to generate the energy needed to make a run at new opportunities.

Executive denial of the normal and natural adaptation process is problematic for a couple of reasons. First, it is difficult to expect employees to let go of outmoded beliefs and practices and replace them with new ones more aligned with the posttransition organization when executives themselves are acting in the same old ways. Second, since movement from the old to the new is always two steps forward and one step back, failing to acknowledge and support the process slows people in their movement through it. Rather than be reassured and supported in reaching for the next ring, they lurch back to the old ring to get a sense of security.

Conveying empathy to transition-fatigued troops helps press the reset button to assist individuals in letting go of undesirable attitudes, perceptions, and behaviors. But the emotional aspect of workplace recovery does not end there. Making the move from the old to the new takes emotional security and self-confidence. People gain energy when they feel well supported—if people feel they have an emotional "safety net" as they move through hang time, they can keep their eyes looking forward rather than down or behind.

There are three dimensions to the emotional agenda of energizing employees to make a grab at the new ring. One is to provide a foundation of *support and reassurance*. People need support as they dangle in hang time between the old and the new, including reassurance that they are on the right track and moving in the right direction. The second is to accept *confusion and backsliding*. People will be tentative as they feel their way through the dark, scary twilight zone between the old and the new—learning through trial and error, watching as others do the same, and forming new mental models. They need to know that the occasional step back in exchange for two forward is to be expected and viewed by their superiors as appropriate progress. The third dimension of the emotional agenda for developing energy is to *communicate and connect*. Communication is essential throughout the recovery process, but it takes on a special value when people need to generate energy to move forward. Aside from the obvious benefit of conveying information, informal communication between leaders and employees keeps the human connection going and in a subtle but important way contributes considerably to the sense of support.

The Virtue of Patience

People need time to move from the old to the new. Certainly, some individuals will be raring to go, but most will move cautiously through hang time. Although clear short-term objectives and opportunities for quick wins are integral to energizing people, the inevitable backsliding and confusion inherent in the twilight zone typically frustrate executives and team leaders who are further along in their adaptation process than their subordinates. Since adaptation is a natural and to-be-expected process, the only alternative to giving people time to move through it is frustration.

Executives and team leaders can "create" time for moving through adaptation in a number of ways. One is just to be patient. This may be foreign to hard-charging leaders, but it is something they can do. More proactively, leaders can factor adaptation into setting realistic expectations for work performance. Timetables, deadlines, targets, and quotas all should take into account that people are not proceeding in a straight line from the old to the new. Leaders can also ensure that the other components of energizing people—conveying an inspiring vision, creating a learning environment, and connecting with and supporting people—occur. You cannot eliminate the need for time to adapt, but you can accelerate it by clearing a path to the new organizational order and by minimizing the disruptiveness of roadblocks.

Support at Pfizer

Despite the good intentions of line leadership and the professional support of staff specialists, there was definite backsliding toward the old comfort zone at Pfizer Global Research and Development. Among the complaints of middle managers and lower-level employees was that too many people were asking for too much. Most people were trying their best to determine and settle into new approaches to doing their jobs, but the impact on employees through the ranks was substantial. Keep in mind that despite everyone's best intentions, these were scientists who never bargained for organizational transformation as part of their work situation.

The strategy at PGRD was to engage managers in supporting people. The delivery of "high-touch" interventions to support employees on the path to the new organizational order was primarily the responsibility of line executives and managers. To begin, senior leaders were intimately engaged in driving the change process. Involving them in its design made them feel responsible for seeing it succeed through careful implementation. They became personally involved in supporting people through one-on-one conversations with individuals, town hall meetings, and published Q&A packages. Modeling this personal involvement set a standard for middle-level managers and front-line supervisors to do the same.

The biggest lesson learned through this process, according to PGRD human resource leader Kym Goddu, was the need to deal with senior management's learning curve. Company leaders had to be committed to the change itself, as true believers, before moving forward with implementation. Supporting adaptation, then, became a component of their personal leadership styles in the new organizational order and not something done as an afterthought or relegated to support staff.

This is not to suggest that human resources, communications, and other staff professionals did not have important roles to play in the transition from the old to the new Pfizer R&D function. Communications specialists produced world-class support materials, and human resource "advocates" were established to support people. One example of an activity to support people through the adaptation process at PGRD was a two-hour workshop titled "Working in a High-Change Environment" designed by organization effectiveness consultant Linda Benner in partnership with human resource manager Elizabeth Sorensen. Through a series of short discussions, it generated understanding and encouraged healthy responses to the changes individuals and work groups were experiencing as a result of the transition. The semistructured, facilitated approach gave valuable content to participants while encouraging them to make the "connections" to their own experience. And it helped group members focus on tangible, concrete actions they could take to help keep the business moving forward.

Sorensen and Benner also developed the on-line "Change Management Resource Guide." It assembled and described the many resources used throughout PGRD to support individuals, managers and supervisors, groups, teams, and the overall organization during and following the transition. An initial screen helped managers identify resources at the appropriate level of intervention and phase of the transition (see Exhibit 8.6). Sorensen and Benner used three phases akin to those of Bridges's transition model to cluster the resources: *transition* (the period of letting go just preceding and following a change), *alignment* (the neutral zone of reorienting to a new reality and redefining goals and roles), and *performance* (the period of acceptance of a new reality when the way forward is clear). A manager wanting to learn about "managing others' performance" during the performance phase, for example, could click

Exhibit 8.6. PGRD "Change Management Resource Guide."

	Transition	Alignment	Performance
Individual	• Dealing with Personal Issues • Managing Personal Change • Understanding the "New Pfizer"	• Clarifying Roles/Expectations • New Employee Integration • Working in a Matrix	• Career Development • Individual Skills Development • Managing Performance
Manager/ Supervisor	• Communication/Involvement • Leading Others Through Change • Retaining Talent	• Leader Transition into a New Role • New Leader Assimilation • Setting Goals for Individuals/ Groups	• Leader/Manager Skills Development • Managing Others' Performance
Group/Team/ Organization	• Communication of Organizational Changes • Understanding Organizational Transitions	• Cultural Integration • Understanding Values • Work Group/Team Start-Up/ Launch	• Improving Processes/ Redesign • Managing Group/Team Satisfaction and Performance • Team Goal Setting • Work Group/Team Building

Source: Pfizer Global Research and Development.

on that option and find support ranging from processes, documents, and workshops available within PGRD to services and products provided by selected outside vendors.

Support in the form of workshops, Web sites, and direct consultation keeps individual managers and supervisors aware of the need to deal with the realities of individual transition. It also provides practical tools for helping leaders—as well as the members of their teams—move forward through workplace recovery. Building on the insights provided to leaders at PGRD for managing transition dynamics, Exhibit 8.7 presents some ways in which executives, managers, and other team leaders can support people during adaptation. Support in this manner generates the energy required to move people through hang time and make a run up the hill for desired organizational results.

EXHIBIT 8.7. Tips for Dealing with Adaptation Dynamics.

- Recognize and strive to accept where you are in the adaptation process. It is not a straight path. You may move forward and backward several times in the process.
- Strive to have empathy for others' progress in the process. People move through the process at different speeds and with different styles.
- Be open about how you feel; expect and accept signs of grieving and confusion.
- Stay focused on the task as much as possible. Keep centered on what has to be accomplished for the next day or week.
- Have well defined objectives or goals with a customer focus. Celebrate achievements, no matter how small.
- Keep your objectives or targets focused and short-term.
- Try not to look for long-term answers. Keep asking questions.
- Forgive imperfections.
- Acknowledge endings—seek closure, say goodbye. This is important to getting on with the new reality.
- Overcommunicate. Keep each other informed.

9

Enforcement

Recall the case of Majestic Enterprises presented in Chapters One and Two. Employees at the electronics company were saturated with the cumulative effects of a series of transitions including acquisition, restructuring, voluntary reduction in force, programs like value-added work analysis and continuous improvement, and finally, an involuntary reduction in force. After six years of ongoing transition, many Majestic employees had become numbed by the dizzying course of events.

While employees were reeling from the organizational MADness, from his vantage point in summer 2001, Majestic CEO Justin Jourdan was growing optimistic about the firm's chances for recovery. Revenues were slowly but surely increasing, and with the savings from the downsizing and other cost containment initiatives, Jourdan fully expected Majestic to return to profitability by late 2001 or early 2002. He also knew that Majestic's two biggest competitors were having serious cash flow problems. Now was the time to make a bold move to wrestle market share away from them. But while Jourdan was looking ahead to new opportunities, he was well aware that his workforce was still looking back, mourning the loss of former coworkers, licking their wounds from six years of transition turmoil, and generally feeling little excitement or optimism about the future.

Jourdan knew he had to help his people recover from the unintended consequences of previous transitions before they could move forward individually and collectively to secure new business and personal opportunities. But he also knew that he had no chance to lay another program on his people and expect them to respond favorably to it. So the CEO employed many of the elements of workplace recovery in a subtle yet effective manner. He expressed empathy to employees for the pain they had been through in recent years and took responsibility for conducting the reduction in force even after he had promised that he would never resort to that kind of tactic. Rather than make a big to-do about his mea culpa, Jourdan used every opportunity he could—big formal meetings, regular staff meetings, and small informal one-on-one conversations—to piggyback his expressions of empathy onto regular business agendas. He acknowledged that employees had every right to distrust him but urged them to consider that they were in this situation together and had to work together to move out of it.

Shortly after the June 2001 involuntary reduction in force, Jourdan freed up the time and resources to engage employees in venting meetings and then sessions to identify how to work smarter in the postdownsizing organization. Throughout the remainder of the year, he communicated changes in the business environment and in October surveyed employees to gain their views on what they needed to achieve desired business results and what they saw as blocking their way toward improved performance. One of the key roadblocks people cited was the absence of a clear sense of direction regarding where the company was headed. Employees were learning that revenues were increasing in a slow but steady manner, but they felt the company was progressing in a haphazard manner. They had many questions: What did the new Majestic stand for? How would it succeed where the old Majestic didn't? How exactly would it regain its stature in the marketplace? What would distinguish it from the competition? Would employees continue to be subjected to downsizings?

With revenues increasing and costs kept in line, Majestic returned to profitability in early 2002. This energized employees, but so did Jourdan's response to their need for direction. He articulated and conveyed a vision for Majestic's new organizational order: "Emerge from the crowd by giving the best customer service while leading the industry in profitability, technology, and employee relations." Majestic was in a highly fragmented industry sector, and the notion of standing out from the competition excited and appealed to employees. It made good sense to them that if they could differentiate themselves from other firms, customers would be directing their business toward Majestic. And the vision clarified the platform on which Majestic would distinguish itself—customer service second to none.

The vision also set a context for the new organizational order. Profitability mattered. Spending had to be kept in line so that the pain of reductions in force and other undesirable transitions were not repeated. With a much more disciplined approach to cost containment, Majestic could weather ups and downs in the business cycle without having to resort to drastic steps. Technology mattered. One area in which the company would make long-term investments, however, was technology. In a business with very slim margins but soaring customer expectations, Majestic had to harness technological advances to get work done as effectively and efficiently as possible. And employee relations mattered. This characteristic of the new organizational order was actually not new to Majestic; it was a carryover from the old organizational order. Prior to the start of its organizational MADness, Majestic was regarded as an excellent place to work with a highly tenured and fiercely loyal workforce. Though it was not always evident through the mismanaged transitions between 1995 and 2001, Jourdan never let go of his commitment to positive employee relations. It was reassuring to veteran employees that this commitment remained consistent from the old organizational order to the new. As a result of the foundation of goodwill developed over the years with employees—as well as the expressions of empathy and actions to engage and energize employees—Jourdan found himself leading a workforce that was confident and ready to move forward.

Enforcement as an Element of Workplace Recovery

Solidify new mental models that are congruent with the desired new organizational order.

Energized by a clear vision, an openness to new ways of doing things, and support by their leadership, employees are ready to march up the hill to capture posttransition opportunities. There will continue to be some uncertainty about the new organizational order and backsliding toward the old as the forces for desired change continue to skirmish with forces for the status quo. The task of the fourth element of workplace recovery, then, is to strengthen the forces for desired change to the point where they contribute to employee mental models that are consistent with the desired posttransition organization. This is accomplished by enforcing the desired new organizational order. As Figure 9.1 shows, the result is a new organizational order that enforces new mental models that in turn support the desired new organizational order.

By enforcement, I do not mean a policing activity like enforcing the speed limit on a highway. I use enforcement in its more positive sense of giving force to or strengthening. That is exactly what needs to happen in the fourth element of workplace recovery—giving force to and strengthening the new organizational order so that people do not retreat to the old or settle into a culture by default rather than by design.

Enforcement contributes to the refreezing phase of Lewin's organizational change model. As noted earlier, some critics say that "refreezing" into a new organizational order is not appropriate for today's business realities. No matter how volatile the business environment, however, people are not machines—they cannot stay psychologically healthy in an unfrozen state, and their ability to perform gets eroded by multiple waves of transition. Instead, people

FIGURE 9.1. The Self-Sustaining Relationship Between the New
Organizational Order and Employee Mental Models.

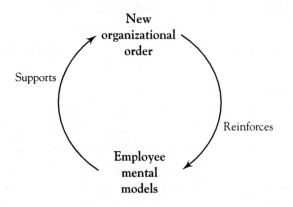

need some degree of stability, security, and support to move forward. That is why I suggest that the desired end state might be more of a slush than a solid ice cube. A slush can maneuver through the turbulence of new workplace realities, but it does have substance.

The good news is that people are extremely resilient and can bounce back from adversity. But they need some foundation on which to do so. After the terrorist attacks of September 11, 2001, Americans pulled together and rebounded on a solid base of patriotism. The post–September 11 world is significantly different from the world before it, and people are adapting to the transition. They are adapting not because they are in a constant unfrozen state but, to the contrary, because of the strong enforcement of key American values coupled with a new vigilance against terrorism.

The Tasks of Enforcement

Enforcing the new organizational order provides the consistency required for true cultural and cognitive change. All of the obvious and subtle components of the organization—systems, procedures, actions, impressions, innuendos, and so on—need to work in harmony to send a clear and consistent message in support of the desired new organizational order. There is no way around the fact that the less consistent these messages are, the less quickly the organization will arrive at its desired posttransition state. Alternatively, the more consistent the messages employees receive about the new organizational order, the more likely they are to develop mental models that support it.

As Exhibit 9.1 shows, three streams of activity contribute to enforcing the new organizational order. To strengthen acceptance of the new business imperatives, *organizational systems and operating standards need to be aligned with the new organizational order*. One reason it takes time for people to abandon the old and accept the new is that systems and procedures often lag behind leadership's intentions. A compensation system that punishes team leaders for short-term declines in productivity when they experiment with new ways of approaching work will not sustain a vision of "innovation." Boring staff meetings plagued by dysfunctional group dynamics will not contribute to a desired culture of "teamwork and respect."

With macro-level systems and standards in place, enforcement of the new organizational order continues by *bringing individual on-the-job behaviors in line with the desired vision*. The best way to do this—both because they know the work intimately and because participation in problem analysis generates ownership of solutions—is to involve employees in bringing the vision to life. Working within the context of the new organizational order, employees "translate" generalities and operating standards into specific work procedures.

Finally, the messages being sent to employees during recovery—both explicit and implied—need to be monitored. *Tracking the extent to which the new organizational order is truly being realized*—that is, the extent to which forces for maintaining the old are being weakened and forces for developing the new are being strengthened—provides feedback regarding the success of organizational recovery. This feedback leads to midcourse corrections that further align organizational forces and individual attitudes and actions with the attainment of the desired posttransition organization.

EXHIBIT 9.1. Transition Realities and Recovery Activities to Create Enforcement.

Reality	Activity
10. The more consistent the forces for the new organizational order are, the more readily people will accept it.	Align systems and operating standards with the new organizational order.
11. People want to identify with their workplace and want a fair chance at succeeding along with the new organizational order.	Involve people in bringing the vision to life.
12. A posttransition culture will emerge—either the status quo or a modified one by design or by default.	Track the development of the new organizational order.

Aligning Systems and Standards with the New Organizational Order

The tenth reality of workplace recovery is that the more consistent the forces for the new organizational order are, the more readily people will accept it. The greater the extent to which structure, systems, standards, policies, practices, and people can be aligned with the new organizational order, the more likely it will be realized.

Aligning Structure

Driving in two lanes during transition—running the business while attempting to manage the merger, acquisition, or downsizing—usually results in an organizational structure that has not been fully fleshed out. An initial "superstructure" is put in place, and it feels good to employees that some basic decisions are being made about the post-merger organization. But people see the weaknesses of the new design. The typical leadership response is, "We'll get around to revising the structure." Of course, this rarely happens, and the temporary structure refreezes into a permanent one.

You have to pull back and critically assess whether the structure in place is contributing to or detracting from the attainment of your desired new organizational order. At Majestic, CEO Jourdan called for "customer service second to none" as a key component of the new organizational order. He meant this for internal customers as well as external ones—every employee was charged with providing the best possible customer service in a cost-effective manner, whether their customers were inside or outside the company. One way Jourdan realigned Majestic's structure to support his new order was to decentralize the firm's human resource organization. In the old organizational order, HR had been centralized because Jourdan (and his senior VP of human resources) thought that staff support services were run most cost-efficiently in a centralized manner. The new organizational order required putting staff in closer touch with internal customers, and Jourdan designated decentralization as the way to do that.

To further enforce the new organizational order, Jourdan moved the role of chief information officer to a more prominent position. In the old order, the CIO reported to the chief financial officer and senior vice president of administration. In the new order, the CIO reported directly to Jourdan. This helped align the structure with the goal of being the industry technology leader.

Aligning Systems

The systems that support the organization also send messages to employees and influence mental models. Systems need to be assessed to determine the extent to which they contribute to or detract from the attainment of the desired organizational order. Organizational systems that are especially pertinent to enforcing the new organizational order include information, compensation, training, and leadership and organization development.

Information. The extent to which information readily flows through the organization influences the development of employee mental models. This includes both formal and informal systems of distributing information. At Majestic, changes in the company's information systems strengthened employees' understanding of profitability and their role in achieving it. In the old organizational order, profit-and-loss statements were disseminated to a small number of executives who used their own discretion with respect to sharing the information with others. In the new order, P&L statements were more widely distributed, and team leaders were expected to discuss their content with employees. This brought the measure of profitability, not just productivity, into the lexicon of employees. Also at Majestic, managers began inviting people from other parts of the organization into their staff meetings. With higher expectations of internal customer service, staff specialists learned much more about the needs of line businesses—as well as about the businesses themselves—by becoming regular participants in weekly meetings.

Compensation. How rewards are distributed sends a powerful message to employees about what the organization values. People will look around and draw conclusions about what is and is not being rewarded in the new organizational order. These perceptions become reality as they get refrozen in new mental models of life after transition. The more explicit you can be in linking who gets rewarded for doing what, the more you can harness the power of reward systems to direct behavior and attitudes in line with the new organizational order.

Rewards should be consistent with the business strategy, management philosophy, employee needs, and financial realities of the new organizational order. At Majestic, the compensation system was revamped to reflect the priorities of the new organizational order.

Whereas in the past, business unit leaders were rewarded for growing revenues, now they were charged with developing or maintaining profitability. The entire performance review system was rewritten to add measures of internal and external customer satisfaction, technology utilization, and employee relations—the foundations of Majestic's new organizational order.

Some basic questions are helpful in designing reward systems for the new organizational order: Can new values and behaviors be rewarded and recognized adequately through existing compensation practices? If not, what changes are needed in incentives, rewards, and recognition? How can the desired values and behaviors be quantified and measured? If they cannot, would recognition programs be a better alternative than financial incentives? What, if any, distinction is to be made between producing desired results at any cost and getting the job done in line with the new order? And what respective weightings will individual, team, and organizational performance receive in compensation equations?

Answers to these questions clarify what really matters in the new order. First, they redefine what "performance" and "results" mean in the organization. A software publisher that wished to increase risk-taking behaviors after a series of downsizings and restructurings earmarked a certain percentage of both merit increases and bonus pay to be based on suggestions for new products, even if they did not come to market. Contrast this with the postmerger consulting firm that espoused the importance of cross-selling in its quest to grow emerging practice areas. Consultants who met their revenue targets despite not introducing colleagues from other practice areas continued to receive pay increases and bonuses in line with those from before the merger. Despite platitudes for cross-selling, office heads who administered rewards were afraid to unsettle senior colleagues who maintained relationships with large clients. The result was that no sanctions were made against those who continued to play by the rules of the old organizational order. Employees learned that making numbers mattered but how they were achieved did not.

Second, the answers to these questions point the way toward modifications in performance management and reward systems. A firm may want to emphasize roles and competencies over jobs and skills, with attention to outcomes like customer service rather than tasks like order processing. If so, there are implications for how people's contributions are measured and rewarded. In addition, there are implications for reward vehicles. Existing plans may be modified by altering the balance between base salary and at-risk pay or by changing weightings of individual, team, unit, and organizational results. Or it may be advantageous to establish new systems like short- or long-term cash incentive awards based on individual or team performance, profit-sharing programs that pay all employees a flat dollar amount or a percentage of base pay at certain milestones, or stock awards that recognize individual or team performance based on the long-term success of the organization. There are also nontraditional and sometimes nonfinancial rewards, such as allowing employees to buy an occasional day off or to qualify for a community service or personal development sabbatical.

Consider also what events or behaviors the organization wants to celebrate. Posttransition organizations often have flatter structures and fewer promotional opportunities than their predecessors, so alternatives to the traditional rewards of promotion up the hierarchy are needed. At a consumer products firm that had been delayered as part of its new organizational order, the celebration and hoopla that heralded promotions now were reserved to acknowledge horizontal moves such as transferring to new departments, learning new skills, and adopting novel behaviors to work across boundaries.

The design of a reward system comes down to the basics of what the organization values, what it wants to pay for, and what it wants to recognize and celebrate. Workplace recovery creates an opportunity for the organization to assess its reward systems to ensure that it is enforcing what leadership intends. This involves the rudimentary steps of asking people what rewards they find *attractive*, making sure that people feel they can influence their *ability* to receive the rewards, making the rewards *timely* so that people see the connection between efforts and rewards, and issuing the rewards *consistently* across various individuals and groups.

Training. Training and development budgets and opportunities have been ravaged during the years of organizational MADness. Whereas Japanese and European firms spend up to 6 percent of payroll costs on training their workers, U.S. companies are investing only 1.5 percent on training theirs, according to the American Society for Training and Development. As a result, just one out of every fourteen employees has received any formal training from his or her employer. One manager put it this way: "We haven't had a training course other than CPR in three years."

Charging up the hill requires a workforce that has the training to pull its weight. In addition to overcoming the bumps and bruises of multiple transitions, organizations are contending with demographic and social dynamics that exacerbate the need for effective training. Aging baby boomers need to retool their knowledge and skills. Many Generation Xers have never known what it is like to work in a setting that offers something more than "learn by the seat of your pants" training. And an increasing number of entry-level employees do not have even the most rudimentary of skills. Near four in ten members of the National Association of Manufacturers say that deficiencies in math, reading, and technical skills are causing serious problems in upgrading factories and increasing productivity.

Many organizations are learning from the MADness and realizing that recovery cannot occur solely—or even primarily—on the basis of cutting away at headcount and other expenses; instead, they must build their productive capacity. As former U.S. Secretary of Labor Robert Reich notes, "American companies have got to be urged to treat their workers as assets to be developed, rather than as costs to be cut." As competitive pressures and customer demands increase, organizations are going to require flexible, responsive delivery of services and products on a global scale, and only highly skilled and well-trained employees can quickly master the dynamics of an ever-changing workplace.

Training aids workplace recovery in some essential ways. First, it helps the organization bolster employee perceptions of the link between effort and performance. An organization may have identified attractive rewards and have every intention of paying out for a job well done, but employees who feel they lack the skills to get the job done will not have the motivation to perform. Second, skills training provides knowledge and tactics to help people align their work with the new organizational order and objectives. Third, awareness training conditions people for ongoing change and transition in their work settings; contemporary organizations need people who can change again and again, not just once. Lifelong learning will be the rule, not the exception. Finally, training regenerates a quality hit hard by years of organizational MADness—it contributes to raising people's self-esteem and self-confidence following transition by equipping them with the skills and ideas they need to contend with the new organizational realities.

Majestic used training to help middle managers and supervisors apply the new corporate vision to their work situations. One workshop was designed around a series of vignettes describing common decision-making situations in the organization, such as a potential conflict between profitability and customer service. Managers and supervisors attending the training workshop offered their views on how they would handle the situation and discussed similarities and differences among one another's approaches. A final discussion centered on how to handle managerial and supervisory issues in the "Majestic way."

Leadership and Organization Development. The prevailing leadership development systems in most organizations created managers in the mold of the old organizational order. Factors that contributed to managerial success in the past, however, may not necessarily do so in the new order. Thus the competencies and capabilities needed to manage and lead people beyond recovery need to be determined, and people having such competencies must be recruited from outside the organization or developed internally.

The best way to develop leaders—as distinct from managers—for the new organizational order is to make leadership an important criterion for promotion. This may involve considering the situations and problems candidates have faced in the past and not just the functions and disciplines they have managed. Leadership development may not benefit recovery immediately, but it will contribute to longer-term adaptability during ensuing cycles of transition and recovery. And the development and selection of higher-caliber leaders is a tangible way in which people see a new and better organization emerging.

Rebuilding organizational effectiveness after a transition requires that barriers to performance be identified and eliminated—just as barriers to adaptation needed to be diagnosed and dealt with—and that work groups develop self-sufficiency in managing future hurdles. This performance-related development relies on a group diagnosis and unifying goals. The assistance of an internal or external organization development (OD) professional helps a work team assess, analyze, prioritize, and confront the truly important issues affecting its performance and to develop and integrate the capacity for doing so on its own. Whereas some managers cast a stigma on team building and other organization development activities, OD—in addition to addressing problems in underperforming teams—is useful for making good teams even better.

To develop internal customer service in its new organizational order, Majestic commissioned a cross-unit organizational development project to enhance intergroup relations. Each session focused on a particular department and included managers from all other departments that interacted with that area. The head of the focal department kicked off the session by sharing her interpretation of the department's role in the new organizational order and, in particular, what other departments could expect from her unit. The manager then expressed her expectations of the other departments. Next, the managers of the other departments voiced their expectations of the focal department and what the focal department could expect from them. Gaps between the expectations were identified and negotiated. The result was a shared set of expectations regarding how departments would support one another in the new organizational order.

Involving People in Bringing the Vision to Life

According to the eleventh reality of workplace recovery, people want to identify with their workplace and want a fair chance at succeeding along with the new organizational order. Despite all of the unintended consequences of mismanaged transitions, the vast majority of employees prefer to care about their workplace and relate to their employer than to just "go to work and have a job." But after years of MADness, they want an opportunity to realize personal success along with organizational recovery.

The Limits of Vision

A well-articulated vision of where the organization is headed plays an important role in revitalizing employee spirit after a transition. When coupled with guidelines for desired values and behaviors, vision can direct employee actions in line with the new organizational order desired by leadership. As important and motivating as vision can be, the "*v* word" is much maligned in business circles today. It's not that visions are bad—as noted in Chapter Seven, people crave direction during and after transition; the problem is that most efforts at vision *implementation* miss their mark. In many organizations, a backlash has formed against the use of vision, denigrating the vision process as nothing more than "navel gazing" resulting in "another Lucite plaque with the vision du jour." In the typical scenario, a CEO or business unit leader goes off-site with fellow senior executives to hash out a vision statement. Upon returning to the office, a message is posted on the company Web site heralding the arrive of the vision, a nice video is made to explain the vision in detail, and posters are ordered so that each employee can have a constant reminder of the vision hovering over his or her work space. Then the top team gets back to the "real work" of running the business.

Employees want to hear more about the vision—in particular, how it will be attained and how they can contribute to achieving it. Once senior executives get the ball rolling in communicating vision, middle managers and direct supervisors must add enough precision to the statement of vision to let employees know how it relates to their specific work area. However, in most organizations, middle managers are themselves unclear on the sprit underlying the words of the vision and, following a transition, do not make a priority of learning more about it and discussing it with their reports. Supervisors, the representatives of management most employees see on a day-to-day basis, are even deeper in the dark about the vision. While newsletters, Web sites, videos, and plaques are important supplements to face-to-face communication, they are not substitutes for the personal touch that employees seek during recovery. Moreover, without ownership of the vision, managers and supervisors are either cynical about it, threatened by it, or both. So they resist vision implementation rather than support it.

Eventually, the senior executive gets some kind of feedback—findings from an employee attitude survey, persistent nudging from the human resource director, sardonic employee comments, or disappointing financial results—that indicates that people in the company are unclear about where the organization is headed and have lost faith in their leadership's ability to move the organization forward. This only serves to frustrate the CEO or business unit leader. "Haven't I already told people the vision?" asks the baffled leader. Yes, perhaps the words have been spoken, but the intentions, spirit, and potential of the vision have not gotten through to the employees on the job.

The process by which the vision is developed is as important to recovery after a transition as the content of what it says. Before any effort was made to broadcast his vision to the overall workforce,

CEO Justin Jourdan used the process of articulating the vision statement as a method for building teamwork within his top team and
for pronouncing his seriousness about having his direct reports carry
the banner in their respective parts of the Majestic organization. I
conducted one-on-one interviews with Jourdan and his top team to
identify issues, concerns, and priorities related to business direction
and vision. At an off-site meeting, I reported the findings from the
interviews and facilitated a discussion with the objective of unifying the senior team members' perspectives about the desired end
state for the firm. Concerns about autonomy versus centralization
and questions about meaning and intent were addressed head-on
through rounds of give-and-take discussions. As he adjourned the
meeting, Jourdan insisted on commitment to using the vision
toward achieving the new organizational order with a passion his
team had rarely seen.

Living the Vision

Statements of vision do little to generate the motivation to charge
up the hill among a workforce recovering from transition; how
those statements are used, however, does much. To motivate people, the vision must come alive. It must be animated and integrated
into people's actions on the jobs, not merely spoken about or
pointed to. This is called *living the vision*.

Figure 9.2 shows a model for living the vision through activity
up and down the organization. It is driven by the vision of senior
leadership at the top of the organization but builds on the support of
each level from the bottom up, thus involving people throughout
the organization. Senior executives articulate a clear direction for
the organization; managers and supervisors link business unit mission statements with the vision and develop guidelines for employee
behavior. Then, in work teams, employees translate the vision, mission, and operating guidelines into on-the-job operating procedures.
This aligns employee activity with the new organizational order and
answers the prominent question of how individuals can contribute

FIGURE 9.2. Living the Vision.

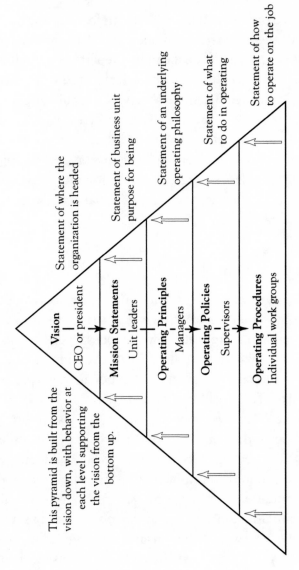

This pyramid is built from the vision down, with behavior at each level supporting the vision from the bottom up.

Vision
CEO or president
Statement of where the organization is headed

Mission Statements
Unit leaders
Statement of business unit purpose for being

Operating Principles
Managers
Statement of an underlying operating philosophy

Operating Policies
Supervisors
Statement of what to do in operating

Operating Procedures
Individual work groups
Statement of how to operate on the job

to overall organizational success. Then, working back up the pyramid, supervisors and managers review proposed new ways of approaching work to ensure that they support the mission and vision and to provide coordination across work areas.

Living the vision aligns employee behavior with the new organizational order not by mandate or directive but by establishing a context for recovery that encourages change at the local level. Living the vision enables employees to transcend their day-to-day work activities and see their contribution to the new organizational order. This process contributes to workplace recovery for a number of reasons:

- *High credibility.* Living the vision directly addresses employees' questions, including, "Where is this organization headed?" and "How do I conduct my work in a manner consistent with the vision?"
- *High validity.* Changes in work procedures are based on employees' own recommendations for aligning work with the new organizational order, not some consultant's suggestion or some program's generic prescription for how to approach work.
- *High involvement.* Care is taken each step of the way to ensure genuine support for suggested revisions before the process goes to the next level.
- *High relevance.* The vision is linked with people's daily work situation.

Living the vision can occur throughout an entire organization or within a business unit or department. Either way, the process converts vision into action through a series of steps down and then up the levels of the organization.

Translating Vision into Mission. After they review and endorse the vision statement, members of the senior team work with their own direct reports to prepare a mission statement for their part of

the organization that supports vision attainment. A mission statement is the business unit's purpose for being, including what distinguishes it from the competition. Each group also prepares work
plans for moving the vision and mission through their part of the
organization and soliciting employee feedback and involvement.
The senior team reviews the mission statements and work plans
before being communicated through the ranks.

*Translating Vision and Mission into Operating Principles and
Policies.* Middle managers take the statements of vision and mission and generate operating principles and policies to guide individuals' work on the job. These are general guidelines on how to
approach work and align it with the organization's direction; they
are not rigid mandates. After developing the operating principles,
middle managers in each unit or department determine how to continue the process into the next levels of the organization. In relatively large organizations, the steps of translating mission into
operating principles and policies can be separated to involve more
people in crafting iterations of the process. In small or flat organizations, it may not be necessary to separate the steps of developing
operating principles and policies; they can be combined in the work
of middle managers. Executives then approve the operating principles and policies before they are communicated to the rest of the
work unit.

*Translating Operating Principles and Policies into Operating
Procedures.* Next comes the work of taking operating principles
and policies and refining them into operating procedures—statements of how to operate on the job. Employee groups, usually regular work teams, meet to discuss the corporate vision, business unit
or department mission, and operating principles and policies. Employees have to understand both the word and the spirit of each
level before they can apply them to their specific work situations. A
manager from the business unit attends the initial meeting to explain the rationale underlying operating principles and policies and

to solicit feedback regarding their relevance and applicability to work activities. If employees do not understand the statements or fail to see their relevance to their work situation, the middle managers have to go back and recraft them. When employees do understand how the statements relate to their work, they meet on an ongoing basis in their work teams to align work behaviors with the operating policies and procedures and, ultimately, the mission and vision. They prepare recommendations, which may include new ways of approaching work or ideas for eliminating unnecessary work, for presentation to supervisors and managers for their review. Superiors then review the recommendations and either accept them or send them back to employees with clear feedback regarding why they do not uphold the vision and mission or are not feasible for implementation.

Through this process, direction comes from the top of the organization, is made more precise as middle managers develop operating guidelines, and is brought to life by employees in the form of recommended new approaches to conducting work. These recommendations are then reviewed up the organization, to double-check for alignment with overall vision and mission. When employees understand that their contributions on the job are aligned with the greater vision and mission of their workplace, they move beyond a recovery frame of mind and start developing a self-reinforcing capacity for creativity and enhancement on the job. This is living the vision in the fullest sense of the phrase.

Living the Vision at Majestic

After the senior team reviewed, amended, and approved the company vision statement, it was rolled out in a special edition of Majestic's company newsletter, placed on the company's internal Web site, and reiterated in a video, large group meetings conducted by Jourdan, and a series of small group meetings conducted by each of his reports in their respective parts of the organization. Each time the vision was presented, Jourdan or one of his direct reports spoke with passion about the importance and urgency of getting the entire company to pull together in achieving it. "If we are to survive in an increasingly competitive industry," implored Jourdan in the video, "we have no choice but to dedicate ourselves to being the best at providing customer service that goes beyond the expectations of the people who use our products and services, becoming innovators in taking current technological capabilities beyond standard applications, providing a work environment and relationship with our employees that goes beyond merely having a job, and generating a return on investment to shareholders that goes beyond what they have received in the past." Every communication of the vision included a caveat that the vision statement was nothing more than the starting point for guiding employee efforts on the job—the vision would be realized only in concert with employee efforts.

Each member of Majestic's top team worked with direct reports to develop a mission statement to support the vision in their area of the business. The operations group, for example, declared its mission to be to "contribute to the attainment of organizational goals through the efficient and innovative organization and execution of product ordering, storing, and distribution"—a vapid statement to be sure, but one that reflected the no-nonsense style of the operations vice president. And according to the results of some focus groups conducted to test employee reactions to the statement, it succeeded at conveying the operations area's reason for being.

Guidelines for employees to use in aligning their work with the vision and mission came next. In the operations area, each department head developed operating principles to clarify the philosophy underlying that department's approach to getting the job done. The head of warehouse operations chose to work independently on this task and came up with several principles. One operating principle in particular caught the fancy of his managers and employees: "Be the easiest company to do business with in our industry." It was simple, relevant, and clearly associated with the vision of enhanced customer service. After reviewing the operating principles with his boss, the head of warehouse operations directed his supervisors to

work as a group to determine operating policies that would go further in establishing guidelines for aligning work activities. The
supervisors were wary of overwhelming employees with what might
be perceived as conflicting policies, so they chose to present just
one operating policy to the head of warehouse operations for his
review prior to sending it down to the next level. Although singular, the operating policy was keenly important to enhancing customer service, highly practical as a guide for aligning work, and
truly challenging to employees: "Any order placed by 5:00 P.M. will
be shipped out the same day."

The warehouse head approved the policy and instructed supervisors to make time and other resources available to employees to
develop operating procedures that aligned their work with it. Each
employee was invited to a one-day training program where they
reviewed the living-the-vision process, learned creative problem-
solving techniques, and gained insight into common pitfalls to
small group decision making. At the program, employees learned
the steps to be followed in reviewing their recommended revisions
in operating procedures. Once a month, a panel of supervisors
would be convened to hear recommendations for operating procedures proposed by teams, individuals, or ad hoc groups representing
multiple work teams. After a discussion, the panel either would
accept the proposal and move it through the regular management
channels with decision-making authority or return it to the sub-
mitter for refinement. In the event that managers rejected a proposed operating procedure accepted by the panel of supervisors,
clear reasons for the decision would be communicated to the
employees making the recommendation. Operating procedures
accepted by management would be assigned to appropriate personnel for implementation, with the understanding that the assignment was to be pushed as low as possible in the hierarchy.

Employees in Majestic's warehouses began meeting weekly in
their work groups to consider how to operate in a way that would
provide for orders placed by 5:00 P.M. to be shipped that day. Some
groups took advantage of coaching and facilitating services provided

by internal support staff, while others worked on their own. Frequently, work groups needed additional business information, such as projections for new business development, to make educated decisions. They could not go off the job to collect the data, so a small number of support staff was designated to help with data collection. In responding to these requests, managers and supervisors shared information historically withheld from employees at Majestic.

Before long, proposals for new operating procedures came forth. These ran the gamut from minor revisions in work shift scheduling to major overhauls in the inventory numbering scheme. Suggestions also cut across traditional boundaries in the company. One work team from the warehouse proposed that telephone order takers mention the availability of same-day shipping but at the same time ask if the products were needed that quickly; orders for customers who did not need them sent out the same day were given a lower priority. An ad hoc team of warehouse employees and order takers refined the proposal, which was presented to a panel of supervisors from the two departments.

As living the vision took hold and stories of successful implementation of enhanced operating procedures circulated throughout the company, Majestic employees at all levels grew more comfortable with the process. Over time, managers and supervisors in the warehouses generated additional operating principles and policies to guide employee groups in their efforts to suggest new ways of operating on the job. Some work teams continued to meet weekly to develop proposals for aligning their work with these guidelines, while others reduced the frequency to biweekly or even monthly.

Did the living-the-vision effort succeed at revitalizing employee spirit and operating results at Majestic? Although no objective assessments were made, some anecdotal signs of improvements emerged. First, several employees met on their own time to augment the weekly work team meetings. Second, many employees incorporated looking for new ways of operating into their daily work routine rather than relegate it to the weekly work group meetings. Bringing the vision to life became not just something to discuss at a meeting but an integral part of their work activities. Third, Majestic people subjectively reported positive changes in their work situations. Noted one warehouse employee, "We all seem to be marching in the same direction." Added a supervisor, "I can't really put it into words, but everybody is more in sync or something. It's like managers, supervisors, and employees are on the same team for the first time in quite a while." Finally, praise from outside the company for Majestic and its people confirmed internal impressions. The most cherished acknowledgment came when a prominent industry magazine awarded Majestic its "customer service provider of the year" honor following the introduction of the living-the-vision process. This external validation of internal feelings reinforced employee pride for their part in making organizational enhancements and nurtured optimism for the company's future. People truly saw Majestic as on its way to "emerge from the crowd by giving the best customer service while leading the industry in profitability, technology, and employee relations."

Tracking Development of the New Organizational Order

The twelfth reality of workplace recovery is that a posttransition culture will emerge—either the status quo or a modified one by design or by default. If the organization tracks the development of the culture—by conducting employee research and obtaining feedback on what cultural messages are being received—it can respond more effectively in steering the culture in the desired direction.

Employees' vigilance is high during recovery—employees crave information as they attempt to make sense of the new organizational order and seek to interpret the clues they receive in the context of "What does it mean for me?" Every manifestation of the organization—every system, procedure, policy, and decision—has meaning. If unattended to, odds are they will be in conflict and result in a new organizational order by default rather than by design. Alternatively, thinking through and deliberately aligning structure, systems, decisions, and actions with the new organizational order will contribute to a posttransition organization headed in the desired direction and meeting its goals. But the job does not stop with messages sent out; rather, it continues by tracking the messages *received* by employees.

Knowing What Is Going On

Workplace recovery benefits not just from skilled leadership but also from *informed* leadership. A constant flow of operational, behavioral, and attitudinal data that report how the business is performing and how people are acting and feeling tracks the extent to which the desired culture is being realized. If it is veering off course, this feedback directs attention and resources to the issues that need to be managed to get back on the path toward the desired culture by design.

Many leaders think they know what is going well and what is not. But when they consult primarily with their peers and direct reports, what they hear is often censored and self-serving. This gives them a distorted picture of progress and false assurance that all is well by staying the current course. Months later, the picture is clearer: the desired culture is not achieved, employee motivation and productivity are not enhanced, and executives have no recourse but to either accept the culture by default or start all over again at unfreezing undesirable perceptions, behaviors, and mental models.

Even in organizations that have a good communication climate under normal conditions, leaders have to go out of their way to collect valid data to assess employee viewpoints during recovery. Trust has yet to fully develop in the posttransition organization, and people do not know the consequences of speaking up. Does the messenger get shot? Will a critical comment come back to haunt someone when pending staffing decisions are made? Will a boss or peers feel betrayed by employees' honest reports about problems in their work teams? Will individuals who are well intentioned by offering their perspective be castigated as naysayers or whiners?

Tracking the development of the new organizational order reaps significant benefits:

- *Determining if the desired new organizational order is being realized.* The primary benefit of tracking is to determine what impressions of the new organizational order are being made on employees and customers. This includes employee views of whether the posttransition culture is by design, by default, or the pretransition status quo and customers' views of their experience in working with the organization.
- *Identifying hot spots before they flare out of control.* The forces against desired change are never fully vanquished. Ongoing monitoring helps identify and address lingering resistance to realizing the desired new organization.
- *Highlighting needs for midcourse corrections.* Even the most successful recovery programs require midcourse corrections. The complexity of contemporary work organizations, competitive environments, technological changes, employee needs, and market conditions makes it likely that the first crack at articulating a new organizational order will need to be revisited and revised as recovery occurs.
- *Continuing opportunities for involvement in the recovery process.* Tracking is a cost-efficient way to keep large numbers of employees—if not the entire workforce—involved in recovery. Seeing that leadership is committed to monitoring the development of the new organizational order sends a message to employees that recovery is not just another fad that will fade away.
- *Ensuring a good flow of multidirectional communication.* Tracking creates a formal mechanism for top echelons to hear from the troops closest to the action. It also creates opportunities for leadership to feed back the findings and engage in conversation with employees about the development of the new organizational order.
- *Sending a message about the posttransition culture.* In addition to the content of what is communicated, tracking sends the symbolic message that the flow of valid information in all directions is

a component of the new organizational order. A formal tracking program reiterates the importance of multidirectional communication and conveys leadership's genuine interest in people's perspectives as components of the new organizational order.

What to Look For

Part of the engagement element of workplace recovery is to diagnose barriers to individual adaptation. The question then was "What barriers are preventing people from ending the old and accepting the new?" Now, as the new organizational order is specified and settles into place, the question is "What impressions of the new organizational order are being received by employees?" It is these impressions that people will use to make sense of the new order and formulate new mental models (or reinforce old mental models).

A starting point in determining what to look for in tracking impressions of the new organizational order, then, is what you are attempting to accomplish with it. This comes directly from statements of vision, mission, and other components of the desired new order. Thus at Majestic, leadership tracked employees' views of customer service, profitability, technology, and employee relations in the emerging organization.

Although the definition of the new order will vary from one organization to another, certain areas to track are relevant to all organizations in recovery. For example, a number of common themes emerge when employees talk about what they consider when drawing conclusions about the posttransition organization and its culture. As summarized in Exhibit 9.2, employees assess the new organizational order from three perspectives: their job, their work team, and their leadership. Tracking these areas helps you assess whether the emerging posttransition organization is by design or by default.

From their jobs, employees draw conclusions based on what short-term rewards and long-term successes are derived from performance. They also consider what opportunities the posttransition

EXHIBIT 9.2. What Employees Consider
About Posttransition Culture.

From Their Job
- What is rewarded over the short term
- What it takes to succeed over the long term
- What opportunities exist to develop new skills and acquire new experience

From Their Work Team
- What opportunities exist for experimentation and learning
- What procedures are predominating
- What matters in achieving work goals

From Their Leadership
- What patterns and styles of communication predominate
- What consistency exists between words and actions
- What consistency exists in how people are treated

organization provides to develop new skills and acquire new experiences. From the perspective of their work team, employees consider the extent to which new methods for accomplishing work are experimented with and adopted. The predominating procedures for how work gets done influence employee perceptions of the new organizational order—the specific work procedures send a clear message of whether a new and better organization is emerging or the old status quo is prevailing. The same applies to what matters in achieving work goals, that is, the choices made when teams confront competing priorities. And from their leadership, employees draw conclusions about the posttransition organization based on patterns and styles of communication, the extent of consistency between words and actions, and the extent of consistency in how people are treated in the new order. Each of these provides the basis for developing measures to track the new organizational order.

How to Look for It

A variety of methods can be used to track the development of the new organizational order—attitude surveys, individual interviews, focus group interviews, observations, and production records are common choices. Some organizations conduct exit interviews to determine what influenced departing employees' decision to seek employment elsewhere. If a repetitive pattern is found, action can be taken to address the causes of voluntary turnover as the new organizational order settles in. And some organizations survey customers and vendors to gain an external perspective on the new order. As with internal stakeholders, this sends a message that the organization is paying attention to customers and vendors as it moves through recovery but also provides solid feedback for making necessary midcourse corrections before the posttransition organization solidifies.

Refreezing the New Organizational Order

Articulating and building a new organizational order is no easy task. Especially in the current environment of rapid change and multiple waves of transition, it is common for inadvertent messages to be sent to a workforce hungry for clues about the evolving work situation. People do not go to work to confront disruption and transition. But that is what they have encountered in the years of organizational MADness. Organizations need good people, but they cannot provide the kind of slow-to-change and paternalistic workplaces that used to favor the development of loyal "lifers." Organizational leaders must try to be as consistent as possible in sending messages to employees. This means ensuring that systems, structures, and jobs are aligned to reinforce the desired end state. It also means understanding employees' needs and issues as the employees adapt to transition.

Tremendous patience is required to recover from transition and revitalize human spirit and work team performance in the workplace. People will not accept the new until they let go of the old.

They need time to pass through denial, anger, and other reactions to loss, as well as to move through the phases of ending the old, dealing with hang time, and experimenting and getting comfortable with the new. However, this time required for adaptation presents a rare opportunity, after people have been unfrozen by the turmoil of transition, to cast a new mold and refreeze attitudes and behaviors congruent with the desired new organizational order. To achieve these opportunities to the fullest extent possible, leaders must proactively help people recover from the unintended consequences of transition and regain the self-confidence and motivation needed to triumph in their charge up the hill to capture the prize that awaits.

PART FOUR

Solidifying the Context for Workplace Recovery

10

Leading and Managing Workplace Recovery

The very natural and normal process of adaptation after transition—and the fact that it takes time for people to end the old and deal with hang time before they can grab the new ring—is increasingly being accepted by organizational leaders. These executives have for the most part learned the hard way—by dealing with the unintended consequences of mismanaged mergers, acquisitions, and downsizings—but some simply have a more humanistic orientation than others. Either way, they accept the need to recover from transition and recognize that they have a job to do in preparing their people for the march toward new economic opportunities.

Executive Support for Workplace Recovery

Whatever their motivation, executives who embrace workplace recovery share some basic orientations. First, they recognize that signs of mourning the loss of the old and coping with hang time may not be apparent in the posttransition organization. They accept that some managers and employees may be afraid of being cast as weak or vulnerable and hide their true feelings, others are stuck in denial, and still others are numbed by the saturation effect of multiple transitions. Second, executives who successfully lead their troops out of transition and on to new opportunities do not assume they know what their people are thinking. They create an environment in which people can express what they are feeling and regularly monitor and track employee viewpoints. Importantly, these executives are able to distinguish between the natural need to vent pent-up emotions and antagonistic bad-mouthing, and they do not take what they hear as a personal attack.

Third, these executives recognize that "you pay now or you pay later" in recovering from the unintended consequences of organizational transitions. Intervening early in the adaptation process, when resistance is relatively weak and minor issues have not yet festered into major problems, requires fewer resources than does addressing stronger counterforces later. They discipline themselves to put aside the typical orientation toward short-term results and quick fixes, recognizing that Band-Aids will not heal the deep wounds experienced by people during transition. Finally, executives who acknowledge the need for recovery after transition are also aware that their behaviors send potent signals to employees regarding the new organizational order. Actions speak louder than words as employees create mental models about life after the transition. Dedicating resources to prepare people for the march up the hill is one of the most compelling ways in which leaders can convey that they recognize what people have been through during transition and are dealing with during recovery.

Creating a Context for Recovery

Workplace recovery does not happen in a vacuum—it is linked with the organization's marketplace proposition, business strategy, and product or service offerings. Nor is it an event or program that happens on the sidelines when people call a timeout from the regular business activity. Rather, recovery helps people move more quickly through the adaptation process precisely because its connection with the core business gives employees a fuller sense of the new organizational order than they might otherwise receive. Recovery is not a free-for-all and does not occur by giving employees a blank slate on which to design their role in the posttransition organization. Rather, employees need to be guided by a clear *context for recovery*. A context provides a template for building the desired new end state—it specifies leaders' framework for the new organizational order and clarifies which aspects of organizational life are "in bounds" and open to review in the recovery process and which are "out of bounds." To create an appropriate context for recovery, leaders should follow six rules of thumb:

1. *Organize work around the new organizational order—direction and guidelines.* Managers and employees contributing to workplace recovery need something with which to align their actions on the job. Two components of the new organizational order—direction and guidelines—give people a sense of what really matters in the posttransition organization and a larger picture to use as a point of reference while conducting their daily activities. Direction is a clear statement of where the organization is headed. Guidelines are more specific indications of the values and behaviors necessary for reaching that destination.

2. *Aim high.* The context for recovery should encourage all members of the organization to search for high-quality answers and not settle for an easy way out. Set clear expectations for fundamental changes in the way work is approached, organized, and managed rather than incremental modifications to the status quo. Compromises and trade-offs are common in posttransition organizations; they provide an immediate sense of moving forward but miss the opportunity to identify and lock in true innovations. Of course, it helps to have priorities—let people know the areas they should be working hard at to craft breakthrough solutions and those that can get by with mere modifications of the status quo. Some organizations call this the 80/20 rule—spend 80 percent of your effort on the 20 percent of the issues that really matter.

3. *Focus on the work itself.* The saturation effect following transition—through which employees' threshold for dealing with stress, uncertainty, and disorientation is taxed up to and beyond its limits—interferes with people's ability to learn and apply new programs or

processes. No matter how conceptually sound or pragmatically applicable an off-the-shelf change management intervention may be, people will perceive it as an irrelevant distraction rather than as a method to help get their work accomplished following transition. An essential condition for developing a context for recovery is to get people to focus on the work itself. Their attention is centered on aligning tasks, roles, responsibilities, and relationships with the critical business needs of the new organizational order.

4. *Emphasize local design.* Senior executives and general managers can articulate the new organizational order, but local managers and supervisors have to direct local change efforts to move their work groups in the desired direction. Local managers are intimately familiar with their work technology and group dynamics. Local design means that managers and employees at the work group level assume ownership of the recovery process. At a time when perceived lack of control is a big issue for employees, local design allows them to feel more like architects of change and less like victims of it.

5. *Encourage coordination and communication.* One of the potential drawbacks of local design is that it contributes to tunnel vision with respect to one's work team rather than to links with other teams. Mechanisms for coordination and communication are therefore needed to enhance workplace recovery. The way one work group deals with an issue provides insight for other groups. Information exchange can occur formally through learning events, small and large group meetings, newsletters, and Web sites, as well as through informal discussions.

6. *Provide resources.* Even when commitment to workplace recovery is sincere, there are always forces acting against desired change in any complex work organization. There are pressures to meet short-term results, frustrations in getting assistance from a support staff that has been downsized, and the persistent feeling of being torn between running the business and managing the transition. Busy managers and employees need assistance in aligning their work with the new organizational order. Three types of resources are especially pertinent to recovery—time, coaching, and prototypes. Lead-

ers have to free up time for people to attend workshops and for teams to go "off-line" on a regular basis to discuss and implement work alignment. Middle managers and supervisors tend to benefit from internal or external coaches who can assist them in articulating operating principles and policies, facilitating meetings, learning creative problem-solving approaches, and using good change management strategies and tactics to implement workplace enhancements. And although workplace recovery stresses learning over copying, it is helpful to provide managers and team leaders with examples of approaches used elsewhere—inside or outside the organization—to facilitate recovery.

Leading Recovery from the Top

Some transition veterans have likened the merger, acquisition, or downsizing process to a kidney transplant: it must be planned and carried through very carefully, and the convalescence must be closely supervised if the organism is to avoid rejection. During the convalescence, the patient goes through a slow and careful process of accepting the new organ, adjusting to lifestyle changes, and recuperating from the debilitating side effects of major surgery. On one level, posttransplant recovery entails the body's physical acceptance or rejection of the kidney and its ability to fight off infection. On another level, posttransplant recovery occurs as the patient psychologically adjusts to life after the surgery and accepts new realities that include both losses and gains. For example, the patient may have to come to terms with the loss of participating in sports or eating particular foods. Alternatively, the better-functioning organ may allow the patient to engage in behaviors and activities not possible before the surgery.

Both the physical and psychological aspects of posttransplant recovery involve considerable learning by trial and error. The physician collects data through extensive presurgery testing and planning and draws from personal experience and insight to devise a program of what drugs to administer and in what dosages to facilitate recovery.

Ultimately, however, it is how the patient's body metabolizes and re-sponds to the drugs that determines the protocol that works, and this is assessed only by ongoing monitoring. Meanwhile, the patient strug-gles with learning how to adapt to new realities through a slow and deliberate process of learning by experimentation. And while the physician, therapists, and family and friends can offer support, it is the patient's own character—his patience, tolerance for frustration, and persistence through the trial-and-error process of learning—that will influence the building of self-confidence and the psychological acceptance of the behaviors in which he can safely engage.

Posttransition recovery mirrors the posttransplant recovery pro-cess. A CEO, president, or business unit leader can steward the process, but it is ultimately the employees themselves who will ac-cept or reject the new organizational order through their own ex-perience of trial-and-error learning. A leader—even with the best intentions and prescriptions—cannot force organizational change, just as a physician cannot compel the body to accept the donor organ. Nor can a leader mandate the adoption of new behaviors congruent with the new organizational order; that comes only from learning the cause-and-effect relationships that prevail in that new order and establishing new mental models.

Much has been written about the senior executive role in the organizational change process, with various characterizations of the "visionary leader," the "transformational leader," and even the "magic leader." Effective senior leadership is essential when people are reluctant to let go of tried and tested mental models and are ten-tative about bringing to life the vision of the new organizational order. Yet traditional calls for "tough turnaround" leadership—that is, "taking the helm" by introducing programmatic change or mak-ing structural changes and hoping that behavior change follows—have proved ineffective.

In contrast, executives who successfully lead the recovery process after transition recognize that they do not change organiza-tions. What they do is create a context within which managers and employees change their own work areas and behaviors. Still, these leaders understand that the stewardship of recovery requires constant give-and-take between flexibility and direction: the flexibility required to allow local change efforts to flourish and the direction required to guide those local changes within acceptable parameters. Effective leadership of workplace recovery requires a number of important actions and behaviors:

- *Be involved without being obtrusive.* Senior leadership must accept responsibility for achieving the new organizational order without imposing it on people. This gets to the heart of what it means to create a context for recovery as opposed to mandating it. Leadership's role is to provide the resources for local change planning and implementation and the guidelines to align work with the new order. In addition, senior leadership actively promotes teamwork and a sense of shared fate to get individuals to pull together toward the organizational good, and it facilitates learning from one unit of the organization to another.

- *Project excitement.* The years of organizational MADness have eroded the feeling of many employees that they are contributing to something special and important as they go about their daily work. Most people want to identify psychologically with their workplace and not just regard it as a place to trade hours on the job for a paycheck. Senior leadership reignites this excitement in the workplace by rallying people, motivating them to act, expressing confidence in their ability to succeed, and rewarding and celebrating their accomplishments along the way to the new organizational order.

- *Direct energy.* It is not good enough to get people excited; their energy has to be directed toward what matters most in the posttransition organization. Creating a context for recovery ensures that employees understand the priorities as well as the fundamental ways in which work is to be approached. During recovery, an atmosphere of give-and-take prevails as leaders and local managers give continual feedback in both directions. Leaders may learn something from a local change effort that modifies their vision and guidelines or should be factored into change efforts in other areas of the organization. Conversely, local managers may need to be reigned in a bit if they interpret leadership's context for recovery too loosely.

• *Motivate from the inside.* Real influence is a matter of winning over people's hearts and minds, not controlling the overt behavior of their muscles and bones. Genuine motivation, the kind needed to make a charge up the hill, comes from people committing themselves to a special cause, not from dangling a carrot in front of good performers or holding a stick over poor ones. The credos of the most successful companies emphasize values that go beyond profitability. Adhered to on a daily basis, they build pride of belonging and meaningful purpose among employees. Leadership's job is to embody the purpose of the new organizational order, not by preaching it, but by making it the basis of all decisions.

• *Accept responsibility.* When things do not go as hoped, it is easy to blame anyone or anything but oneself—the business environment, the decisions made by previous top management, the failure of current middle management to implement correctly, and so on. Although there may be some validity to this finger pointing, it detracts from the true issues at hand. A new organizational order occurs only when executives, managers, and employees accept that fundamental change is needed and that they—and only they—are responsible for the organization's failures in the past as well as its success in the future. This is a matter of getting people to stop placing blame for the past and to start accepting responsibility for the future and what it will take to get there.

• *Say it again and again.* Nothing has been more overcommunicated than the need to overcommunicate to employees. But the message still has not been heard. A *Wall Street Journal* survey of 164 chief executive officers found that although they acknowledged that personal communication helps create more employee commitment to change, 86 percent said other demands prevented them from devoting more time to communicating. Communicating during recovery goes beyond formal channels of newsletters, Web sites, videos, and large group meetings orchestrated by staff specialists to a more personal commitment and involvement to ensure that messages are being heard as well as sent.

- *Show empathy.* Even when they are willing to let go of the old, employees suspended in hang time grapple with a changing work situation and with making sense of the new order. It is naïve to think that employees will embrace the new order without some experience of threat or hesitation. Beyond merely acknowledging this reality of human adaptation, leaders must display genuine empathy for the situation of others in the organization—a gut-level understanding of what it is like to be an employee during and following a difficult transition. Doing this requires staying in touch with employees' concerns and viewpoints. Understanding what concerns them about transition and recovery means knowing what they worry about, what excites them, what frustrates them, and what they are thinking, feeling, hoping, and needing as they do their work.

- *Be patient.* Meaningful and desired change does not happen overnight. To create a new organizational order is to fundamentally change the organization's culture, and cultures change slowly. Of course, this cannot happen until people first let go of the old order, itself a time-consuming process. Executive disdain for this slowness contributes to the customary preference for programmatic or structural change. Mandating a change gives leadership the illusion that its wishes have been implemented and supported when in reality, forces for the status quo create substantial resistance. Recovery after transition may take substantially more time up front, but it eliminates the back-end resistance that so often defeats organizational renewal.

- *Anticipate mistakes.* Ask people to discuss the most potent learning experiences in their careers, and they are likely to talk about learning from mistakes. This is a stressful yet powerfully effective way to learn. Leaders set expectations: "We will stumble and fall down on the road to recovery, and it will hurt sometimes. But we are in this together, and we will do what we can to pick ourselves up, learn from our mistakes, and move forward."

- *Model vulnerability.* Leaders will make mistakes along the way, too. "Walking the talk" here means that senior executives own up to their personal missteps and miscalculations. They model vulnerability and the effective process of learning from mistakes. Anything less strengthens cynicism and suspicion of leadership's true intentions. An organization cannot adopt a learning mode unless its most senior executives do the same.

- *Implement change at the top.* Senior leadership has to be willing to put its own team in play and align it with the new organizational order. New skills, capabilities, styles, and value orientations may be required at the top to nurture the recovery process as well as to manage the new organizational order. A change in the top team is a dramatic move but one that may be essential for recovery and enforcement of new ways of doing things. If senior people—who may very well be products of the old organizational order—do not embrace the new, neither will people in the ranks. Past loyalty and performance are difficult to overlook, but there comes a time of reckoning when the leader must either end the old and embrace the new or somehow rationalize not doing so. Either action sends a clear, strong, and obvious message to the overall workforce.

Managing Recovery in the Middle

Workplace recovery can truly be a mixed bag for middle managers. Some are especially threatened by the creation of a new organizational order. Like others in the organization, they must align their work with the new order and adapt to transition. To a greater degree than most, however, middle managers are likely to experience a sense of loss as they see some of the planning and implementation responsibilities they held in the old order shared with others in the new. They may have worked hard at advancing in the organization but now feel frustrated by what appears to be a stall in their ascent up the hierarchy and may resist giving up the traditional trappings of their position.

Middle managers also see at first hand the pain of mismanaged transitions, however. When engaged in recovery after transition, they quickly warm to a process that acknowledges employee concerns and actively works to help people let go of the negativity while embracing a new organizational order. Middle managers can prepare themselves for their role in workplace recovery in a few key ways:

- *Seize the opportunity.* Workplace recovery relies on the contribution of middle-level managers. They must seize the opportunity presented to bring the new organizational order to life at a local level. Rather than keep their head in the sand or run around like a chicken with its head cut off— common reactions of middle managers after a difficult transition—in recovery, they have the courage to take risks and experiment, ask for needed information and resources, and have the common sense and loyalty to contribute to the organizational good.

- *Trust in oneself.* Even though they themselves are often among the key dissidents and naysayers who thwart programmatic change, middle managers feel insecure without a format to follow when given the responsibility for contributing to desired change. Certainly, middle managers need the contributions of senior executives, staff specialists, and external consultants, but they must also pull from their own knowledge, experiences, values, and creative processes. Middle managers who play their roles well in workplace recovery see themselves and their reports as powerful and creative individuals.

- *Learn new ways of doing things.* One way to build self-confidence in one's ability to manage during recovery is to acquire new skills and insights, especially in the area of team management. Managers are often well versed in technical skills but lacking in managerial skills. Successful middle management during recovery relies on harnessing the power of groups to solve problems, removing barriers to group performance, and helping groups resolve conflict.

- *Be proactive.* A middle manager who sees the need for recovery after transition but works in a setting where superiors deny or ignore the need will have to risk being proactive in building the context for positive change. There are instances in which middle managers have initiated recovery without a sanction from the top. Savvy middle managers recognize changes in the competitive environment or company strategy following transition and align their work teams accordingly, even though senior leaders have not formally articulated a new organizational order. Sometimes these middle managers act in covert ways, keeping recovery activities low-key until enhancements can be documented. At other times, middle managers act overtly, lining up resources and support before launching their local efforts. Either way, middle managers take proactive action because they accept that the old ways of approaching work cannot meet the posttransition challenges to their areas.

• *Keep perspective.* Managers who rebound after a transition develop a singular ability to keep things in perspective. They distinguish between what they can and cannot control; they spend their energy on doing the former well and do not waste it on trying to do the latter. They have listened closely to the explicit and implicit messages from senior leadership and understand what about the status quo in their work area is consistent with the new order and what is not. This focus buffers them from criticism—from their subordinates and from themselves—when confronted with matters beyond their control or when faced with competing demands and potentially overwhelming time and resource pressures.

The Critical Period for Workplace Recovery

The rapid pace and massive scope of transitions in today's work organizations—often coming in multiple, overlapping waves—make it difficult to prescribe exactly when to initiate a recovery program. In some organizations, the best timing might be right after a major transition that stands out from others in terms of its pervasiveness or intensity. In others, recovery may be warranted when the saturation effect has left the workforce listless and unable or unwilling to garner the physical and psychological energy to make a run at business opportunities. No matter what prompts the call for recovery, one thing is for certain: recovery and the building of a new organizational order are most likely to produce desired results when people remain at least somewhat unfrozen following the disruptiveness of transition. This is when employees' mental models aligned with the old organizational order have been confronted and begun to break down and are most inclined to be replaced by new ones aligned with the desired new organizational order.

This relatively unfrozen state provides a tremendous opportunity for impression management with employees, comparable to the critical period for the imprinting of baby ducklings in psychologist Conrad Lorenz's famous studies. Lorenz found that at a certain time in their development, ducklings would psychologically attach themselves to and follow whatever large figure was in their midst. If no impression was made during the critical period, the ducklings wandered aimlessly, never able to make a psychological connection in their later years.

Mature employees are substantially more cognitive than baby ducklings, yet they have their own critical period after transition when their attitudes and behaviors are relatively unfrozen and subject to change. Once this critical period for psychological attachment to the new organizational order passes, the only way to recapture employees' commitment and align their behavior with new business objectives is to repeat the entire process of unfreezing, changing, and refreezing. Inevitably, breaking down the old diverts much more time, energy, and resources away from core business operations than workplace recovery does.

There is no doubt that the organizational order of paternalistic cultures, womb-to-tomb employment relationships, and predictable upward mobility and base pay increases is a thing of the past. Senior executives in all but a few companies let go of these assumptions a long time ago. Only more recently have employees at middle and lower levels begun to loosen their grip on these old expectations. And while senior executives have benefited from a vantage point from which they could see transitions coming and exert control over them, other employees learned about changing work realities only when they arrived and by then had few, if any, ways to control them.

What has especially hurt employees during the years of organizational MADness is that their leaders did not warn them that this powerful locomotive of transition was speeding down the tracks and heading right at them. Many saw former coworkers who did not have the deftness to jump out of the way become casualties. Others managed to survive but suffered the fright of their lives and are wary of going down that path again. No one argues against the need for change and transformation in business, yet employees hold on to the angst and anger over why they were not prepared for what came their way.

Commitment to Recovery

The elements of workplace recovery are derived from sound theory and practice of individual adaptation to transition and organizational change management (see Figure 10.1). They are fairly straightforward, but their implementation is made very difficult by the many forces that prevail following transition. These counterforces come from both within the organization (such as lingering distrust, prevailing politics, and scrambling work teams reeling from the effects of reduced headcounts) and outside (including ever-increasing global competition and changing social and demographic realities). Therefore, the commitment to workplace recovery must be strong.

A genuine commitment to workplace recovery can be the starting point to revitalize an organization and its people bruised and battered from organizational MADness. Recovery can forge a new working relationship between an organization and its people that considers contemporary realities, workplace requirements, and human needs. It is an opportunity to clarify that layoffs, increased use of temporary or contract employees, and reduced benefits and career develop opportunities are a fact of organizational life today and not the evil doings of insensitive corporate fat cats. A new

FIGURE 10.1. The Elements of Workplace Recovery.

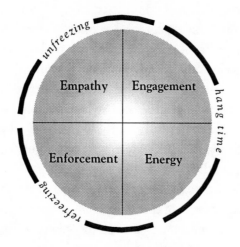

meaning of what the organization and worker are willing to commit to one another in the pursuit of shared goals must be and can
be specified. Recovery can also accelerate the rate at which people
end the old and accept the new by clarifying a new psychological
work contract, joining people in a common pursuit for success, inspiring excitement at the workplace, restoring individuals' perceived
and real capacity to act, and ultimately, enhancing the organization's
competitiveness and performance.

Mergers, acquisitions, and downsizings are here to stay in the
managerial repertoire of contemporary work organizations. But they
have eroded the psychological bond between employer and employee and have diminished loyalty and the motivation to act. A
workforce with one eye looking out for the next swoop of the downsizing ax or looking back in anger at what are perceived as past
injustices is simply not going to be focused on enhancing organizational performance and capturing new business opportunities. Organizational leaders cannot expect to charge back up the hill and
capture business opportunities with a bunch of out-for-themselves
mercenaries or with a raggedly equipped, poorly trained, and under-
motivated militia.

Success in today's organizational battlefields depends on developing a ready-to-act core of committed troops. This implies a tremendous opportunity for executives—along with work team leaders, human resource professionals, and others who have or create the ability to act—to become social engineers by designing new molds for the mental models that are aligned with the desired new organizational order. A new forward-looking human spirit and sense of organizational achievement are possible in the workplace of the twenty-first century, but only after acknowledging and working through the pain of the past.

Once the economic recovery is in full swing, it will be too late to begin thinking about workplace recovery. By the time it takes to end the old, articulate the new, and get people to bring that vision to life on the job, a competitor will have charged up the hill and grabbed every prize in sight. In contrast, the organization that today owns up to the unintended consequences of its MADness is taking the essential first step in recovering from the past and developing a committed, excited, and motivated workforce that is ready and willing to charge up hill after hill in pursuit of mutually rewarding prizes and is confident in its leaders' and its own ability to succeed.

Selected Bibliography

The models of organizational transition and individual adaptation that form the conceptual foundation for this book are described in Kurt Lewin's "Frontiers in Group Dynamics," *Human Relations*, 1947, 1(1), 5–47, and William Bridges's *Managing Transitions* (Addison-Wesley, 1991). Although the expectancy theory of motivation does have limitations in terms of applicability to different types of people (the theory is most predictive among individuals who have an internal, as opposed to external, locus of control), no other motivational theory matches its consistent support or generalizability. For a discussion, see Lyman Porter and Edward E. Lawler III, *Managerial Attitudes and Performance* (Irwin, 1968). Elisabeth Kübler-Ross's stages of loss are presented in *On Death and Dying* (Macmillan, 1969). The three stages of the letting-go process are detailed in Robert Tannenbaum and Robert Hanna, "Holding On, Letting Go, and Moving On: Understanding a Neglected Perspective on Change," in Robert Tannenbaum, Newton Margulies, Fred Massarik, and Associates, *Human Systems Development: New Perspectives on People and Organizations* (San Francisco: Jossey-Bass, 1985). Current perspectives on managing downsizings and related organizational transitions can be found in Kenneth P. De Meuse and Mitchell Lee Marks (eds.), *Resizing the Organization: Managing Layoffs, Divestitures, and Closings—Maximizing Gain While Minimizing Pain* (Jossey-Bass, 2002). More classic research on managing the downsizing process is reported in Joel Brockner, "Managing the Effects of Layoffs on Survivors," *California Management Review*, 1992, 34(2), 9–28. Finally, the experience of Philip Mirvis and myself in consulting and researching more than seventy-five cases of organizational transitions is reported in *Joining Forces: Making One Plus One Equal Three in Mergers, Acquisitions, and Alliances* (Jossey-Bass, 1998), which reports the sources and symptoms of employee stress, management crisis, culture clash, and transition mismanagement, along with methods to help combinations meet their financial and strategic objectives.

Index

Printed in the United States
110042LV00002B/103/A